ROME AND THE MAKING OF A WORLD STATE, 150 BCE – 20 CE

In the century following 150 BCE, the Romans developed a coherent vision of empire and a more systematic provincial administration. The city of Rome itself became a cultural and intellectual center that eclipsed other Mediterranean cities, while ideas and practices of citizenship underwent radical change. In this book, Josiah Osgood offers a new survey of this most vivid period of Roman history, the Late Republic. While many discussions focus on politics in the city of Rome itself, his account examines developments throughout the Mediterranean and ties political events more firmly to the growth of overseas empire. The volume includes a broad overview of economic and cultural developments. By extending the story well beyond the conventional stopping date of Julius Caesar's assassination in 44 BCE, Osgood ultimately moves away from the old paradigm of the fall of the Republic. The Romans of the Late Republic emerge less as the disreputable gangsters of popular imagination and more as inspired innovators.

Josiah Osgood is Professor of Classics at Georgetown University, Washington, DC, where he teaches Roman history and Latin literature. He has published numerous books and articles, including *Caesar's Legacy: Civil War and the Emergence of the Roman Empire* (Cambridge University Press, 2006) and *Turia: a Roman Woman's Civil War* (2014). Osgood's academic interests include civil war, the figure of the Roman emperor, and ancient biography, historiography, and satire. He lives in Washington, DC.

ROME AND THE MAKING OF A WORLD STATE, 150 BCE – 20 CE

JOSIAH OSGOOD

Georgetown University, Washington, DC

CAMBRIDGE
UNIVERSITY PRESS

CAMBRIDGE
UNIVERSITY PRESS

University Printing House, Cambridge CB2 8BS, United Kingdom

One Liberty Plaza, 20th Floor, New York, NY 10006, USA

477 Williamstown Road, Port Melbourne, VIC 3207, Australia

314–321, 3rd Floor, Plot 3, Splendor Forum, Jasola District Centre, New Delhi – 110025, India

79 Anson Road, #06–04/06, Singapore 079906

Cambridge University Press is part of the University of Cambridge.

It furthers the University's mission by disseminating knowledge in the pursuit of education, learning, and research at the highest international levels of excellence.

www.cambridge.org
Information on this title: www.cambridge.org/9781108413190
DOI: 10.1017/9781139342698

First published 2018

Printed in the United States of America by Sheridan Books, Inc.

A catalogue record for this publication is available from the British Library.

ISBN 978-1-107-02989-7 Hardback
ISBN 978-1-108-41319-0 Paperback

CONTENTS

FIGURES

MAPS AND TABLES

Maps

Tables

ACKNOWLEDGMENTS

Writing a survey of more than 150 years of Roman history for a general audience proved far more challenging than I anticipated, and I am much in debt to my Georgetown colleague Carole Sargent for helping me get started. In the spring semester of 2014, Andrew Meshnick, Georgetown College class of 2017, read early drafts and gave me essential advice. Since then Andrew has shared in the research and continued to edit all of my writing with great intelligence and sensitivity, even in the dog days of DC summer. I thank him for all of this and many entertaining conversations along the way. Three other enterprising Georgetown students – Andreas Niederwieser, Diana Chiang, and Annee Lyons – have also done valuable work in editing the manuscript and preparing the illustrative material. Thanks to them as well.

Dave Espo and Ron Bleeker made the mistake of auditing my Age of Augustus class in the spring semester of 2016. I shamelessly asked both to read large portions or all of the manuscript. As a journalist, Dave tightened my prose and has helped me become a clearer writer. Ron brought to the text a deep familiarity with Roman history and a lawyer's attention to detail and suggested a number of substantive improvements. I could not have asked for better editors, and I thank them both for their extraordinary generosity and good cheer.

I also gratefully acknowledge the help of Elizabeth Meyer, Tim Brannelly, Catherine Daun, Rebecca Frank, and Kevin Woram at the University of Virginia, who read all or part of the final manuscript a few weeks before submission and sent me many suggestions for improvement.

Any remaining faults should be ascribed entirely to my own oversight or stubbornness.

At Cambridge University Press it was a pleasure to work with Beatrice Rehl on developing the initial proposal for this book and then preparing the manuscript for publication. I am grateful for her advice and support. I also am indebted to the referees of the initial proposal as well as of the final manuscript for their helpful suggestions. Thanks finally to copyeditor Lois Tardío and to Katherine Tengco-Barbaro, Allan Alphonse, and Sathish Rajendran for their work on producing the book.

I

FROM WORLD POWER TO WORLD STATE:

AN INTRODUCTION

In the late 40s BCE, a disillusioned politician and officer of Julius Caesar named Sallust withdrew from public life and began writing history. His first work was a short account of a plot to overthrow the Roman Republic two decades earlier by a disreputable senator, Catiline. Sallust found the topic agreeable because it illustrated his belief that there had been a total deterioration in the values that underpinned public life. To get ahead in Rome at the time, Sallust claimed, you had to lie, bribe, sleep around, steal, and use violence. He admitted that even he had been less than pure. He offered no details. But a contemporary of his, Varro, alleged that Sallust was caught with another senator's wife, flogged, and let go only after paying a bribe.

Having introduced Catiline early in his work, Sallust next traced the rise of the Roman state to its greatness and then the means by which it "became the worst and most shameful." By his account: after the Romans threw out the kings who ruled them and established a republican government around 500 BCE, the newly won freedom inspired men to seek glory. They took pleasure in armor and warhorses rather than "prostitutes and parties." Every soldier wanted to be the first over the enemy walls. Men honored the gods and cared for their families. But once Rome destroyed its imperial rival Carthage in 146, Sallust wrote, individual greed and ambition were ascendant. Roman soldiers became more interested in love affairs and drinking. Their generals robbed temples and built villas the size of cities. Lust for conquest fueled the expansion of the overseas empire, but the greed that accompanied it led to the civil war that eventually destroyed the Republic.

For the nearly two millennia since Sallust's time, it has been hard to shake his pessimistic view of Rome after the fall of Carthage. Modern historians regularly write articles and books on the century ending in Julius Caesar's assassination in 44 BCE and focus on the factors that led to the end of the Republic. So entrenched is the idea of the "fall of the Roman Republic" that it recurs in political debate and popular culture. Critics of the Vietnam War spoke darkly of a nascent "American empire" and suggested that the fate of the United States would be that of republican Rome's. Similar claims were made during the presidency of George W. Bush. In his 2007 book, *Nemesis: The Last Days of the American Republic*, Chalmers Johnson argued that Bush's militarism had placed America on the path to dictatorship. Meanwhile, the first season of the HBO/BBC miniseries *Rome* (2005) presented viewers with a semifictionalized history of the end of the Republic dominated by brutish soldiers and sexually voracious women. One episode was called "How Titus Pullo Brought Down the Republic."

Accounts like these resonate powerfully in an era of anxiety, but they overlook a series of remarkable achievements that followed swiftly after Sallust first laid out his interpretation. Just 20 years after the historian began his dark work, Vergil was finishing what all agree is the singular masterpiece of Latin literature, his epic *Aeneid*. In this poem, Rome's empire is reconceived as a force for good, spreading peace over the world. Indeed, by the time of Vergil's death in 19 BCE – a quarter century after Caesar's assassination – there was an unprecedented level of peace across the Mediterranean and in the lands beyond. New cities were springing up in western Europe, with bustling marketplaces, marble temples, theaters, and heated baths. Roads and bridges were built to connect them – feats of engineering still used today in some cases. All this was possible because Julius Caesar's heir, Augustus, commonly regarded as Rome's first emperor, ushered in a new era of stable government able to administer the vast empire more effectively than it had been before. Augustus himself went on extended tours of inspection throughout the empire. He ensured that revenues were collected as efficiently and fairly as possible, and used them to fund a standing army that was essential for maintaining peace. Commerce flourished as never before.

Throughout this book, in a sort of shorthand, I refer to the Roman state of Augustus' day as the "world state." Obviously Rome did not literally embrace the entire world. But it did encompass all the main centers of ancient Mediterranean civilization and areas farther north, which was unprecedented. What is more, in the lifetime of Augustus, hundreds of thousands of men and women gained Roman citizenship, and tens of thousands of them lived as far away from Rome as Spain and the Middle East. This huge network helped work out new answers to the question of what it meant to be Roman. People read the *Aeneid*, dined off of fine Italian pottery, celebrated Augustus' birthday as a holiday, and sacrificed to the gods on his behalf. Noncitizens joined them in these activities, and in the process started to become Roman too. The new customs knitted the world together in ways that older traditions of citizenship, focused on city-state activities like listening to speeches in the main square of Rome, could not.

To focus obsessively on the "fall of the Roman Republic" not only minimizes all of these political accomplishments and related innovations in literature, commerce, and religion. It also obscures the fact that much of Rome's transformation into a world state happened in the century leading up to the widely known Ides of March in 44 BCE. We need to recognize that it was during the long "fall of the Roman Republic" that a more ambitious provincial administration was being developed, along with a more coherent vision of empire that promised lasting peace in exchange for loyalty to Rome and the payment of taxes. It was during "the fall of the Roman Republic" that the city of Rome itself became a cultural and intellectual center that eclipsed other Mediterranean cities and could rightly proclaim Roman power. This book starts in the year 150 BCE and continues to the year 20 CE, soon after Augustus was peacefully succeeded by Tiberius. It traces achievements that have gotten too little notice from Sallust and others since him, who have concentrated on the fall of the Republic.

THE TRANSFORMATIONS OF ROME

At the outset, it will be helpful to offer a brief sketch of Rome in 150 BCE, the changes it underwent in the next century or so, and an overall framework for thinking about those changes. We can focus on the overseas empire, culture, and then politics.

In 150 BCE, Rome was the dominant state in the Mediterranean. The Roman Senate regularly sent out military commanders to oversee parts of Spain and the islands of Sicily and Sardinia. To other areas, it issued instructions drafted in Rome or by delegations of senators on the spot. Overall, administration was minimal. During the following century, Rome gained tighter control of a much vaster territory that stretched from northwestern Europe to Africa, Asia Minor, and the Middle East. By 50 BCE there were more than a dozen provinces across three continents, with Roman governors who ensured that taxes were collected and that basic order was maintained. They defended the interests of thousands of Roman citizens living overseas. There was, however, no standing army. Legions were raised as needed and then disbanded, and soldiers increasingly looked to their commanders for rewards upon discharge, especially grants of land and money.

Throughout the same century, there was profound cultural transformation. In 154 BCE, a stone theater with seats was under construction in the city of Rome. Before it could be completed, though, the Senate voted to demolish it. Conservatives thought it was all too Greek: real Romans, they said, should be tough enough to stand. A hundred years later, Rome had a massive marble theater. Attached was an art-filled portico that served as a favorite pickup spot,

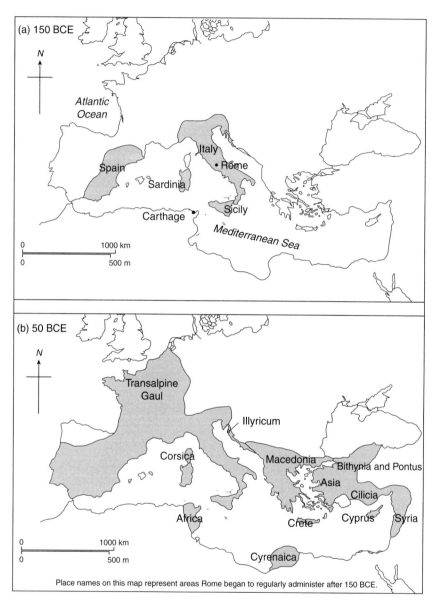

Map 1 Growth in Areas Administered by Rome, 150–50 BCE

according to contemporary poets. Houses, too, were decorated with Greek-style sculptures, paintings, and marble columns that proclaimed the taste of their owners. Romans were now embracing the flamboyance and individualism that characterized Greek culture after the conquests of Alexander the Great. By 44 BCE, they were writing autobiographies and even poems about their love affairs.

As for politics, in the mid-second century BCE, Rome was a republic, governed by its people. In fact, the official name of the state was the "Roman People." Treaties by other states were always made with the Roman People. Among themselves, Romans referred to the state as the *res publica*, a phrase that literally meant "commonwealth." Power ultimately resided with the Roman People – which in practice meant the male citizens who came together in assemblies held in the city of Rome. There they would elect magistrates and vote on legislation presented to them by magistrates currently in office. Past and present magistrates, numbering altogether a couple of hundred men, formed the Senate, which set much of the Republic's policy. Senators, who typically served for life, managed Rome's budget, guided relations with other states, and determined which magistrates would have military command and where. Because of the Senate's importance, the government was often conceived of as the "Senate and People of Rome" (*senatus populusque Romanus*), conveniently abbreviated "SPQR."

Despite a seeming continuity, government by SPQR went through many changes in the century following 150 BCE. The Senate more or less doubled in size, and the rules governing admission to it changed. The number of magistrates increased too. A bedrock principle of Rome's republic was that magistrates should only hold office for a term of one year and that power should always be shared with at least one fellow magistrate. But from the late second century BCE onward, the principle was increasingly violated. The great general Gaius Marius held the top office of consulship five years in a row, from 104 to 100 BCE. Later, Julius Caesar's rival Pompey was granted extraordinary power for most of the 60s BCE in order to fight pirates menacing the Mediterranean Sea and then one of the most dangerous foreign enemies Rome ever faced, King Mithridates of Pontus in northern Asia Minor. Along with individuals gaining unprecedented levels of power came another change: even as the institutions of SPQR endured, for extended periods of time their legitimacy was directly challenged. Leaders relied on soldiers and street fighters in Rome to get their way. Swords and daggers replaced speeches, laws, and voting.

In 44 BCE, citizens still gathered in their assemblies and the Senate still met. In reality, though, Rome was ruled by Julius Caesar, who held the ominous title of Dictator for Life. It was Caesar, along with his personal staff, who managed finances and set foreign policy. Caesar would convene the People to "elect" the men he chose. At the end of 45, one of the consuls died and Caesar had an officer of his appointed for a single day in a sham election. Caesar's enemy, the great orator Cicero, darkly joked, "When this fellow was consul, no crime was committed. His vigilance was extraordinary! Throughout his whole consulship he didn't sleep a wink!" A few months later, Caesar was assassinated. Cicero, who sympathized with the assassins, hoped he could bring back traditional republican government but failed. Instead, 15 years of civil war followed, in the midst of which Sallust wrote his pessimistic histories.

Throughout his published works, Sallust tied political developments firmly to moral decline. Given that the Roman state was its People, there was logic to this approach. His argument was that the fear of Carthage had united Romans. Once the fear was removed, nobles and ordinary men alike began grabbing what they could for themselves individually. On the whole, the nobles did much better, taking the lion's share of the profits of the growing empire, but a few nobles were willing to challenge their peers and stand up for ordinary people. The politicians' violent quarrels soon descended into armed violence, in a dangerous spiral.

Modern historians have tended to be skeptical of Sallust's emphasis on morality. For one thing, there already were voices of doom in the second century BCE. The historian Lucius Calpurnius Piso lamented the collapse of sexual morals and the influx into Rome, before the destruction of Carthage, of such dangerous Greek luxuries as one-legged tables. If morality had already declined by then, how did the Republic survive as long as it did? Still, it is important to take into account voices like those of Piso and Sallust to gain insight into how Romans understood the profound changes their society was undergoing. Moreover, Sallust deserves respect for attempting to give a coherent theory of how Rome's acquisition of an empire, its cultural development, and its political revolution were intertwined. Like Sallust, most practicing historians today will never be content to see Rome's development after 150 BCE as just a series of more-or-less accidental events.

THE SPOILS OF EMPIRE

Ultimately, students should decide for themselves how to explain the transformations of Rome, including the "fall of the Roman Republic." The narrative that follows is meant to help in that task. But no narrative can be written without its author having some view of what really matters, and so I briefly set out my own here. Too often, historians have limited themselves to just one of the strands described above: politics, cultural affairs, and foreign affairs. I believe they were intertwined, and I try to bring them together by developing an insight by the historian Keith Hopkins that the wealth flooding into Rome and Italy from the growing empire led to structural differentiation in society. Distinct new groups arose, such as financiers, a large urban population, and a wealthy ruling class in the towns of Italy. These groups clashed over the spoils of empire, as did the senators themselves.

While modern historians can isolate interest groups such as financiers in their analysis, we should note that the Romans themselves divided society into a hierarchy of groups with officially defined status. These groups were sometimes referred to as "orders," a concept that survives today in the idea of a religious or fraternal order like the Masons. A fundamental status distinction separated those with full Roman citizenship from those without. Although only men could vote, women could be citizens. All slaves lacked citizenship, as did free members of other communities. By 150 BCE, some Italian communities had been granted Roman citizenship; the rest, whether they liked it or not, were "allies" of Rome, required to fight Rome's wars. This would change with a great rebellion that began in 91 BCE and ended a few years later with the granting of citizenship across Italy. This was one of the most momentous developments in all of Roman history, crucial for the later spread of citizenship in the world state.

Among male citizens, there were two distinguished groups. One was made up of senators – basically current or former magistrates. Since all magistrates had to be elected, there was no formal hereditary aristocracy in Rome, although some families were successful generation after generation. These were the "nobles" Sallust writes about so scathingly. A select group who claimed descent back to Rome's earliest days were the patricians. Everybody else, including, by 150 BCE, some highly distinguished families, was plebeian.

The second distinguished group was the Equestrians. In earlier times Rome's cavalry (hence their name), these were men who met a high property requirement. It was really in the 120s BCE that they became an order in society distinct from the Senate. Many were involved in executing the massive contracts the Roman government issued to supply armies or collect revenues in the empire, in lieu of a civil service. The growth of the Equestrians into a distinct constituency particularly associated with lucrative government subcontracting is an excellent example of structural differentiation.

Other large, distinctive groups developed, such as the inhabitants of the city of Rome. There were much smaller groups too, including new specialists who did not exist when Rome was a small city with access to few resources. We could consider here the rise of legal experts, teachers of rhetoric, architects, and even love poets.

Hopkins' point about structural differentiation was that as Roman society grew more complex, government by SPQR had difficulty coping with the change. Italians thought they deserved greater recognition for their contribution to the growth of empire; the inhabitants of Rome thought that with all the wealth coming into Rome, they should get grain at a fair price. But the Senate and the People did not always agree, and they often became split over what to do. Senators' fights with one another were the most devastating to peace, because it was really only in the Senate that compromises could be hammered out. The People, able only to pass laws presented to them, could not make deals to end deadlock. In their struggles, senators enlisted the support of new groups or specialists, like the rhetoric teachers and the architects. Battles were fought in speeches and building projects, parades and festivals. All of these lent splendor to the age. But to the extent that these endeavors increasingly supported great leaders, they undermined the republican principle of limiting individuals' power.

If empire brought fights over spoils and heightened competition among politicians, it also was more directly destabilizing. In toppling or weakening other Mediterranean powers without investing many of their own resources to maintain security, the Romans precipitated a series of foreign crises. These included pirate raids, two slave rebellions in Sicily, and ultimately the major revolutionary movement in Asia Minor in the 80s BCE initiated by the opportunistic King Mithridates. At times of civil war, the sprawling empire allowed rival Roman leaders to carve out alternate states for themselves, such as in Spain. Empire fostered and fueled political conflict of the most dangerous sort. On this point, Sallust was essentially correct.

BEYOND THE "FALL OF THE ROMAN REPUBLIC"

Already it should be starting to become clear that there are advantages to thinking of the period from 150 BCE to 20 CE as a whole rather than accepting the traditional split of "The Last Age of Roman Republic" and "The Augustan Empire." Understanding the successes of government by emperors can reveal the weaknesses of SPQR, such as its inability to deal with army veterans and its difficulty in stopping the uncontrolled use of armed force. Yet we can also see more clearly how late republican leaders, however much they might have upset their contemporaries, were innovators of lasting importance, perhaps none more so than Pompey. To go back even further, the famous Gracchus brothers of the 130s and 120s BCE always loom large in accounts of the "fall of the Roman Republic." As politicians, both pushed through reforms dealing with the distribution of land and the sale of grain. Both aroused fierce controversy. Tiberius Gracchus and several hundred of his supporters were clubbed to death by a mob led by Rome's chief priest. Tiberius' younger brother Gaius and Gaius' supporters met a similarly grisly end. It is traditional to emphasize how the violence of these years undermined republican government. But from a longer view, we can also see that the brothers' ideas about finance and empire started a century-long process of reimagining the Roman state to suit an increasingly complex social and political reality.

FURTHER READING

Good surveys of the century or so of change from 146 to 44 BCE are *The Cambridge Ancient History* (2nd ed.) Vol. 9 (with a helpful preliminary chapter); P. A. Brunt, *Fall of the Roman Republic* (1988); M. Beard and M. Crawford, *Rome in the Late Republic* (2nd ed.; London, 1999); C. Steel, *The End of the Roman Republic, 146 to 44 BC* (Edinburgh, 2013). For a detailed political narrative that goes through the death of Augustus, see C. S. Mackay, *The Breakdown of the Roman Republic* (Cambridge, 2009). Older, but still valuable for politics and war, is H. H. Scullard, *From the Gracchi to Nero* (5th ed.; London, 1982). T. P. Wiseman's *Remembering the Roman People* (Oxford, 2011) is a series of typically vivid essays by a master in the field. T. Holland's *Rubicon: The Triumph and Tragedy of the Roman Republic* (London, 2004) and its sequel *Dynasty: The Rise and Fall of the House of Caesar* (London, 2015) are unmatched for their portraits of the major personalities.

Broader works on the Roman Republic are H. I. Flower (ed.), *The Cambridge Companion to the Roman Republic* (2nd ed.; Cambridge, 2014), and N. Rosenstein and R. Morstein-Marx (eds.), *A Companion to the Roman Republic* (Oxford, 2006, with a good chapter by the editors on "The Transformation of the Republic"). H. I. Flower's *Roman Republics* (Princeton, 2011) emphasizes discontinuities in an original fashion.

Rome's economic history has been boldly reinterpreted in recent work; two valuable guides are W. Scheidel (ed.), *The Cambridge Companion to the Roman Economy* (Cambridge, 2012), and W. Scheidel, I. Morris, and R. P. Saller (eds.), *The Cambridge Economic History of the Greco-Roman World* (Cambridge, 2008). For the cultural history treated in this book, A. Wallace-Hadrill's *Rome's Cultural Revolution* (Cambridge, 2008) is foundational. "Structural differentiation" is discussed by Keith Hopkins in his pioneering work *Conquerors and Slaves* (Cambridge, 1978), and its importance is emphasized in penetrating remarks by M. H. Crawford, "States Waiting in the Wings: Population Distribution and the End of the Roman Republic," in L. de Ligt and S. Northwood (eds.), *People, Land and Politics: Demographic Developments and the Transformation of Roman Italy, 300 BC–AD 14* (Leiden, 2008), 631–43 (the whole collection is useful).

More sweeping works usefully situate late republican Rome: G. Woolf, *Rome: An Empire's Story* (Oxford, 2012); D. S. Potter, *Ancient Rome: a New History* (2nd ed.; New York, 2014); M. Beard, *SPQR: A History of Ancient Rome* (London, 2015); and the picturesque R. Lane Fox, *The Classical World: An Epic History from Homer to Hadrian* (London, 2005).

On the history of Rome in popular memory see T. P. Wiseman, *The Myths of Rome* (Exeter, 2004), especially chap. 10, "The Dream That Was Rome"; P. Burton, "Pax Romana/ Pax Americana: Perceptions of Rome in American Political Culture, 2000–2010," *International Journal of the Classical Tradition* 18 (2011), 66–104; M. Wyke, *Caesar in the USA* (Berkeley, 2012).

2

THE NEW WORLD POWER: THE EMPIRE

AND IMPERIAL AFFAIRS (150–139 BCE)

It was late June 168 BCE, and with sudden urgency a delegation of three Roman senators sailed from the small Aegean island of Delos to Alexandria, on the coast of Egypt. There, on the outskirts of the magnificent city, the energetic king of the Syrian-based Seleucid Empire, Antiochus IV, was waging war. As the Roman delegates approached, he greeted them and extended his hand to the delegation's leader, a grim-faced man named Popillius Laenas. Popillius, instead of shaking, placed in the king's hand a decree of the Senate that instructed him to end the war in Egypt immediately. The king read it and said he would have to discuss it with his advisors. With his usual harshness, Popillius proceeded to draw a circle around Antiochus with a walking stick and told him that he must remain in the circle until he answered. Hesitating for a moment, the king finally replied, "I shall do what the Senate decrees."

Popillius' humiliation of the king demonstrated Rome's dominance, and was meant to. Just before his delegation left Delos, it had received word that the Romans had decisively defeated their strongest rival, the kingdom of Macedon, with whom war had broken out several years earlier. The Senate could now see itself as the undisputed arbiter of world affairs, and it sent to Macedon a delegation of 10 of its members with instructions for the victorious Roman general Aemilius Paullus on what to do with the defeated kingdom. These instructions also put Rome's dominance on display. The monarchy itself was to be abolished and the king's territory split into four republics, each to be governed by a separate council. The lucrative gold and silver mines were closed (they might fund a rebellion), but the new republics were responsible for paying tax to Rome.

Reprisals came for Macedon's allies and others judged to have been insufficiently loyal. By decree of the Senate, seventy towns of Macedon's neighbor Epirus were given over to plundering by Paullus' army, and 150,000 souls are reported to have been sold into slavery as a result. The Senate's 10 commissioners heard denunciations of individuals throughout Greece alleged to have helped the Macedonians secretly. In the federal state of Achaea alone, a thousand men were implicated, and the commissioners arranged for all of them to be brought to Italy for trial. There they would remain for 16 years, with charges never heard.

Among the detainees was the politician and historian Polybius. By striking up a friendship with Aemilius Paullus' son, Scipio Aemilianus, he was able to live in the city of Rome. Overwhelmed by Rome's successes, and impressed by the grim Popillius Laenas and other senators he came to know, Polybius began work on a new type of universal history – one that would explain how "the Romans succeeded in less than 53 years in bringing under their sole rule nearly the whole of the inhabited world." His main narrative would begin in 220 BCE and end in 167, chronicling each year's events across the Mediterranean, from Spain to Syria. Because of Rome's supremacy, Polybius argued, with some justification, that the history of the world (or the world he knew, anyway) was now "an organic whole."

Although parts of Polybius' history are lost, what survives – including descriptions of the Roman army, political institutions, and customs – is invaluable. Moreover, whereas by 167 BCE Polybius believed that it was "universally accepted as fact that the whole world must submit to Rome and obey her orders," he decided later on to explore how the new world power was acquitting itself. Extending his history by 10 books and bringing the narrative to 145 had the added benefit of allowing him to write about events in which he and his patron Scipio Aemilianus had a major part to play.

For all its dominance, Rome was experiencing problems. In practice, Roman power was strongest in areas bordering the Mediterranean Sea. The Senate administered them through a mixture of regular military commands and instructions it issued in Rome or by seaborne delegations like that of Popillius. But highhandedness, inconsistent policy, and reluctance to commit resources to administration resulted in Rome having to fight an overlapping series of wars in Spain, North Africa, and (once again) Macedon from the mid-150s, some of them quite protracted. Romans could ask themselves just how competent the Senate was. If foreign kings found senators to be arrogant, at least at times some Romans did too.

ROME'S *IMPERIUM*

When Polybius wrote his history, he was in no doubt that Rome had an empire. The word he used, as a writer in Greek, was *arche* (the root of such English words as *monarchy*). The same word had been used centuries earlier by Greek

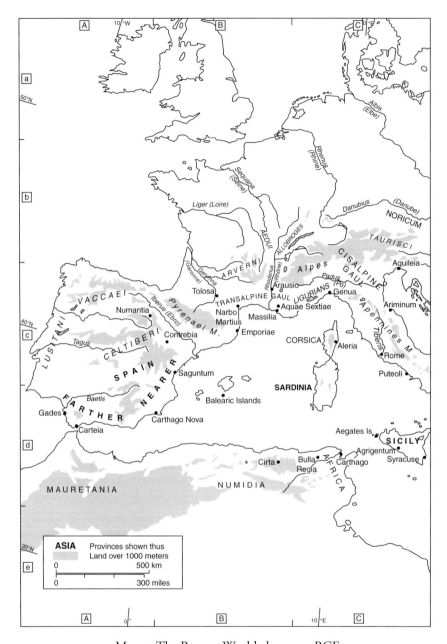

Map 2 The Roman World about 150 BCE

historians to describe the sprawling empire of Persia. Over time, the Latin word *imperium* (the source of the English "empire") came to have a similar meaning. In 150 BCE, though, *imperium* referred primarily to the power that the Roman people delegated to their magistrates, allowing military command. *Imperium*

Map 2 (cont.)

could also refer, more abstractly, to the power of the Roman People (i.e., the Roman state), including the power to command obedience overseas.

This overseas *imperium* was exerted in part by military commands. Every year, the Senate would give each of the senior magistrates, the two consuls, and the six lower-ranking praetors, a specific assignment – or, in Latin, *provincia* (pl. *provinciae*). While the word later came to mean a geographic entity to be administered on an ongoing basis (similar to the provinces of modern Canada), it did not initially imply any claim to permanent possession. Thus, during the war with Perseus, Macedon was for a time assigned as a *provincia*, but after the settlement of 167, it no longer was, even though the four new republics were expected to pay tax. In the thirty or so years after 200, one or both consuls regularly had *provinciae* in northern Italy, which was gradually brought under Roman control, with colonization and road building as key tools (Chapter 7).

By the 150s, while *provinciae* were still primarily military in nature, in the western Mediterranean some were being assigned by the Senate on a regular basis. Each year commanders were sent to Sicily, Sardinia, Nearer Spain, and Farther Spain. All four regions had been part of Carthage's maritime empire, and Rome's commitment to them was the result of its epochal wars with Carthage in the third century BCE – the so-called First and Second Punic Wars. (*Punic* was another word the Romans used for "Carthaginian," referring to the Phoenicians who first settled Carthage.) Commanders in Sardinia and the two Spains were fighting wars with local populations throughout the second century, especially in the vast Iberian Peninsula. Increasingly they had other jobs as well, such as adjudicating disputes between local communities, defending the interests of Roman settlers, and supervising payment of taxes. In Sicily, for example, with its splendid fields of grain, a tithe (i.e., one-tenth) of the harvest was collected.

In the east, with its more fully developed city-states and kingdoms such as those of the Seleucids in Syria and the Ptolemies in Egypt, the Romans exerted their *imperium* less directly. In 150 there were no regularly assigned eastern *provinciae*. Rather, while states had a fair degree of internal autonomy, when disputes arose with their neighbors, they would send delegations to Rome to speak before the Senate. The Senate, in turn, periodically sent out delegations, as Polybius explained, "to settle differences, to offer friendly advice, to impose demands, to receive submissions, or to declare war."

After the Seleucid King Antiochus IV died in 164 and was succeeded by his infant son, Antiochus V, for example, the Senate took the opportunity to dispatch three commissioners. They were to burn the fleet and hamstring the war elephants that the kingdom had for some time possessed, in violation of its treaty with Rome. Upon their arrival, an uproar ensued, and the head commissioner was killed in a riot. Meanwhile, defying the Senate, a rival claimant to the throne living in Rome, Demetrius I, snuck out of the city, sailed from Italy on a Carthaginian ship, and back in Syria executed the infant king and seized power. Polybius, a friend of Demetrius who hunted wild boar with him in the Italian countryside, later wrote that the Senate had initially refused to enthrone Demetrius because the senators thought that the weakness of a child king would better suit Roman interests. But after Demetrius' return, the Senate allowed him to stay in power.

The story is typical of the Roman *imperium* of this era. While demanding obedience, the Senate was eager to commit as few military or financial resources as possible, especially in the east. As a result, senatorial policy was often totally opportunistic, aiming for maximum power at minimum cost. But the Senate also aimed always to be in the right, at least technically (by not violating treaties, for example). To an outsider, this all might have seemed capricious. It was one function of Polybius' history to explain to his Greek readers the logic behind the senatorial decision making of his day – and to suggest ways of coping with it.

SPAIN CATCHES FIRE

After the Second Punic War (218–201 BCE), Rome had a permanent presence in Spain, and commanders fought wars for nearly two straight decades (197–179). The vastness, fragmentation, and unfamiliarity of the Iberian Peninsula made the Romans vulnerable, especially to the Lusitanians in the mountainous west (modern Portugal) and the Celtiberians living in the high plains of central Spain. In the early 170s, Rome's two commanders coordinated their campaigns, one of them, Tiberius Gracchus, father of the famous tribune of the same name, winning the confidence of the Spaniards sufficiently to settle treaties with many of the Celtiberian communities. This brought 20 years of relative peace, although complaints about the conduct of Rome's commanders arose and went largely unheeded when brought to the Senate.

In 154 a new cycle of war broke out when independent Lusitanians invaded the territory of Farther Spain. Meanwhile, when the peoples of one Celtiberian group were found enlarging their primary settlement and erecting walls around it, the Senate ordered them to stop, while also suddenly demanding taxes that they had not been required to pay for some time. The Celtiberians resisted, and in response the Senate sent one of the consuls of the year 153 with a large army, although normally the two Spanish *provinciae* went to praetors. It is hard to avoid the conclusion that with no other major wars to fight at this time, the Senate was willing to foment one in Spain, so that the consul would have something to do.

Polybius reported that the ensuing conflict with the Celtiberians was called "the fiery war." This was because it spread like a fire, and like a fire it kept flaring up after seemingly being extinguished. When the Roman army arrived, the resistant Celtiberians found powerful allies and ambushed the

Romans. The consul, Q. Fulvius Nobilior, failed to take Numantia, a major settlement with a strategically important location in the Duero River valley. His successor, the consul of 152, M. Claudius Marcellus, managed to negotiate peace terms with the Celtiberians, but the Senate was unwilling to ratify them when the Spanish representatives reached Rome. The consul of 151, L. Licinius Lucullus, was sent to replace Marcellus, and he found that peace prevailed anyway. Lucullus proceeded to attack another people, the Vaccaei, unprovoked, and then treacherously massacred a town that had surrendered.

Meanwhile, the minor war with the Lusitanians had escalated. Lucullus joined the praetor of Farther Spain, Ser. Sulpicius Galba, and together they invaded Lusitania. Following Lucullus' example, Galba lured several tribes away with the promise of land, and then massacred them. One of the few to escape was a shepherd named Viriathus, who became a war leader. Taking advantage at first of Rome's distraction by other wars in Africa and the Balkans, and exploiting his knowledge of the Iberian landscape, he enjoyed a run of victories over Roman commanders through the year 141. The Senate assented to peace with him but then was persuaded by the consul of 140 that it could break it. Taking to the field again, Viriathus was finally abandoned by his exhausted troops and murdered in his sleep by agents bribed by Rome.

While the Lusitanians soon capitulated entirely, Viriathus' revenge outlived him. His successes had inspired another flare-up of the "fiery" Celtiberian war, and through 133 the settlement at Numantia managed to hold out against the Romans. Back in Rome, this, and the Spanish wars more generally, were nothing short of a scandal, with major long-term political consequences (see Chapter 4). In the eyes of ordinary Romans, including the soldiers drafted to fight in Spain, the ability of the Senate and certain senatorial commanders was seriously open to question – especially in the later 150s and then again in the later 140s and 130s. At the same time, the earlier humiliations may help explain the Senate's own humiliating treatment of Carthage in 150 and 149.

"CARTHAGE MUST BE DESTROYED!"

After the Second Punic War, Carthage was not only required to renounce its Spanish empire but also agreed to pay Rome an indemnity for 50 years and not to wage war without Rome's consent. By intensifying the agriculture of its hinterland, Carthage quickly regained its economic health. But it had ongoing problems with its neighbor King Masinissa of Numidia. Rewarded in 201 for his help to Rome with an enlarged kingdom, for the next 50 years the wily monarch expanded it further, eventually lopping off pieces of

Carthaginian territory. Carthage made repeated protests to the Senate, commissions were sometimes sent out, and the decision was always against Carthage. The elderly Senator Cato returned from one commission to offer dreadful warnings of Carthage's revival. He made it his habit to conclude every speech he gave, whatever the subject, with the words "Carthage must be destroyed!"

Not all agreed. Scipio Nasica – the senator who successfully blocked the building of a stone theater in Rome (Chapter 1) – thought that the fear of Carthage kept the Romans disciplined. But in 151 the hardliners had their chance. The Carthaginians' patience had finally snapped. They waged war on the eighty-eight-year-old Masinissa – with no success, and in violation of the treaty that ended the Second Punic War. When the Carthaginians meekly sent delegations to the Senate in 150, they were given brief and menacing replies. The Senate expected a full capitulation, and when it did not come, the senators began assembling on Sicily a massive expeditionary force under the two consuls of 149. Carthage now capitulated, agreeing to turn over 300 hostages and to obey whatever demands the consuls issued, in exchange for Carthage's liberty.

After the consuls reached Africa, with their legions, the demands were revealed. First Carthage was required to hand over all of its war material, which it did. And then an ultimatum was issued: the Carthaginians had to abandon their city and move at least 10 miles inland. As the Romans knew full well, to do so would cripple Carthage. The city's splendid commercial harbor, with its docks, ship sheds, and warehouses, was its economic lifeline, shipping out the region's olive oil and grain – sometimes to Roman armies – along with hides and wool, ivory and ebony, slaves from the African interior, and wild animals for staged beast hunts in Rome.

Perhaps the Senate thought the Carthaginians would accept this last humiliation, but instead they resisted ferociously. The city had a tremendous set of fortifications, behind which its men and women took refuge, heroically contriving new weapons. Women even cut their long hair to make it into cords for catapults. For several years Rome's consular commanders made almost no headway, and at one point a senatorial commission was sent to investigate why. The only bright spot, it seemed, was the leadership shown by a junior officer, Polybius' friend Scipio Aemilianus. Back in Rome, Cato praised Aemilianus by quoting a line of Homer: "Only he has wits; the rest are fluttering shadows." (The put-down of more-senior colleagues was vintage Cato.)

Defying the Senate, Roman voters demanded Aemilianus as consul for 147, even though he was technically ineligible. Legislation was passed permitting his candidacy, Aemilianus was elected, and then – in another departure from normal procedure – he was selected by voters for the command in Africa. Aemilianus managed to tighten the blockade of Carthage, and as the city's residents starved, they literally lost their strength. Finally, he breached the walls and after some appalling street fighting forced surrender. The surviving Carthaginians were sold into slavery. Although old Cato was now dead, his wish had been fulfilled: Carthage was destroyed. A solemn curse was pronounced on the site, forbidding future inhabitation.

THE GREEKS ARE BURNED

As the Senate precipitated war with Carthage, a crisis crept up in the east. In 150 the Senate finally allowed the surviving Achaean detainees of 167, fewer than 300 now, to return – as if it mattered, Cato said in debate, where "some wretched old Greeks" were buried! But in fact their return proved a destabilizing influence on Achaean politics, already embroiled in a dispute between Sparta and the other members of the federal state (the city of Corinth being the most dominant). And then a pretender to the old Macedonian throne suddenly appeared, "fallen from the sky" as Polybius put it. So weak were the four separate republics the Senate had created that the pretender, named Andriscus, easily reunited the kingdom and amassed many supporters. The Roman commander sent in 149 was defeated and killed. A larger army was sent under the praetor of 148, Q. Caecilius Metellus, and captured Andriscus.

In the meantime, in the absence of any response from the much-preoccupied Senate on the Achaean dispute with Sparta, that imbroglio worsened. Finally, a senatorial delegation arrived in Corinth in the summer of 147 and informed the Achaeans that Sparta was to be detached from the federal state, and Corinth too. Infuriated, the Achaeans began to arrest every Spartan in the city, who sought refuge with the senatorial delegation. Over the winter of 147/146, Achaean politicians rallied their cities for war against Sparta – and defiance of Rome's orders.

From Macedon, Metellus tried to negotiate a peace in Greece, but in vain. He went on to enjoy victories in central Greece and then turned the command over to the consul of 146, Mummius, who showed up with an army, as well as the fleet just freed up from the war with Carthage. Routing the remaining Achaean forces, Mummius advanced to Corinth. The Senate had given orders to plunder the city, renowned for its artistic heritage, and then burn it to the ground. Polybius travelled to the site and witnessed the destruction. He wrote in his history that he saw masterpiece paintings lying on the ground, with Roman soldiers playing games of checkers on them.

EMPIRE, ENVIRONMENT, AND ECONOMY

To understand the Senate's decision to destroy Corinth along – in the very same year – with Carthage, and to understand the development of the *imperium* overall, it is essential to consider the physical environment of the Roman world.

Even a cursory glance at a map shows that in 150 BCE Rome's imperial interests were focused on the coasts of the Mediterranean Sea and its islands (Map 2). The reason for this is clear. Travel by sea was, in general, far more efficient than over land. Armies, generals, and senatorial commissions routinely crisscrossed the waters – and they were not the only ones. The same Cato who worried about Carthage's prosperity wrote a book, *On Agriculture*, that advised large landowners to locate their estates "near to the sea or a navigable river" – precisely so that their surpluses could be sold without transportation costs absorbing the profit. In the year 150, cargo vessels of all sizes were plying the Mediterranean, some traveling short distances, others going great lengths, hopping the islands, and hugging the coasts. From Alexandria a ship might sail up the Levantine coast, to Cyprus, to Rhodes, to the Aegean Islands, and beyond, conveying from even farther away Egyptian papyrus or luxuries such as Arabian incense. The eastern Mediterranean, in particular, had developed an elaborate infrastructure for trade, including ports, independently of Rome.

The sea cut travel time and costs, but there were other ecological factors at work. The lands of the Mediterranean are associated with long, hot summers and rainy winters, a climate that favors the growth of grain as well as two more distinctive plants – olive trees and grape vines. Like the Greeks, Romans viewed olive oil and wine as markers of civilized life, and as they made their way into Mediterranean hinterlands, they cultivated these crops wherever they could. The fact is, though, that there really was a great deal of diversity even within the Mediterranean basin. The Nile valley, for instance, with its extraordinarily fertile soil, was its own ecological zone. The grain fields that blanketed Sicily were not easily achieved in more mountainous regions like southern Greece. (Other resources were distributed unevenly too, such as silver, which abounded in Spain.)

Moreover, even within a particular region there could be spectacular variations in climate year to year. There were years of glut and years of dearth, and while individual farmers or whole cities might store grain in good years as a hedge against bad, shortages frequently developed. Rome was not immune to these shortages, and the city magistrates did not entrust the food supply entirely to the free market. An inscription discovered in the 1970s, for example, shows a magistrate in Rome arranging for surplus wheat from Thessaly in northern Greece to be shipped to Rome, perhaps around the year 130 BCE. Such was the regionalism of the Mediterranean, and the pattern of boom and bust, that there were strong imperatives to redistribute. Wheat, olive oil, and other foodstuffs and resources sometimes moved across vast distances.

The physical environment encouraged redistribution and the sea fostered it, but there were real limits even on maritime commerce. The sea's currents and winds favored some routes over others, stormy winters deterred sailing at that time of year, and there were other major hazards such as hidden rocks and shoals or narrow straits with fast-moving waters. Mythology immortalized some of these: to sail the straits separating Sicily from mainland Italy was to be "between Scylla and Charybdis," two menacing monsters. Furthermore, information could only spread as fast as a ship could travel, meaning that traders could not always discover the best markets for their goods. For this reason, trade favored larger settlements with ambitious governments. This leads to a familiar paradox from ancient and also medieval Mediterranean history: despite their small sizes, islands often had large populations supported by trade. The Italian Peninsula itself, with its long coastline and central position in the Mediterranean, was well situated to benefit from exchange.

The power of water was not confined to the Mediterranean. Rivers extended the connectivity of the sea well inland, even if goods or passengers had to be transferred onto barges or rafts. It was no accident that the city of Rome was located not only near a coast, but also on a river – the Tiber. Rivers were highways.

Where rivers failed, Romans laid down the roads for which they are still justly famous. By the year 150 BCE, Italy had a network of major roads, built up as the Romans achieved dominance over the peninsula. In time, the Romans would carry the practice overseas, since they needed to be able to move armies efficiently. After the defeat of the pretender Andriscus, Macedonia became a regularly assigned *provincia*, and work soon began on a great road, the Via Egnatia, originating on the Adriatic coast. Armies and commanders, after a brief sea crossing from the increasingly busy port at Brundisium in Italy, would have a route to Thessalonica, and ultimately all the way to Byzantium. Even before Gaul was a regular *provincia*, garrisons (another method of control) were established and a road built – the Via Domitia – furnishing a good land route to Spain. Roads were named after the commanders who built them. Thus the Via Domitia perpetuated the glory of its builder, Cn. Domitius Ahenobarbus (consul in 122 BCE). While their origins were military, Rome's great roads facilitated interregional commerce as well as better communications overall.

TRADERS AND PREDATORS

Clearly, in 150 BCE the Roman Republic depended on the sea. The sea allowed the Romans to project power, whether by transporting huge armies or senatorial delegations. By the sea, armies were supplied, and increasingly the city of Rome. Like many other ancient states, Rome did not develop elaborate commercial policies, but it did invest in port facilities, on the coast of Italy and on the Tiber River in Rome itself. Furthermore, its actions had a major impact on the movements of goods and peoples. Perhaps most significantly, the spread of Roman power to the western Mediterranean opened up new markets for Italian traders. They used the Rhône River to ship wine from Italian estates to thirsty Celts who had not yet developed the wine culture France is now famous for. In turn, another commodity – slaves – was sent back.

Exact statistics are lacking, but material evidence shows an increase in trade and new trade patterns resulting from Rome's increasing presence in the Mediterranean, especially after the Second Punic War. Through underwater archeology, shipwrecks have been discovered, some of whose contents (especially pottery) survive, providing indications of what was being carried, in what quantities, and approximately when (since the pottery can be dated). Of ships wrecked prior to the year 1500 CE, the vast majority discovered date to the classical Roman period (200 BCE–200 CE). Many have been found in the western Mediterranean, and of increasing size over the last two centuries BCE. Furthermore, around the year 150 BCE, a new type of clay storage vessel came into production, designed to carry in bulk products such as wine, oil, and the salty fish sauce that was an essential ingredient in Roman cooking. The jars could be stacked horizontally in cargo holds. Italian goods were traveling farther and farther, and in greater quantities.

Italian products were even starting to penetrate the eastern Mediterranean, while eastern goods, including luxuries such as vintage Greek wines, Egyptian glassware, and works of art, were imported back with increasing ease. For this, some credit should go to the senators, however limited their commercial policy in general. During Rome's war with King Perseus of Macedon, the Aegean island of Delos – famous for its sanctuary of Apollo – was, like other states, judged insufficiently friendly to Rome. The Senate expelled the ruling class, including the priests, and handed the island over to Athens, on condition that all trade there should be customs-free. This made the island a magnet for traders from as far away as Arabia as well as Italy. A community of increasingly wealthy Italians flourished on the island, building elaborate commercial facilities as well as grand houses for themselves. Meanwhile, Rhodes – another state deemed not friendly enough during the war with the Macedonian king Perseus – lost commercial traffic, and the customs it collected at its harbors to pay for its navy dwindled.

Tiny Delos was like a turntable for goods, linking the east to burgeoning ports in Italy, such as Puteoli (sometimes known as "little Delos"). One of the main commodities trafficked on the island was slaves. According to the geographer Strabo, at its peak, Delos "could admit and send away ten thousand slaves a day." He added that they were supplied by pirates, especially pirates based in Cilicia, on the southern coast of Asia Minor, who captured free peoples and enslaved them. The Romans, Strabo hinted, turned a blind eye, so eager were they for slaves.

Throughout history, piracy has been endemic to the Mediterranean, and again geography is important for understanding why. Mountainous coastlines like those of Cilicia or the eastern coast of the Adriatic, characteristic too for its hundreds of small islands, encourage predation. Agriculture is difficult in such regions, while their fragmented landscapes offer all too many convenient spots for concealing ships and launching raids. Only an unusually well-organized state could succeed in controlling the region. It is not implausible to relate, as ancient sources do, the rise of Cilician piracy in the mid-second century BCE to Rome's weakening of eastern powers like the Seleucid kingdom and Rhodes.

There are problems with taking these sources totally at face value, however. Traders from the Black Sea, with its access to the vast Eurasian steppe, were likelier to have supplied more slaves. Moreover, the label of "pirate" was a loaded one, used sometimes by Greeks and Romans to dismiss small states with which they were at war. To its enemies, subject to mass enslavements after military defeat, Rome itself must have seemed like a pirate. The systematic plundering of cities and the imposition of taxes also led to accusations that Romans were little better than bandits. Whomever we call pirates, there can be no doubt that Rome's rise to Mediterranean-wide power, taken with the Senate's parsimonious administration, had some paradoxical results. Trade increased, but so too did predatory activity, sometimes creating challenges for traders. Pirates interrupted commerce in the Adriatic already in the third century BCE, Delos later became the victim of more than one pirate raid, and the problem of piracy ultimately became a major issue in Roman politics.

THE DESTRUCTION OF CARTHAGE AND CORINTH AND ITS AFTERMATH

When the Senate ordered Carthage to move at least 10 miles from the Mediterranean coast, it showed once again a clear appreciation of economic power. Glowering at its rival's prosperity, the Senate wanted not just to humiliate Carthage but also to proclaim the dominance of the Roman state – military and economic at once. The seas were now subject to the *imperium* of the Roman People. The message was broadcast even more clearly three years later, when, by order of the Senate, Carthage was abandoned and cursed after being plundered.

Cities had been destroyed by Rome before, as well as by other victorious states. The destruction of Troy by the Greeks at the end of the Trojan War was a turning point in the Roman (mythical) past. Still, the events of 146 shocked contemporaries – and are still shocking. Not only Carthage was destroyed; wealthy Corinth was too, and with the same solemnity as Carthage. In the east and the west, the Romans were supreme. Treaties were not to be violated, nor delegations flouted – ever. Just like Popillius Laenas back in 168, the Senate meant to awe, even overawe, contemporaries. The ruins of the cities, visible to travelers by sea, were the ultimate assertion of Roman *imperium*.

Beyond the destruction of the two great cities, the wars of the 140s resulted in some other important changes. The Senate sent a delegation of 10 to assist Mummius in the reorganization of Greece. The federal states, including Achaea, were dissolved; local democracies were discouraged in favor of pro-Roman oligarchies. Macedonia was now to be a regularly assigned *provincia*, with its commander to keep an eye on Greece. With Carthage gone, Africa also was now to be a regularly assigned *provincia*, with taxation imposed. Much of its territory, like Corinth's, became the property of the Roman people, meaning that it could be rented out at a profit. Enterprising Romans and Italians started to take over the land. The Senate commissioned a translation into Latin of a multivolume treatise on agriculture by the Carthaginian Mago – a sign, once more, that Rome was concerned with economic power.

Before he traveled to Corinth, where he acted as an intermediary between Greeks and Romans, Polybius had been with Scipio Aemilianus and witnessed the destruction of Carthage. By extending his history to include the events of 146, he was affirming what the Romans had asserted through the destruction of cities. An epoch in Mediterranean history was over. But as a Greek, committed to a cyclical view of history, Polybius could only imagine that after its spectacular rise, Rome too must decline. According to Polybius, as Aemilianus contemplated the fall of the once-glorious Carthage, he shed tears. He had a foreboding that the same doom would one day be pronounced on Rome.

FURTHER READING

There are masterly discussions in *The Cambridge Ancient History* (2nd ed.) on Rome's management of its empire in the second century (in Vol. 8, see chap. 5 by W. V. Harris, chap. 9 by P. S. Derow, and chap. 10 by C. Habicht; in Vol. 9, see chap. 2 by A. Lintott and chap. 15 by J. Richardson; chap. 16 by C. Nicolet on the economy is also relevant). On the changing idea of *imperium*, J. Richardson, *The Language of Empire: Rome and the Idea of Empire from the Third Century BC to the Second Century AD* (Cambridge, 2008), is essential. On the *imperium* of magistrates, two innovative, and sometimes contradictory, works are F. J. Vervaet, *The High Command in the Roman Republic* (Stuttgart, 2014), and F. K. Drogula, *Commanders and Command in the Roman Republic and Early Empire* (Chapel Hill, 2015); I have followed more-conventional views. B. C. McGing, *Polybius' Histories* (Oxford, 2010), introduces the historian and his work well, as does the collection of essays by F. W. Walbank, *Polybius, Rome and the Hellenistic World* (Cambridge, 2002).

The wars are well described and analyzed in J. Richardson, *The Romans in Spain* (Oxford, 1996); R. M. Errington, *A History of the Hellenistic World, 323–30 BC* (Malden, MA, 2008); and the lively B. D. Hoyos, *Mastering the West: Rome and Carthage at War* (New York, 2015). Consult also P. De Souza, *Piracy in the Graeco-Roman World* (Cambridge, 1999).

For the empire and the economy, works mentioned in Chapter 1 are helpful – in particular, W. Scheidel (ed.), *Cambridge Companion to the Roman Economy* (chap. 7 by A. Wilson, chap. 8 by G. Kron, chap. 10 by P. F. Bang, and chap. 11 by C. Adams), and G. Woolf, *Rome: An Empire's Story* (especially chap. 4 on ecology). N. Morley's *Trade in Classical Antiquity* (Cambridge, 2007) usefully brings in ecology. On the environmental setting, a landmark study is P. Horden and N. Purcell, *The Corrupting Sea: A Study of Mediterranean History* (Oxford, 2000), while D. Abulafia's *The Great Sea: A Human History of the Mediterranean* (London, 2011) gives a linear narrative.

N. Purcell's essay "On the Sacking of Carthage and Corinth," in D. Innes, H. Hine, and C. Pelling (eds.), *Ethics and Rhetoric: Classical Essays for Donald Russell on His Seventy-Fifth Birthday* (Oxford, 1995), 133–48, is characteristically exciting.

3

THE CITY OF ROME: SCENE OF POLITICS

AND GROWING METROPOLIS

By the mid-140s BCE, Rome was in desperate need of more water. Only two aqueducts supplied the city, both were in bad repair, and individuals were believed to be diverting water from them. Rather than wait for a new pair of censors (the magistrates elected only every five years who typically awarded contracts for public works), in 144 the Senate took the unusual step of commissioning the praetor Q. Marcius Rex to repair existing water lines and bring in a new supply. He did so, probably reviving an earlier abandoned project to create his new aqueduct, and named it (after himself) the Aqua Marcia. It ran an impressive length of 56.5 miles and was the first to use arches on a grand scale, springing across the landscape. Not surprisingly, work was incomplete by the end of 144, and the Senate had to extend Marcius' official authority.

In 143, he faced a new, unexpected challenge. A college of priests entrusted with the Sibylline Books, a collection of Greek oracles allegedly dating from the time of Rome's pre-republican kings, insisted that it was improper to extend an aqueduct to Capitol Hill, with its ancient and important temple of Jupiter. They shared their finding with the Senate, which ordered Marcius to stop. It was a couple of years later, when the matter was reopened, that he was allowed to finish the line all the way to the Capitoline and so take full credit for it.

But was the aqueduct entirely his? Coins issued around the year 114 BCE by a mint official named Aemilius Lepidus appear to show an aqueduct, and arguably it is the one started by the censor of 179, also named Aemilius Lepidus, and then revived by Marcius in 144. Lepidus' coin could be an attempt to restore to his family some credit for the project. A later member of Marcius' family, in turn, issued coins in the 50s BCE with a similar design – and clearly labeled AQUA MAR (abbreviating "Aqua Marcia"). Intriguingly, on the opposite face of this same coin is Rome's early king Ancus Marcius,

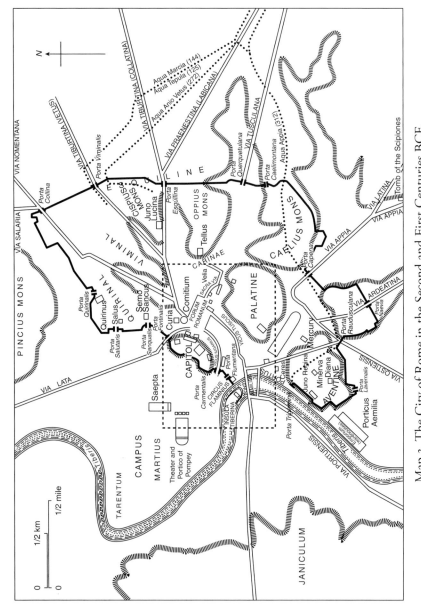

Map 3 The City of Rome in the Second and First Centuries BCE

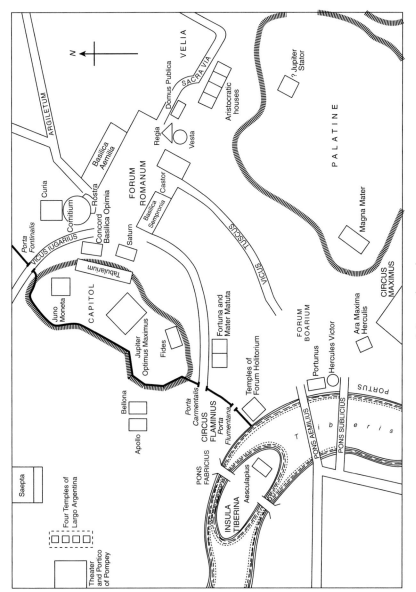

Map 3 (cont.)

Figure 3.1 A silver coin of mint official Mn. Aemilius Lepidus, issued around 114 BCE. The three arches below the equestrian statue have been interpreted as showing the aqueduct begun by the great censor of 179, M. Aemilius Lepidus. (Photo © The Trustees of the British Museum.)

Figure 3.2 A silver coin of mint official Marcius Philippus, issued in the mid-50s BCE, showing the Aqua Marcia. On the obverse is Rome's legendary king Ancus Marcius, his headband denoting royal authority. (Photo © The Trustees of the British Museum.)

from whom the family was proud to claim descent – even though Romans were supposed to hate kings! It was King Ancus Marcius, the family was now maintaining, who built the first (then lost) Aqua Marcia, leaving any claims for priority by the Aemilii in the dust.

The debate over the new aqueduct, its construction, and the coins cast much light on Rome in the 140s and beyond. Thanks especially to Rome's burgeoning empire, as well as to expanding trade networks and the ability to manage resources, including water, the city was growing. Eventually it would become the largest in the Mediterranean, with a population perhaps of a million people by 50 BCE. This was an urban giant without parallel in European history until the nineteenth century. Those living in it had new, distinctive needs arising from the city's risk-filled environment. Able to mass in the thousands, residents also found new ways to exert pressure on politics.

Despite Rome's expansion overseas, politics remained entirely based in the city, with citizens required to assemble in large open spaces if they wished to vote. Other important rituals took place in Rome, such as the census held every five years and the routine games that honored the gods whose temples and shrines filled the city. Extraordinary spectacles such as triumphal parades and funeral processions also brought the people together and were a showcase for senatorial families. In spectacles as well as in buildings, illustrious families like the Aemilii and Marcii competed for power and prestige, with the empire bringing in the resources to make this possible.

COUNTING THE PEOPLE

The census was an institution at the heart of the Roman state in the second century. This was because it not only counted the Roman People, but it also categorized them, determining each man's military role and voting rights. Every five years, adult male citizens were required to make a declaration to the censors in Rome or to local representatives. The first requirement was to state your full name. Each male citizen had a family name (usually ending in "ius" like Marcius) and a first name (such as Quintus) to distinguish himself. Since there were very few first names, these were frequently abbreviated (e.g., Q. = Quintus). Increasingly, male citizens also had an additional name, to distinguish branches of the family (Rex meant "king"). The end result was the distinctive threefold name (Q. Marcius Rex). Women, by contrast, customarily only had a single name, the feminine form of the father's family name (so any daughter of Marcius was Marcia). In addition to giving his name, the declarant in the census would state his age, the name of his father (or, if he was a freed slave, the man who freed him), his place of residence, and the property he held.

The censors used the information to register the male citizen into two important divisions: the voting tribe and the century (*centuria*). The tribe was a division based on locality; altogether there were 35, with just four, the so-called urban tribes, representing the city of Rome. The other voting group, the century, was based essentially on the amount of property held. Early in Rome's history, this was directly linked to one's role in the army. The wealthiest men, for example, formed the 18 centuries of cavalry (the *equites*, or Equestrians). Note that each century could have well more than 100 men, the original number. Altogether there were 193 centuries, the vast majority of them assigned to one of five property classes. Those without significant property formed a single century, called the *capite censi* ("counted by head"). While the military purpose of the centuries was mostly obsolete in the mid-second century BCE (*equites* were not really the cavalry, for example), the landless *capite censi* were still normally excluded from army service.

In addition to conducting the census, the censors supervised the community's morals, and this too had consequences for individuals' status. Censors could examine men physically and morally; since it was the citizens who made up the state (the Roman People), bad men should have limited roles. The censors could remove a man from his voting tribe. They could banish a man from the Senate, and in fact it was they who formally admitted men to the Senate – usually younger magistrates, priests, or other members of distinguished families. Men could also be banished from the *equites* – if, for example, they were too fat to ride properly in the horseback parade that was now a ceremonial part of each census. After the whole census was over (about 18 months), the censors purified the city in a religious ceremony.

Censors went on moral crusades, and none was more famous for this than Cato. Serving in 184, he set out "to cut away the hydra-like luxury and effeminacy of the age." He placed steep taxes on items he judged extravagances, such as jewelry. He cut the pipes by which Romans were illegally conveying public water to their houses and gardens. He ruthlessly expelled members of the Senate he deemed unworthy. Why, one of them had dared openly to kiss his wife, with their impressionable young daughter looking on! For his part, Cato said, he never kissed his wife unless there was loud thunder, which at Rome meant that public business could not go forward.

Literary sources report for many censuses the total number of adult male citizens counted (Table 1). These statistics might fail to include soldiers serving overseas and also fluctuated according to how assiduous the censors were. They also excluded women and children. As a very rough estimate, we could slightly triple the figure of male citizens to get the overall citizen population. Also excluded are non-Romans – notably the Italians allied with Rome and expected to contribute militarily. In 225 BCE, we happen to be told, they outnumbered the Romans roughly two to one. Excluded, too, were slaves, a rapidly expanding group in the second century.

A surprise in the surviving statistics is the declining number of male citizens after the census of 164/163. As we shall see (in Chapter 4), there may be reasons for this other than population loss, yet Roman politicians had real concerns about dwindling manpower – it could impact Rome's ability to win wars. Censors urged men to marry, and even contemplated requiring it. "If we could exist without a wife, Citizens, we would all free ourselves of

Table 1 Roman Census Totals, 252/251–70/69 BCE

252/251	297,797
247/246	241,212
241/240	260,000
234/233	270,713
209/208	137,108 (237,108)
204/203	214,000
194/193	143,704 (243,704)
189/188	258,318
179/178	258,294
174/173	269,015
169/168	312,805
164/163	337,022
159/158	328,316
154/153	324,000
147/146	322,000
142/141	328,442
136/135	317,933
131/130	318,823
125/124	394,736
115/114	394,336
86/85	463,000 (963,000)
70/69	910,000

Note: Most scholars have interpreted these tallies as referring to the total number of adult male citizens. For a full discussion, concluding that the tallies refer only to adult male citizens who were legally independent heads of their own families, see S. Hin, *The Demography of Roman Italy* (Cambridge, 2013), especially chap. 7. The figures in parentheses are proposed corrections to the immediately preceding figures transmitted in the manuscript tradition of the literary sources.
This table is based on P. A. Brunt, *Italian Manpower* (Cambridge, 1971), 13–14, and S. Hin, *The Demography of Roman Italy* (Cambridge, 2013), 351–53.

that annoyance," one of them argued, perhaps not too persuasively, "but . . . we must give thought to our survival rather than transitory pleasure."

If the count of male citizens declined, what does this mean for the city of Rome itself? There are far fewer numbers here, and plotting population shifts even decade by decade is impossible. In the 50s BCE, when an entirely free grain dole was introduced in the city, 320,000 recipients (adult male citizens) are said to have received it. Adding women, children, and others who were excluded (e.g., foreigners and slaves), we could easily bring the overall total to one million. Subsidized grain began much earlier, in the 120s, and almost certainly was a magnet for immigrants. Still, an overall population for the city of Rome of 250,000 is entirely plausible for 150.

There were other magnets to draw men and women to Rome, including jobs – especially jobs in construction. A major project like the Aqua Marcia must have employed thousands, but there was steady work on smaller commissions such as houses or the temporary theaters built for annual games. Teachers, doctors, and artists came from the Greek world. Many came involuntarily, to work as slaves in the households of the well-off. In exchange for income they brought in, they could be freed and gain citizenship, being registered in one of the four urban tribes. Ex-slaves were an important component of the urban population (see Chapter 10).

THE LAYOUT OF THE CITY AND THE PEOPLE'S ASSEMBLIES

A map of Rome in the late republic gives a useful orientation to the city's topography, including its famous hills, the Tiber River, and the large floodplain at the Tiber's bend, known as the Campus Martius (the Field of Mars). The Campus was where boys did physical training, an essential activity in Rome's martial culture. Along the riverbanks were clustered port facilities, marketplaces, and warehouses, including an immense structure traditionally assigned to the same Aemilius Lepidus whose aqueduct was never finished. Altars and temples important to sailors stood near the river too.

Everywhere in Rome there were temples, none more important than Jupiter's on the Capitol. The area around it was sacred (meaning it belonged to Jupiter) and was filled with statues that reminded the Romans of their history. There were representations of the early kings and also L. Junius Brutus, who drove out the last of these kings and helped found the Republic. On other hills, such as the Palatine, lived wealthy senators, enjoying the more salubrious air. Poorer Romans crowded together on the lower ground – for example, in the valley between the Quirinal and the Viminal, known as the Subura, a neighborhood with plenty of bars and brothels.

In another valley, between the Capitol, Palatine, and Velian Hills was the very heart of Rome, the Forum. It was lined on its long sides by two basilicas, large halls (named after similar structures in the Greek world) where business and legal proceedings were transacted. One of them was built by the busy censor of 179/178, Aemilius Lepidus. Networking was at its easiest in the Forum, and citizens could come to learn all the latest news. The Forum was a political center too. At its western end was the Curia (Senate house) and also one of the traditional meeting places for the voters, the Comitium. Statues scattered around here – including a representation of Rome's founders, Romulus and Remus, suckling a she-wolf – also helped teach history. A clear sign of Rome's growth was the decision in 145 to move voting out of the Comitium, which might only have had room for three thousand men, into the Forum itself.

Voting assemblies were the core of the Roman political system. They elected all magistrates, and only they could pass laws. There were four distinct

Table 2 The Voting Assemblies

	Curiate assembly (*comitia curiata*)	Centuriate assembly (*comitia centuriata*)	Tribal assembly (*comitia tributa*)	Plebeian assembly (*concilium plebis*)
Voting units	30 *curiae*	193 centuries: 18 *equites* (cavalry), 170 *pedites* (infantry), 5 unarmed	35 tribes, divided into 4 urban and 31 rural tribes	
Citizens attending	In late Republic, each *curia* represented by a lictor	Open to all	Open to all	Open to plebeians (patricians restricted)
Presiding officer	Consul or praetor	Consul or praetor, or if no consul at the beginning of the year, an *interrex* to hold consular election	Consul, praetor, or curule aedile	Tribune of the *plebs* or aedile of the *plebs*
Election		Of consuls, praetors, censors	Of curule aediles, quaestors, lower magistrates	Of tribunes and aediles of the *plebs*
Bills	Passed law confirming appointment of magistrates	Rarely passed laws after 218 BCE except for declarations of war and confirmation of the censors	Legislation of any type except that restricted to the centuriate assembly (most laws were proposed by the tribunes of the *plebs*)	
Meeting place	Comitium	Outside sacred boundary of Rome, almost always the Field of Mars	For elections, the Field of Mars (or, very rarely, the Capitol) For legislation, the Forum (the Comitium before 145 BCE) or the Capitol	

Source: This table is closely based on the one in L. R. Taylor, *Roman Voting Assemblies from the Hannibalic War to the Dictatorship of Caesar* (Ann Arbor, 1966), 4–5.

assemblies (Table 2), but all were similar in that the voter always voted only as part of a group. For example, in the curiate assembly, one voted in a *curia*, or neighborhood group. This was Rome's oldest assembly and almost purely ceremonial in the late Republic, mainly serving to pass laws confirming certain magistrates elected by the other assemblies and also to witness adoptions.

The centuriate assembly, also quite old, was in origin an assembly of the army. Even in the late Republic it had to meet in Campus Martius, beyond the sacred boundary (*pomerium*) of the city that armies were forbidden to cross. This assembly could only be called by a senior magistrate to pass laws, to vote formally to go to war, and – most important – to elect the next year's senior magistrates, consuls, praetors, and censors. The voting unit here was the century, described earlier.

On election day, voters would gather by the huge rectangular structure known as the Sheepfold or Pens (Saepta), because it was divided into discrete alleys. The Equestrians and also the seventy centuries that made up the first property class voted first. Men would proceed up the individual alleys, several abreast, but then individually walk over wooden gangways called "bridges" to cast their vote. Voting was oral until 139, when a secret ballot was introduced in all electoral assemblies. Votes for each century were tallied. As soon as a candidate had a majority (97 centuries), he was declared a winner, and once a full slate of magistrates was elected, voting stopped altogether. This meant that the centuries in the lower class, including the single landless century that voted last, might not vote at all. In this assembly, the votes of wealthy citizens were valued much more highly than those of the nonwealthy.

Passing a law in the centuriate assembly proceeded along the same cumbersome lines, with the result that in the late Republic most legislation was enacted in one of the remaining two assemblies. The tribal assembly consisted of the 35 tribes described previously, with just four assigned to the city of Rome and the remaining 31 to communities of Roman citizens beyond. Seventeen of the 31 tribes had at least some territory within a day's travel from Rome, but citizens living far away were seriously disadvantaged.

Figure 3.3 A toga-clad Roman citizen is shown on this silver coin voting. He has crossed the wooden gangway or 'bridge' and is dropping the tablet with his vote into a wicker basket on the right. (Photo © The Trustees of the British Museum.)

The plebeian assembly was a near twin of the tribal assembly and actually was born first, out of social struggle. In the early years of the Republic, a small number of established families (the patricians) were dominant. The mass of citizens (the plebeians) began meeting and passing their own resolutions; they also had their own officers – eventually 10 tribunes – who were to protect the plebeians. In 287, plebeian resolutions were made legally binding on the whole community, and plebeians had overall attained equality with the hereditary patricians (who dwindled in number but always had the cachet of their ancestry). The plebeian assembly used the same 35 tribes as the tribal assembly but simply excluded patricians from voting. It passed much legislation in the late Republic, and it also elected annually 10 tribunes as well as two aediles (junior magistrates in charge of the fabric of the city). The tribal assembly elected two more aediles, as well as the quaestors (junior magistrates with financial responsibilities).

Both electoral and legislative meetings of the tribal assemblies were typically held in the Comitium, until the year 145. Traditionally the Comitium was also where citizens – and perhaps others too – came together for the *contio*, a meeting called by a magistrate to discuss new legislative proposals or other matters of importance. As the people stood, he would address them from an elevated platform decorated with ships' beaks (*rostra*) captured in a naval battle and therefore called the Rostra. Like other magisterial platforms, this was sacred space and thus offered the speaker some protection. While those attending could express their views through cheers, catcalls, or gestures, ordinary citizens could not ordinarily gain recognition to speak individually as they could in the more genuinely democratic assembly of Athens.

Topography was not just the backdrop for Roman political life but was intrinsic to it. Just as voting moved from the Comitium into the Forum, so did the *contio*, allowing an audience of perhaps 6,000 or even 10,000 rather than 3,000. To hold such a meeting effectively, the magistrate would need to turn around on the Rostra, and thus he would no longer be facing the Senate. An ancient biographer suggested that Gaius Gracchus, a tribune in the 120s, was the first to do so. By just slightly pivoting his body, Gracchus "stirred up a great question." Were the magistrates, including the tribunes, too subservient to the desires of the Senate?

THE THREE BRANCHES OF GOVERNMENT: MAGISTRATES, SENATE, AND PEOPLE

The Roman People passed laws in assemblies, but they needed an agent to execute their wishes, and this was the function of the annually elected magistrates (Table 3). Each of the magistrates had at least one colleague, to prevent a monopolization of power the Romans associated with kingship.

Table 3 The Magistrates about 150 BCE

General Principles and the "Career Path" (*cursus honorum*)

1. The magistrates were elected annually by voting assemblies for terms of one year (except for censors, elected only every five years). They entered office on January 1 (except for tribunes, who did so on December 10).
2. Office was always shared with at least one colleague; distinct spheres of activity (*provinciae*) might be assigned to each.
3. By 150 BCE, the praetorship was required before the consulship; a quaestorship was usually held first and became mandatory under Sulla, creating the standard career path of quaestor/praetor/consul. The aedileship and tribunate were optional steps before the praetorship. Censors usually were former consuls.

Title and Number	Main Functions
Censor (2)	Censors took the census, revised the Senate membership, had oversight of morals, awarded public contracts.
Consul (2)	Consuls were the heads of state; granted *imperium*, they levied armies and commanded in war abroad; in Rome they presided over the Senate and enforced laws.
Praetor (6; after Sulla, 8; by 44 BCE, 16)	Praetors, also granted *imperium*, could command abroad and regularly did so in Sicily, Sardinia, and the Spains; in Rome they oversaw the legal system and were the head of state in the absence of the consuls abroad.
Aedile (4)	Aediles oversaw the grain supply and festivals in Rome and maintenance of Rome's buildings.
Tribune of the *plebs* (10)	Tribunes presided over the plebeian assembly and proposed legislation to it; because of their sacrosanctity, tribunes could aid other citizens and veto legislation, most Senate decrees, and elections (except elections of other tribunes).
Quaestor (at least 8; after Sulla, 20)	Quaestors administered the treasury in Rome; abroad, they assisted more senior magistrates with financial administration and military and judicial tasks.

The consuls – the top executive officers – could veto one another's actions. Both consuls had *imperium*, the supreme power that allowed them to command in war and also (according to the standard view) to execute laws and inflict punishments in the city of Rome itself. *Imperium* was powerfully symbolized by the bundle of rods (*fasces*) carried by the magistrates' attendants. The symbol was appropriated by the totalitarian politicians of 1920s Italy, giving rise to the word "fascism." The six praetors had *imperium* also: in the mid-second century BCE, normally four were given overseas commands while two served as judicial officers in Rome. Aediles handled the city of Rome's games, food supply, and buildings. Quaestors were junior financial officers. A still-more-junior board of three was elected to run the mint and influenced the design of coins. Laws set minimum age limits for some of the magistracies and also limited repetition of office, especially the consulship.

An utterly distinctive post was that of the tribune of the *plebs*. Ten were elected yearly, and in addition to presiding over the plebeian assembly, they were, at least by tradition, supposed to protect the lives and property of the people – especially from actions by other magistrates. Tribunes individually could veto legislation, end most official business, stop the other magistrates from carrying out punishments, and bring magistrates to trial. They had no special insignia like the *fasces*; they were supposed to be available day and night, at their houses with the doors open or sitting on special benches in the Comitium. Their power lay in their inviolability: anyone who laid a hand on a tribune was accursed, meaning that he had to be killed as a sacrifice to the gods.

The Senate's role was to advise current magistrates, including tribunes, by issuing decrees understood as binding but not legal. In the mid-second century BCE, the Senate had perhaps 300 members, mostly ex-magistrates. We have already seen the Senate's crucial role in shaping foreign policy and assigning commands. The Senate also concerned itself with the maintenance of order in Rome and Italy. Through its control of state funds, it could arrange for major new building projects, even if the censors themselves normally issued the contracts for these. Taking advice from the major colleges of priests, all of whom were senators, the Senate ruled on religious matters too – for example, when the dispute arose over the Aqua Marcia.

The Senate always met indoors, in the Senate house near the Comitium or in a temple. Meetings could be behind closed doors and decisions kept secret. Far more than in *contiones*, it was here that genuinely free debate might take place. The presiding magistrate, often a consul, would introduce a topic for discussion, and senators were called on to state their views. The first to speak was the *princeps senatus*, the senator chosen by the censors to head the list of members. The *princeps* was almost always a senior patrician. Open voting preceded the issuing of decrees. Fixed procedures like this helped resolve debates among its members (who were quite competitive) over allocations of command and resources.

From Polybius on, historians have been fascinated by the interactions among the three branches of Roman government: the People, their magistrates, and the Senate. Polybius argued that at least at the time of the Second Punic War (218–201 BCE), each was powerful but that if one became too powerful, it would be blocked by the others. This neat system of "checks and balances" was to be hugely influential 17 centuries later on the founders of the United States of America. Polybius himself was aware, though, that despite continuities, the balance was always subject to renegotiation. In his view, the influx of wealth was a destabilizing factor. We could add the growing size of the city of Rome, since it changed the dynamics of how magistrates and ordinary citizens interacted.

By the mid-second century there were some clear limits on the magistrates' executive power. Not only could tribunes veto their actions, but a series of laws had been passed concerning "appeal" (*provocatio*, in Latin, meaning "crying out," as in crying out for help). These laws stated that magistrates could neither put citizens to death without a trial before the assembled people nor flog them. The laws were guarantees of *libertas* – the freedom from arbitrary action by magistrates, or kings – that Roman citizens tended to take very seriously. The introduction of the secret ballot in 139 – an act with real significance for the balance of power in the Republic – was viewed as a further enhancement of popular liberty.

A particularly important question was how much the Senate (and senators) deferred to the citizens as a whole. In his analysis, Polybius claimed that "the Senate stands in awe of the masses and takes heed of the People's will." Yet prior to the Second Punic War, the Senate tried unsuccessfully to stop a tribune from passing legislation that distributed to Roman citizens plots of land conquered in northern Italy.

Conflict between the Senate and tribunes revived around the year 150. In 138, for example, two tribunes pressed the consuls to have the Senate

Figure 3.4 A silver coin from around 110 BCE that illustrates the precious right of appeal. A swaggering general threatens the toga-clad citizen on the left. The citizen cries out *PROVOCO*, "I appeal!" (Photo © The Trustees of the British Museum.)

authorize special purchases of grain for the city because of a price spike. Called to a *contio*, one of the consuls – Scipio Nasica, son of the man who blocked Rome's stone theater – stopped the crowd shouting by saying, "Citizens, please, be quiet; I understand better than you what is in the public interest" (or so a later source records). Reports such as this one may be less objective testimony than salvoes in ongoing political controversy.

An essential part of the debate about the nature of the Roman Republic, then and now, is the electoral success enjoyed by a relatively small number of families, both patrician and plebeian, over multiple generations. Members of these families came to be identified as the *nobiles* (literally "the well known"). The historian Sallust claimed that in the second century "the nobility passed the consulship from hand to hand among themselves."

Modern research at least to some extent agrees with Sallust. Examination of known officeholders clearly shows that it was extremely hard for newcomers to the Senate to achieve election to the consulship even though the Senate itself was constantly refreshed with members from new families. Some modern researchers have argued that the reason for the nobles' success was their creation of relatively small factions of families who would secure prizes for one another – not just political offices but priesthoods and commands. A further part of this thesis is that the well-established families could mobilize electoral support directly through ties of patronage. A far better explanation, however, can be found by returning to the original meaning of *nobiles*.

PUBLIC SPECTACLES: THE REAL BASIS OF ARISTOCRATIC SUCCESS

Senatorial patronage was an important tradition. Each morning senators opened their houses to even the humblest Romans and would offer meals, gifts, legal advice, and more. In exchange, these "clients" might accompany the senator around Rome, to suggest his importance and support him with their votes. To facilitate visits by clients, senators lived near the Forum.

But personal patronage alone cannot explain why well-established families enjoyed so much success, down to the year 50 BCE. After all, newcomers to the Senate often had a great deal of wealth to share. Even more important, as Rome had grown, so had the number of voters. Senators' houses were growing bigger as well, but they could not receive thousands. It was, therefore, at public spectacles that senators could impress large numbers of citizens.

One of the most important of these was a funeral, which struck Polybius so much that he left a detailed account of it. After a man who had attained at least the rank of aedile died, his body would be carried in a procession to the Forum. There, from the Rostra, his son or another young family member would deliver a eulogy. Actors portraying the ancestors of the deceased who had also held political office joined the procession. They wore wax masks of the dead family members (normally stored in the main hall of the family house) as well as magisterial robes. These "ancestors" would listen as the eulogist recited not just the dead man's accomplishments, but also those of earlier generations. Later there might be a public banquet and games, which often featured gladiatorial combat – sure to draw a large crowd.

For noble families, the funeral was a golden opportunity to remind the community, including its newest members, of their names. In the later second century, noble families even regularly began holding such public funerals for their women. Polybius writes of how moving these events could be, as the Roman People saw the heroes of their early days almost brought back to life. The funeral did not just help the political fortunes of the young eulogist. As Polybius saw, it was an institution that helped inculcate core aristocratic values, such as military valor. Funerals burnished the reputation of the nobility by demonstrating their commitment to public service.

Another hugely important spectacle was the triumph. This was an honor voted on by the Senate to pay tribute to a commander who had earned a notable military victory. Assembling on the Campus Martius with his army, the commander would parade through the streets of Rome. Spoils taken in war were carried on litters – weapons, precious metals, works of arts. Paintings showed highlights of the campaign. Captured enemies stumbled along in chains. The general, dressed in purple and silver, rode in a chariot to the Capitol, where he sacrificed white oxen to Jupiter. Again, a banquet and games followed.

Triumphs usually lasted only a day, but their glory was perpetuated in many ways. At a funeral, an "ancestor" who had won a triumph wore the special triumphal costume. The Senate and People often erected public statues for those who had celebrated triumphs. And the triumphant general used the plunder he had taken to enhance the city of Rome. After his victory in Macedon in 148 for which he earned a triumph, Caecilius Metellus used some of the spoils to fund a new temple for Jupiter, the first in Rome built entirely of marble. A twin for a temple of Juno, it was enclosed in a portico – essentially a covered walkway – within which Metellus put on display his most prized plunder, including a famous statue group of Alexander the Great and his companions.

Over the years, triumphing generals transformed Rome with buildings and displays like this one – and in doing so helped future generations of their families. Other types of buildings monumentalized families. Although censors used public funds, they gave their own names to the grand basilicas or infrastructure

Figure 3.5 A Roman holding portraits of two of his ancestors. The busts are not the wax masks worn by actors at the aristocratic funeral but their warts-and-all realism is typical of Republican portraiture and the style might have been influenced by the masks. Museo del Palazzo dei Conservatori, Rome, Italy. (Photo Album/Art Resource, NY.)

projects they constructed – structures that thousands would see and use. No wonder, then, if the Marcii and the Aemilii fought over "naming rights" for the great aqueduct of the 140s. Even a house could become a monument: victorious generals decorated their doorways with glittering arms and armor captured from the enemy. Cato once gave a speech reminding Romans that the spoils had to be captured – and not, for example, purchased.

While nobles skillfully displayed their inherited glory, spectacles reinforced the power of even regular magistrates. The sight of them walking around Rome with their attendants – and, yes, their clients – was impressive. Moreover, they presided over regular games in honor of the gods who protected Rome, held each year according to a fixed schedule. Statues of the gods would be brought out of the temples and paraded on floats through Rome to the Circus Maximus, the vast racetrack that filled the valley between the Palatine and Aventine Hills. There, along with thousands of Romans – men and women, rich and poor – the gods would watch professional chariot racing. All sorts of dramatic performances were shown on temporarily erected stages. There were tragedies, comedies, and even a racy genre called mime in which women were allowed to perform, without masks, and perhaps without much clothing either. The magistrate in charge could win extra glory if he supplemented the regular entertainments with his own resources, bringing in exotic animals for a staged beast hunt, for example. The games that Rome is still so famous for in the popular imagination had their origin in religion, and in the politicians' never-ending quest for publicity.

CIVIC RELIGION AND RELIGIOUS PLURALISM

Polybius was stunned at how much religion permeated public and private life at Rome. Unlike the Greek world, here politicians were also priests, and it seemed to Polybius that they used religion almost consciously to bind society together. Certainly the gods were ubiquitous. Their temples filled the city, in addition to which there were many statues of them, and they were honored not just with grandiose games that did indeed bring citizens together but also by small gifts left at their altars. In part, the sheer number of deities worshipped was a reflection of Rome's growth. As the Roman state fought foreign powers, it tried to win over those powers' gods by offering them a new temple and cult at Rome.

Gods were, in a sense, the most powerful members of Roman society, and senators took their wishes seriously. Rome had four major priesthoods, each of which cultivated a distinctive expertise and had specific duties (Table 4). Particularly important was the pontifical college, which advised the Senate and individual citizens on matters of sacred law (example: How should you treat statues of gods seized as plunder in war?). This college

Table 4 The Major Colleges of Priests

	Pontiffs (*pontifices*)	Augurs (*augures*)	Board of 10 (later 15) for sacred actions (*decemviri sacris faciundis*)	Board of three (later seven) for public feasts (*tresviri epulones*)
Members	Nine pontiffs from 300 BCE; 15 pontiffs after Sulla, 16 after Caesar; there were additional members, including 6 Vestal Virgins	Nine augurs from 300 BCE; 15 augurs after Sulla; 16 after Caesar	Ten from 367 BCE; 15 after Sulla, 16 after Caesar	Three from 196 BCE; 7 after Sulla
Functions	General supervision of public cult; control of sacred places and calendar; advice to Senate and individual citizens on sacred law	Supervision of and advice concerning auspices, divine signs of approval or disapproval for particular actions	Custodianship and consultation (on request of the Senate) of Sibylline Books	Supervision of festivals
Selection	Priests were selected by members of the colleges until the Domitian Law of 104 BCE, and again from the reforms of Sulla to 63 BCE; at other periods they were elected by 17 out of the 35 tribes (chosen by lot), with candidates nominated by the colleges. The head of the college of pontiffs, the *pontifex maximus*, chose the additional members such as the Vestal Virgins.			

This table is based on Table 1 in J. A. North, *Roman Religion* (Oxford, 2000).

included, in addition to the pontiffs, the Vestal Virgins – six women who, on pain of death, had to guard their celibacy and tend the flame that represented Rome's continuity. The head of the college was called *pontifex maximus*, a title later borrowed and still used by the popes.

Relying on the advice of priests, the Senate was the ultimate decider in religious matters. Reports of unusual, even sinister, events known as prodigies – thought to be signs of divine anger – were sent to the Senate. An ancient book collects these reports for the years from 190 BCE onward and gives a sense of how such reports were resolved. For example, an entry in the year 142 explains that "since there was famine and an epidemic, offerings were made by the board of 10." Priests advised in the face of military disaster too. It was very likely a Roman defeat in the Alps that prompted the board of 10 to consult the Sibylline Books, leading to trouble for Marcius Rex.

The role of priests extended well beyond the Senate, and at the same time the priests could be challenged. All public actions, including voting, the census, and even war making, were preceded by the taking of auspices. This required the magistrate to watch for signs from the gods, such as thunder and lightning. A bad sign meant that the contemplated action should be deferred to another day (luckily for Cato, this did not include kissing!). The college of augurs had special expertise in auspices. But the People in their assemblies also passed a series of laws concerning auspices. In 145, a tribune proposed that future vacancies in the priesthoods be filled by election (the practice was for each college to appoint its members). This bill failed to pass, but a similar measure would succeed 40 years later. The intertwining of religion and politics makes a certain type of skeptic, like Polybius, suspect that religion was manipulated for political purposes. A more compelling view of the evidence is that the Roman People and the Senate alike cared for the gods who had made Rome so powerful.

Roman religion never stood still – and it went beyond civic religion. Already by the early second century BCE there was a steep decline in the number of new gods officially recognized, while private religious associations proliferated, some with secret rites. If mighty gods like Capitoline Jupiter held sway over Rome's imperial destiny, there were other deities, and other experts like astrologers, who could speak to the concerns of ordinary Romans – their health and material well-being. A sign of the times was a decree issued by the Senate in 139 that expelled astrologers from Rome, at once showing senatorial conservatism and proliferating religious activity. Despite such actions, which were justified on the grounds of public order, the Senate did not really concern itself with matters of individual belief. The polytheistic nature of Roman religion enabled a pluralism that usefully complemented shared rituals like the games and allowed individuals to find a place in smaller communities.

GETTING BY IN THE CITY

The city of Rome was full of risks. One of the worst was epidemics. Epitaphs recording the day or month of death have revealed a pattern of seasonal mortality, with a high concentration of deaths in August through October. The cause, in part, was mosquito-spread malaria, endemic to Rome but peaking at this time of year. Malaria itself could kill, or it could weaken people susceptible to other infectious diseases such as tuberculosis. Along with flows of human beings, animals, and goods, new pathogens regularly made their way into Rome. The high population density helped spread disease. Waters, including the Tiber, provided breeding grounds for malaria-infected mosquitoes. Overall, the death rate in the city was high, even for young adults and especially for immigrants with less resistance to malaria.

There were other sources of misery. Floods of the Tiber – which helped spread diseases, including malaria – were also devastating to property and life. Fires, too, were a constant threat. While ordinary Romans might live in shops or apartments attached to the houses of the wealthy, the less fortunate crammed into rickety buildings of many stories that were firetraps. Add to this recurring, if not chronic, grain shortages and price spikes, and life could be quite difficult.

Public services around the year 150 BCE were quite limited. There were no firefighters, no public health officials, and no police. Theft was only a civil offense, requiring victims to sue for the recovery of stolen property, or to take the law into their own hands. However, magistrates did take action in the face of acute food shortages. The Senate made investments in major infrastructure projects like the Aqua Marcia, which brought vital drinking water into Rome. There were the public games, increasingly outdoing any other city's, and these could feature ever-popular free food.

Inhabitants of the city found support in one another. Funerary monuments reveal that freed slaves – not necessarily related – formed such strong emotional bonds that they were buried together. There were formal groups as well that linked citizens, organized along sometimes-overlapping lines of profession, neighborhood, and religion. They would ensure burial for their members – welcome assurance in a world where death could strike so suddenly. Familial ties were often essential, such as those of husbands and wives, parents and children. Censors might have celebrated an old-fashioned ideal that the good wife was the obedient wife, but epitaphs show men far more often calling their wives "very dear" and "well deserving" – just as wives described their husbands. In addressing citizens, politicians would appeal to men's desire to protect their families. When a tribune proposed a bill to investigate Sulpicius Galba for his treacherous attack on the Lusitanians in Spain (see Chapter 2), Galba brought his young sons into the Forum to arouse pity for himself – with great success. Obligations to kin were taken seriously.

As the metropolis grew, so did the threats posed by epidemics, fires, and food shortages. Still, the wealth of empire, as it poured in and paid for massive projects like the Aqua Marcia and lavish houses for senators, attracted migrants. Spectacles like the triumph and the games became more extravagant, entertaining thousands – while also confirming the power of the senatorial nobility. The city of Rome was the stage of politics, where citizens identified themselves as citizens, through the census, at voting assemblies,

Figure 3.6 An early Augustan funerary monument of a Roman, Lucius Vibius, who married an ex-slave, Vecilia. With her veiled head and serious expression, Vecilia is the height of respectability. In between the couple floats a young boy, almost certainly their son; he has the same jug ears as his father. Vatican Museums, Rome, Italy. (Photo Alinari/Art Resource, NY.)

and to an extent in *contiones*. They asserted their freedom with pride. The increasing number of citizens below the Equestrian class who resided in the city, referred to as the *plebs urbana*, were emerging as a distinctively powerful force – a good example of Rome's structural differentiation. Their interests did not necessarily correspond with those of citizens in the countryside, much less of Italians who lacked the vote altogether. This was to be one of the greatest issues facing Romans in the late Republic.

FURTHER READING

A splendid introduction to the ancient city of Rome is P. Erdkamp (ed.), *The Cambridge Companion to Ancient Rome* (Cambridge, 2013), including chapters by N. Morley on population size, W. Scheidel on disease, E. A. Dumser on topography, A. Ziolkowski on civic rituals, N. Purcell on games, and A. Bendlin on religion. On demography, see also W. Scheidel, "Human Mobility in Roman Italy, I: The Free Population," *Journal of Roman Studies* 94 (2004), 1–26.

The relationship between politics and topography is well described in J. Patterson's *Political Life in the City of Rome* (London, 2000); see also his articles "The City of Rome" and "The City of Rome Revisited," *Journal of Roman Studies* 82 (1992), 186–215, and 100 (2010), 210–32, respectively. Topography is also a theme of C. Nicolet's *The World of the Citizen in Republic Rome* (London, 1980), which attaches great importance to the census. Other works helpful for thinking about politics in the mid-second century BCE (and beyond) are a classic article by L. R. Taylor, "Forerunners of the Gracchi," *Journal of Roman Studies* 52 (1962), 19–27; A. W. Lintott's "Political History, 146–95 B.C." in *The Cambridge Ancient History* (2nd ed.) Vol. 9; various essays in F. Millar, *Rome, the Greek World, and the East – Vol. 1* (Chapel Hill, 2002, especially chaps. 3–5); R. Morstein-Marx, *Mass Oratory and Political Power in the Late Roman Republic* (Cambridge, 2004); and K.-J. Hölkeskamp, *Reconstructing the Roman Republic* (Princeton, 2010). Refer also to the works mentioned in Chapter 1.

H. I. Flower makes clear the importance of the aristocratic funeral in *Ancestor Masks and Aristocratic Power in Roman Culture* (Oxford, 1996); see also her excellent chapter on spectacle in her *Cambridge Companion to the Roman Republic* (2nd ed., Cambridge, 2014). On religion, a landmark study is M. Beard, J. North, and S. Price, *Religions of Rome* (2 vols., Cambridge, 1998), while J. North, *Roman Religion* (Oxford, 2000), is a good, and briefer, introduction. For spectacle, religion, and much more see the splendid essays in E. Rawson, *Roman Culture and Society* (Oxford, 1991).

There are many good studies of Roman marriage and family life, including S. Treggiari, *Roman Marriage: Iusti coniuges from the Time of Cicero to the Time of Ulpian* (Oxford, 1991); S. Dixon, *The Roman Family* (Baltimore, 1992); and K. R. Bradley, *Discovering the Roman Family: Studies in Roman Social History* (New York, 1981). A comprehensive introduction to slavery is K. Bradley and P. Cartledge, *The Cambridge World History of Slavery* Vol. 1 (Cambridge, 2011).

On coins and monuments, including the aqueducts, see A. Meadows and J. Williams, "Moneta and the Monuments: Coinage and Politics in Republican Rome," *Journal of Roman Studies* 91 (2001), 27–49. The Aqua Marcia is discussed (rather differently than in this chapter) by M. G. Morgan, "The Introduction of the Aqua Marcia into Rome, 144–40 B.C.," *Philologus* 122 (1978), 25–58. In general, see P. J. Aicher, *A Guide to the Aqueducts of Ancient Rome* (Wauconda, IL, 1995).

4

THE STRUGGLE FOR REFORM (150–104 BCE)

"The wild animals that roam over Italy have every one of them a den or hole to lurk in, but the men who fight and die for the country enjoy the common air and light but nothing else." It was with words like these, according to the Greek biographer Plutarch, that a tribune of the *plebs* named Tiberius Sempronius Gracchus persuaded voters in 133 BCE to pass a law to help citizen soldiers who had lost their farms. Son of a noble senator with an impressive record of command, Tiberius was a man of great courage himself: when the final assault on Carthage began in 146, he was the first – along with his friend Fannius – to scale the immense city walls. Tiberius believed that lands seized by Romans in war, which belonged to the state, should be given to the brave peasants who were the backbone of the army. Soldiers should not be fighting just to protect "the wealth and luxury of others."

With this and subsequent proposals, Tiberius started a contentious debate on the division of the profits of war and empire, and his political techniques aroused even fiercer controversy. Senators felt that Tiberius was taking away their power, and before the year was out Tiberius and his supporters were massacred in the sanctuary of Jupiter on the Capitol. The mixed constitution Polybius so admired, with equilibrium among Senate, People, and magistrates, had proved unable to resolve peacefully the dispute over where power lay. Moreover, as the Greek historian Appian wrote of the bloodshed in his *Civil Wars*, "this foul crime, the first that was perpetrated in the public assembly, was not the last." In hindsight, the tribunate of Tiberius ushered in a willingness to use violence that would grow worse in later years, ultimately undermining republican government.

The politics and violence of Tiberius' tribunate provoked an outpouring of history writing as well as more-popular mythmaking. Tiberius' younger brother Gaius made key contributions, publishing a short book about

Map 4 Italy and Sicily

Tiberius after his death. In passionate speeches, Gaius bewailed the fate of the martyr: "Those scoundrels, they slew Tiberius, my noble brother!" The accounts on which we mainly rely, those of Plutarch and Appian, written in the second century CE, often reflect stirring rhetoric like this. For Plutarch, Tiberius and his brother were heroes – courageous, generous, idealistic – with Tiberius' opponents motivated by sheer greed. This picture of a clash between the defender of the poor and the rich is too simple. Tiberius' reforms had much to do with the dragging on of unpopular wars in Spain and a growing willingness of tribunes to challenge the Senate's management of the empire.

For all the violence of Tiberius' tribunate and the decades that followed, these years had a political creativity that is easily overlooked. Romans were taking steps that would help make Rome the world state it was by the age of Augustus. In the tribunate of Tiberius' hard-working brother Gaius, for example, voters passed innovative legislation that would maximize and allow advanced projection of tax revenues in the recently acquired province of Asia. The money raised would help fund another law, which made grain available at a fixed price for citizens in the city of Rome. Legislation like this contributed to the structural differentiation of Roman society and the strain on the traditional institutions of SPQR. Yet it also was at the heart of new conceptions of a more ambitious and powerful Roman state that ran its overseas empire with greater efficiency.

THE POLITICS OF EMPIRE

For years after Carthage was destroyed, war in Spain persisted. The assassination of the shepherd-turned-general Viriathus in 139 finally more or less ended the long Lusitanian war (see Chapter 2). But the "fiery" war against the Celtiberians was still alight, with the hilltop fortress of Numantia holding out. Over the winter of 140/139, the Roman commander Q. Pompeius, who was camped nearby, was himself put under siege and forced to negotiate a peace on terms favorable to the Numantines. Not surprisingly, the Senate rejected the peace, before the People could even vote to ratify it. In 138 the consuls proceeded to hold a military levy for another year's fighting, at which point something shocking happened.

At a levy, citizens of military age were required to appear in Rome or other designated locations. From this group, the strongest candidates would be selected by the magistrate(s) or officer(s) in charge. An initial posting overseas could last up to six years. The yearly pay was 480 sesterces, but money was deducted to cover living expenses and equipment. If plunder was taken in campaigning, though, soldiers could expect a share. Thus when a good general held a levy for a war that promised loot, many might volunteer, including those with battle experience. Finding men to fight in the often-lucrative wars fought in northern Italy after 200 BC seems to have posed little problem. Conversely, at the levy for an unpopular war, many men would have to be compelled to serve – or might even fail to appear.

At the levy of 138, two tribunes threw the consuls into chains and dragged them to Rome's small prison. One of the consuls, the abrasive Scipio Nasica, also happened to be *pontifex maximus*. Ostensibly the tribunes acted as they did because they had not been allowed to exempt certain men from the levy, a right they customarily enjoyed. But in all likelihood they were actually protesting the way the Senate, and senatorial commanders, had been using war in Spain to glorify and enrich themselves, while failing to bring victory and sometimes harming ordinary soldiers.

The crisis of 138 was built on earlier frustrations. Already in 151 tribunes had briefly imprisoned both consuls for carrying out the levy for Spain too strictly. One of the consuls, L. Licinius Lucullus, was determined to fight, and when he made it to Spain, he attacked several peoples unprovoked. In 149, a tribune proposed trying Lucullus' perfidious colleague, the praetor Ser. Sulpicius Galba, and releasing those Galba had enslaved. Arousing great pity with his speeches of defense, and also perhaps by distributing bribes, Galba just managed to defeat the tribune's proposal. It was probably in response to this debacle that another tribune, C. Calpurnius Piso, passed a law setting up a permanent court to try senatorial magistrates for extortion (the stealing of money from those subject to Roman power). Verdict was to be given by small juries of senators, and the punishment for the guilty was payment of damages. By delegating some of their judicial authority, the People hoped to make magistrates more accountable.

Hand in hand with greater scrutiny of senators' conduct came a renewed emphasis by tribunes on the individual citizen's liberty. In 139, the People passed into law the secret ballot for elections, replacing oral voting. The new measure made it harder for senators to coerce (or bribe) more-vulnerable citizens. Two years later, a secret ballot went into effect for most trials before assemblies. A bill extending the citizen's right of appeal to active-duty soldiers may also have been passed around then – and would make perfect sense amid the ongoing wars in Spain.

Although the imprisoned consuls of 138 were quickly released, problems continued – as Tiberius Gracchus was to see firsthand. In 137, yet another general, C. Hostilius Mancinus, was defeated by the Numantines and trapped. Forced to make a peace, he and his officers were required by the wary enemy to swear oaths that it would be upheld. Serving on Mancinus' staff as quaestor was Tiberius Gracchus, and in fact it was Tiberius who negotiated the peace. The Spaniards, fondly remembering Tiberius' father, who had himself negotiated a long-lasting peace in 178, trusted him. By his efforts, Tiberius "clearly saved the lives of twenty thousand Roman citizens," wrote Plutarch.

Yet back in Rome there was a storm of protest. Insisting on the unconditional surrender of the Numantines, the Senate refused to ratify the peace. Mancinus agreed with the Senate and blamed his defeat on the poorness of his army. Meanwhile, relatives of the soldiers in Spain flocked around Tiberius, rejoicing at how he had saved their loved ones. While under normal circumstances the Senate did not have to honor a commander's agreements, there was the problem of the oaths that Mancinus and his staff had sworn. To break them could bring the gods' wrath on Rome. A Senate panel found a solution, based on a precedent from Rome's ancient history: the general and his staff would be stripped naked and surrendered to the enemy. Legislation was presented to the People on the matter, and they voted to hand over Mancinus but spared all the other officers. Tiberius was saved.

But the war had to continue. A law against second consulships then in effect was suspended to allow the election of Scipio Aemilianus in 135, and he was then given command in Spain. He did not bother to hold a levy and relied instead on volunteers, including some sent by foreign kings friendly to him, such as the king of Numidia. Just as he wore down Carthage by a blockade, Aemilianus now threw up massive fortifications six miles in circumference around Numantia. The city fell and was razed to the ground in 133.

Meanwhile, there was an unexpected calamity in another part of the large empire. In 135, a slave rebellion broke out in Sicily. Workers on estates and shepherds, used to defending their flocks with arms, joined together and defeated several Roman armies. A major granary for Rome was now in jeopardy – and at a time when supplies were needed for Spain. Prices must have soared in the city of Rome. Thus when Tiberius Gracchus embarked on his tribunate, citizens were in the midst of ongoing debates – about Rome's military preparedness, the competency and ethical standards of the Senate, and the distribution of imperial profits.

TIBERIUS GRACCHUS CHALLENGES THE SENATE

The reform that Tiberius proposed in 133 concerned Rome's "public land" (*ager publicus*) in Italy, territory seized in war or confiscated from rebellious allies. It belonged to the state (that is to say, the Roman People), but from the fourth century on was often distributed to poorer citizens, who together formed new colonies with their own local identities. As war in northern Italy came to an end, colonization there and elsewhere stopped in 177 BCE.

Remaining public land was leased out and cultivated by individual proprietors. According to Appian and Plutarch, over the second century certain landowners had come to view much of this public land as their own, taking advantage of the absence of men overseas on military service. Smaller farmers, these two writers assert, were displaced, and gangs of foreign slaves replaced them. The result was a decline in the number of free peasants who could serve in Rome's army. Reported census figures may corroborate this account, since they trend downward after 164/163 (see Table 1) – although it must be remembered that they give the overall number of male citizens, not just those eligible for military service.

Modern historians have attempted to build on Appian's and Plutarch's cursory narratives. Some have argued that long terms of military service, as well as the influx of slaves able to work on large plantations, drove many poorer citizens off private land as well as public. Yet more recent research suggests that this picture of agrarian crisis is overdrawn (see Chapter 6). Survey archeology suggests that small farms still existed alongside plantations, and it also has been observed that military service took men away for lengthy terms long before the 130s.

How then to explain Tiberius' sense that something was badly wrong? According to Gaius Gracchus, his brother grew alarmed when, traveling through Etruria on his way to serve in Spain, he saw a countryside filled with slaves. Likely he did see some large estates on the Etrurian coast, and perhaps he generalized from these. Adding to his worries was the slave rebellion in Sicily. There also was the conspicuous problem of recruitment during the Spanish wars, as well as the falling census count. As fewer men showed up for service, evading levies, even perhaps the census (hence the falling count), Tiberius grew convinced that Rome's military dominance was endangered. And so, just as in earlier times humbler citizens could gain a fresh start on state-founded colonies, now they could do so on reclaimed *ager publicus*.

Tiberius tried to draft as moderate a bill as possible. He was helped by some powerful allies in the Senate, including the *princeps senatus* Appius Claudius, who happened to be Tiberius' father-in-law, and one of the consuls of 133, P. Mucius Scaevola (Table 5). The proposal that they came up with allowed current occupiers of public land outright possession of up to 500 Roman acres, and improvements made to holdings beyond that – which would be returned to the state – would be compensated. Then a commission of three senators would redistribute the excess to new colonists, in lots that they could not sell. These colonists would be eligible for military service, and, perhaps even more important, they would be able to support families. Their sons would grow up into the strapping soldiers Rome would need to ensure military dominance into the future.

Table 5 The Family of the Gracchi

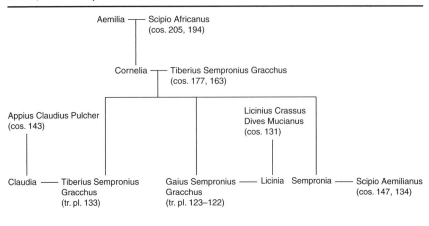

Despite the concession to current occupiers, Tiberius knew that there would be opposition. Rather than allowing the Senate to debate the proposed bill – as was often done with legislation – Tiberius took it straight to voters, publicizing it in a series of *contiones*. Tiberius was a skilled orator and used words, probably like those quoted earlier, to stir his audience, which included men who came in from the countryside to support him. At least initially, his critics in the Senate seemed less interested in arguing publicly, although at one point some of them walked around the Forum dressed in mourning, as a protest. Their plan was to have a tribune who was a friend of Tiberius, M. Octavius, veto the bill. Usually such a veto (or a veto threat) was used simply to delay proceedings until a compromise could be reached. But in a major departure from tradition, Octavius made it clear he would not back down, despite strong popular support for Tiberius' bill.

Matters soon reached an impasse. Tiberius decided to simply ignore his colleague's veto and gathered the plebeian assembly to vote on his law. His opponents appeared and knocked over the urns from which lots were to be drawn to decide the order in which the tribes would vote. Two former consuls begged Tiberius to refer the whole matter to the Senate. He agreed to do so, but the Senate, which alone had the power, proved unable to broker a compromise. The People in their assemblies were not permitted to modify pending legislation.

Now it was Tiberius' turn to again flout convention. He proposed a bill depriving Octavius of his tribunate and proceeded to have it passed in the plebeian assembly. Refusing to recognize it, Octavius was dragged away from the Rostra by supporters of Tiberius – a shocking action, since tribunes were supposed to be inviolable. While the agrarian bill now passed, many were disturbed by Tiberius' methods. A former consul named T. Annius Luscus challenged Tiberius in the Senate, leading Tiberius to summon a *contio* at which Annius was forced to appear. There Annius asked the key question: What if Tiberius injured Annius and Annius appealed to another tribune for help? "Will you then depose that man from his office?" Tiberius could not answer. Annius had suggested that Tiberius had undermined the office of tribune. Tiberius' removal of Octavius, with physical force that violated Octavius' sacrosanctity, certainly was a departure from the practice of earlier tribunes.

After the bill's passage, Tiberius' opponents were able to resume their obstruction by having the Senate refuse to fund the commission of three (comprising Tiberius, his younger brother, and Appius Claudius). An envoy then arrived from Pergamum, a wealthy state in western Asia Minor whose kings for decades had done the Senate's bidding. The envoy told Tiberius that King Attalus had died and that he had left his kingdom to the Roman People. Tiberius proceeded to present a bill to the People recognizing the inheritance, which could be used to fund the commission. As for the fate of the cities in the kingdom, which Attalus intended to have at least nominal freedom, that was no business for the Senate, Tiberius said coolly. He would submit a plan to the People.

In usurping the Senate's traditional control of foreign policy and finance, Tiberius had gone too far. The denunciations of him redoubled, and all that had happened before took on a more sinister appearance. Tiberius, his opponents felt, was aiming for kingship. This was in violation of a law that Romans believed was established when the Republic was founded; according to this law, aspiring tyrants should be sacrificed to the gods.

BLOODSHED IN JUPITER'S SANCTUARY

Fearful of what would happen to him after his term of office ended, Tiberius shifted tactics. In another break with convention, he announced that he would run for a second term as tribune. To his critics, it was just more regal behavior. Since his rural supporters were busy with the harvest, Tiberius decided to appeal to the large population within the city of Rome itself. It was much easier for them to hear Tiberius' ideas at *contiones*, or elsewhere in the city. Tiberius' new supporters could vote for him and also help control voting spaces – to prevent any more obstruction by his opponents there.

The night before Tiberius hoped to be reelected, his supporters occupied the sanctuary of Jupiter on the Capitol, where voting would take place. As proceedings began the next morning, a disturbance broke out and word of it reached a Senate meeting in progress. The *pontifex maximus* Scipio Nasica – who as consul in 138 had been thrown in prison by the tribunes – demanded that the consul Scaevola put down the "king." Scaevola refused. For there was another ancient law, the law of appeal, that held that no magistrate could put to death a citizen unless the People had ordered it. Nasica was thus forced to assemble his own forces. Veiling his head with his toga, he ran to the steps of the Temple of Jupiter. By doing so, he was asserting that Tiberius must be sacrificed to the gods. Tiberius, along with many of his supporters, was then killed in the sanctuary.

As Plutarch later wrote, it was "the first outbreak of civil strife in Rome to end in bloodshed . . . since the abolition of the kings." Behind the struggle was no simple clash of rich and poor, although money was definitely at stake. Hoping to solve what he perceived as a social crisis, Tiberius had reminded the Roman People that the wealth of empire should be theirs. In doing so, he unleashed some powerful forces in politics, perhaps more powerful than he realized. From this point onward, the plebeian assembly, with its tribunes, would repeatedly challenge senatorial management of the empire. Urban crowds in the growing metropolis again would be rallied, to control space. And violence again would be used to try to settle quarrels – both political and, as time went on, personal.

In the years immediately following his death, Tiberius' legacy was contested. While the Senate decided that it would allow Tiberius' agrarian commission to continue operating, in 132 it established a panel chaired by the consuls to seek out and punish Tiberius' supporters. Some, including Tiberius' Greek teacher of rhetoric, were put to death. Others were simply banished – perhaps especially citizens, so that the law of appeal would technically not be violated. High-ranking supporters of Tiberius seem to have escaped punishment. One of them, Papirius Carbo, became tribune (perhaps serving in 130) and tried to strengthen both the People's power and the office of tribune. He introduced, successfully, a secret ballot for all legislative assemblies and proposed, unsuccessfully, indefinite reelections to the tribunate. Scipio Aemilianus, back from Numantia, opposed the latter bill. Questioned at a *contio* by Carbo about Tiberius' murder, Aemilianus said that the deed was justified if Tiberius had aimed to overwhelm the Republic. When the crowd hissed, Aemilianus snapped back at them. Aemilianus died unexpectedly soon after that, and adherents of Tiberius – including even Tiberius' sister, who was married to Aemilianus – were suspected of murder. These suspicions showed how high feelings still ran about Tiberius.

Overseas, there was rebellion to contend with in Pergamum. It was led by a resourceful man named Aristonicus, who claimed to be the son of the late king Attalus' predecessor. In 133, the Senate had decided to acknowledge

Attalus' will, accepting the royal lands as property of Rome while allowing the cities freedom. Five commissioners, including Scipio Nasica, whom the Senate thought it prudent to send from Rome, went to make a settlement. Upon their return (minus Nasica, who died), the Senate decided that a consul would need to take an army in 131 to put down Aristonicus. With the treasures of Pergamum awaiting and the chance of a triumph, it was a command to make senators' mouths water.

One of the consuls of 131 was P. Licinius Crassus Mucianus, one of Tiberius' distinguished senatorial sponsors in 133 and father-in-law of Gaius Gracchus. He managed to wrest the command away from his colleague, exploiting a point of religious law (he was now *pontifex maximus*). A better lawyer than general, he was captured and killed in Asia. His successor turned the tables, and it was left to the consul of 129, M. Aquillius, along with a senatorial commission, to make a settlement. Following the recent precedent in Macedonia, Asia was to become a regularly assigned *provincia*. New roads were built, and the territory (really just western Asia Minor) was organized, with some lands given to local kings who had supported Rome in the recent war. Gifts of thanks flowed to Aquillius. After his return to Rome in 126 and the celebration of a triumph, he was put on trial for extortion. The new *provincia* was clearly a goldmine, and citizens could well ask who should benefit from it.

THE SCANDAL OF THE WINE JARS

The memory of Tiberius weighed on his brother, Gaius, who grieved at how Tiberius and his supporters had been killed. Gaius also saw how the Roman People could enjoy more of the fruits of imperial success with tribunes acting on the People's behalf, pushing through reform. Gaius worked hard to develop a style of speaking that could electrify huge audiences in the Forum. According to Plutarch, he would stride up and down the Rostra as he spoke and wrench his toga off his shoulder, freeing his left hand to make dramatic gestures. A specially trained slave signaled if he became too high-pitched and emotional.

Thanks to the biography of Gaius by Plutarch and to Appian's *Civil Wars*, Gaius' career is fairly well known, especially his two consecutive terms as tribune (123–122). Reconstructing politics in the earlier 120s is more difficult. The annexation of Asia, as we have seen, was one major issue; another was the question of the Italian allies bound to Rome by treaty.

By 129 some of the allies were complaining about the land commission established by Tiberius' law. To judge by the jump of 75,000 census declarations between 131 and 125 (see Table 1), the commission had been successful. The problem was that wealthy Italians were losing public land they had laid claim to (perhaps unjustly), while poorer ones gained nothing since they were not Roman citizens. Eager to undermine Tiberius' legacy, Scipio Aemilianus, shortly before his death, seized on the complaints and persuaded the Senate to shift responsibility for adjudication to the consul. A war across the Adriatic conveniently then took the consul away, leaving the commission stymied.

Could Italian objections be overcome? In 125, a stalwart supporter of Tiberius, Fulvius Flaccus, was consul and proposed offering Roman citizenship to the Italians. This would make them eligible for land – and also of course service in the legions, something not all might have sought. Those who did not desire citizenship would receive instead the same protection against Roman magistrates that citizens enjoyed. The allies, it seemed, were increasingly subject to abuse. In one of his speeches, Gaius Gracchus told a shocking story of a consul who showed up in an Italian town along with his wife, who wished to bathe in the men's baths. When the baths were not cleared sufficiently quickly, the consul had the local official publicly beaten. Before Flaccus could pass his Italian legislation, however, the Senate sent him to Gaul to help Rome's ally Massilia in a struggle with its Celtic neighbors.

Probably after Flaccus' bill died, there was an uprising against Rome, by the people of Fregellae. Fregellae was one of Rome's so-called Latin colonies – settled mostly with Romans who had given up full citizenship for land but retained certain "Latin rights." Even in the darkest days of the Second Punic War, the Latin colonies had stayed loyal to Rome, and so the revolt of 125 was shocking. The Senate responded by destroying the city to the ground. No source explains the revolt's origin; if not linked directly to Flaccus' bill, it might have been in response to the increasing harshness that the Roman Senate and magistrates were evidently showing.

Gaius was out of Italy from 126 for a couple of years, serving as quaestor in Sardinia. The army he was with had a terrible winter, suffering from a shortage of grain even though the island normally was a grain exporter. After Sardinian towns complained to the Senate of forced requisitions, Gaius persuaded them to provide voluntarily; he also had the king of Numidia send grain for the army. As Gaius' term of office was extended, he grew impatient and returned to Rome in advance of his governor. A complaint was made to the censors then in office, and Gaius skillfully defended his record, showing his regard for those subject to Roman *imperium* and for the People's money. "I brought back empty from my province the purse that had been full when I got there," he said. "Others took out full jars of wine, and brought the jars back home overflowing with money." No bribes were going to him, he paid his own way, and he was tough enough to drink the awful local wine!

Winning the tribunate for 123, Gaius quickly sought passage of two laws. One would disqualify a man deposed from a magistracy from all further political office. The other affirmed that the People could prosecute a magistrate who killed or banished a citizen without trial. The second law, which passed, was clearly aimed at Popillius, the consul of 132 who had enthusiastically led the inquisition of Tiberius' supporters. Even before its passage, Popillius fled Rome. The first law was aimed at Tiberius' fellow tribune and opponent, Octavius. Gaius let it drop, but the hint of what he could do to an obstructive colleague had been made.

GAIUS GRACCHUS: THE COMPREHENSIVE REFORMER

Gaius had a bold political program, focused on the overhaul of the Roman state's finances. Other senators, he said, were using office to enrich themselves. "You should increase your revenues," he told the citizens, "to meet your own needs and manage the state more easily." Over his two years as tribune, Gaius pushed through a raft of laws to these ends, sometimes getting his fellow tribunes to formally propose the bills to help win support. Distribution of public land was to resume, and also new colonies were to be established, in Italy and in the fertile lands around Carthage seized in 146. For the inhabitants of Rome, a law was passed making grain available at a fixed price, and public granaries were established, thus removing one of the great uncertainties of life. Gaius initiated other public works projects that offered jobs, including road building.

Costs for all this exceeded existing revenues, which is where the new province of Asia came in. The People passed a law by which a contract to collect taxes there, including customs duties, was to be auctioned every five years by the censors. The state had long relied on such concessions – for collecting customs dues at ports, for example, or to supply armies. Wealthy men organized themselves into companies, which for revenue contracts paid up front what they expected to collect. These men, called *publicani*, sent agents to collect the amount bid, along with some profit for the company. With Gaius' law, a huge and predictable revenue stream was in principle now guaranteed.

Ordinary Romans benefitted, and so too did the wealthy *publicani*. The businessmen were not members of the Senate, but Gaius created a new role for them politically. To prevent senatorial commanders from benefitting financially from their service overseas, Gaius had a tribunician colleague pass a new extortion law, large portions of which survive on bronze tablets. Along with his oratory, these yield insights into his views. The law concerned itself with crimes such as accepting unsolicited bribes or demanding money for favorable judgments. In the court that would hear such charges, jurors would no longer be senators – who might be too lenient on one another – but the wealthy men were still classified by the censors as Equestrians even though they no longer actually served in the cavalry. Later sources suggest that Gaius was trying to create an Equestrian order to undermine the Senate, but this is anachronistic. He was trying to improve senatorial administration.

Apparently without controversy, Gaius was elected to a second term as tribune. He then tried to pass a bill reviving his ally Fulvius Flaccus' Italian proposal of 125. Those with Latin rights were to receive full Roman citizenship, and the other allies, Latin rights. Some Italians came to Rome to support Gaius (those with Latin rights could vote, but they were all assigned by lot to just one of the 35 tribes). The consul Fannius, a one-time supporter of Gaius who had scaled the walls of Carthage with Tiberius, cleverly stoked opposition by asking citizens "If you give citizenship to the Latins, I suppose you think that you will still find somewhere to stand to listen to a *contio* or to attend games and festivals as you do now?" Gaius' opponents co-opted more of his supporters by having a tribune, Livius Drusus, put forward – on the authority of the Senate – a set of reforms to benefit the People, even outdoing Gaius in the number of colonies proposed. Away in Africa, trying to establish his own colony at Carthage, soon to be abandoned, Gaius fell from favor and failed to win a third tribunate.

Efforts were soon under way to undo Gaius' measures, led by the consul of 121, L. Opimius. Along with Fulvius Flaccus, Gaius recruited supporters who would resist Opimius if he resorted to violence. At an assembly on the Capitol, one of Opimius' attendants was killed, and his body was conspicuously displayed in the Forum the next day. The Senate passed a decree instructing Opimius to take action to preserve the safety of the state, and he soon had Cretan archers and other special forces at his disposal. This was virtually military mobilization, far exceeding the use of force in Tiberius' tribunate.

Gracchus and Fulvius were summoned to appear before the Senate, but instead they fled with their supporters to the Aventine, a hill associated with the much-earlier struggle of the plebeians against the patricians. Opimius' forces advanced, and his archers routed the Gracchans. Fulvius was found in hiding and killed, while Gaius took his own life. Altogether, 3,000 are reported to have died, many of them executed by Opimius after being cast into prison. The corpses were thrown into the Tiber River like garbage, as they had been in 133, and Rome was then ritually purified.

The following year, out of office, Opimius was put on trial before the People by a tribune, on the grounds of taking citizens' lives without trial. He was acquitted. Implicitly at least, the legality of the novel type of Senate decree he had acted on was affirmed, and it would be used again – controversially.

Borrowing a phrase from the writings of Julius Caesar, modern historians refer to it as the "ultimate decree of the Senate."

Gaius' legacy was enormous. To be sure, some of his measures were rescinded. A tribunician law allowed Popillius, convener of the inquisition of 132, to return from exile. By 111, the work of Tiberius' land commission, revived by Gaius, was ended, and large amounts of what had once been *ager publicus* were now legally recognized as private. But the Asian tax law endured, and the extortion law, while subsequently modified, left a lasting footprint. More than Tiberius, Gaius had welcomed new forces in politics: the Italians, the wealthy Equestrians, and city dwellers reliant on subsidized grain. Temporarily defeated, his supporters would not forget the fate of the martyrs. Politicians would be willing to challenge the Senate even more directly in the years ahead.

"AT ROME, EVERYTHING IS FOR SALE"

Political history after 120 is again poorly documented. Thanks to Plutarch's biography of the great general Marius, we do know that already in 119 a tribune (Marius) was clashing with the Senate again. Marius came from a wealthy Equestrian family and so was a "new man" (*novus homo*) in politics; he had no masks of his ancestors to show off, nor could he boast of their triumphs. As a junior officer he had the luck to serve at Numantia, where his toughness impressed Scipio Aemilianus. This led to further military postings and connections with other nobles, including the powerful and prolific Caecilii Metelli. Q. Caecilius Metellus, the conqueror of Macedon and consul in 143, left behind four sons, all of whom became consuls and two, censors. With help from this family, Marius won election as tribune for 119. When Marius introduced a law to guarantee the secrecy of voting, Consul Cotta had the Senate decree that it was opposed and summoned Marius to appear. Marius refused to back down. He threatened to imprison Cotta for threatening the People's interests. And he then did the same to the other consul, who happened to be one of Macedonicus' sons, L. Caecilius Metellus. After Metellus vainly appealed to the other tribunes to defend him, the Senate withdrew its opposition. The new man had out-muscled the nobility.

Another victory over the Senate concerned the colony at Narbo Martius (in southern France). The background to this was Roman campaigning in Transalpine Gaul in the later 120s. After victories over major Celtic tribes, the consul of 122, Cn. Domitius Ahenobarbus, began constructing a road from the Pyrenees to the Rhône River. Probably in 118, a Gracchan-style law was passed establishing a full-citizen's colony on the road, at Narbo. When the Senate tried to overturn the law, L. Licinius Crassus, a forceful young speaker who was destined to be one of Rome's best, spoke against the Senate and saved the colony. With many non-Roman settlers, it flourished.

Crassus was soon involved in another display of the People's rights, one that more directly challenged several key nobles. In 114, the daughter of a wealthy Roman was reported to have been struck by lightning and stripped naked. Religious experts had no doubt that this was a sign from the gods that the Vestal Virgins, the six priestesses who tended the flame of the hearth goddess Vesta, had failed to maintain their sexual purity and had thereby endangered Rome. By year's end, three of them – Aemilia, Licinia, and Marcia – were on trial before the pontiffs. Only Aemilia was found guilty. Outraged at what seemed a cover-up, the People passed a tribunician law to censure the *pontifex maximus* – none other than L. Caecilius Metellus, the consul whom Marius had crossed in 119 – and to appoint L. Cassius Longinus as special investigator. Cassius had a reputation as a strict judge and convicted Licinia and Marcia, as well as their alleged lovers, despite a plea of defense by Licinia's relative Crassus.

From 112 an increasingly important issue in domestic politics was the situation in Numidia, the North African kingdom that had goaded Carthage to war and then ruin. King Micipsa, a faithful ally to Rome, had died in 118, leaving three sons, Adherbal, Hiempsal, and Jugurtha, the last of whom was illegitimate. A physically powerful man who was famous in Numidia for his feats of hunting and horsemanship, Jugurtha had also won over Roman senators by his energetic service under Scipio Aemilianus at Numantia. After Micipsa's death, Jugurtha's soldiers had Hiempsal murdered and Jugurtha began plotting to take over Adherbal's portion of the kingdom. In 116, Adherbal sent envoys to the Senate, and then appeared himself, while Jugurtha only sent envoys – with bribes for important senators, according to the historian Sallust.

Along with Plutarch's *Marius*, Sallust's monograph *The War with Jugurtha* is the major historical source for this period, and it is not without its problems. In powerful prose, Sallust convincingly shows how, after the Gracchi, tribunes rallied voters angry at the Senate's conduct. But it is harder to accept at face value Sallust's portrayal of most senators as totally corrupt. According to Sallust, Jugurtha had learned from his high-ranking Roman friends at Numantia that "at Rome, everything is for sale," and this was why he had his envoys bribe the senators. But in truth, the Senate responded to the envoys much as would be expected even without the bribes. It decreed that 10 commissioners should go to divide the kingdom between the two rivals. The commission's head was L. Opimius, the consul who had destroyed C. Gracchus and his supporters in 121. Sallust alleges that he and some of the other envoys, once in Africa, were bribed by Jugurtha. But in truth, Jugurtha got the worse part of Numidia. This fact helps explain why Jugurtha then attacked Adherbal, driving him to the hilltop capital of Cirta in 112, which was put under siege.

Jugurtha's war with Adherbal proved a turning point. Envoys went back and forth between Rome and Africa, but the Senate initially refused to help Adherbal militarily. While Sallust claims once again that senators had been bought, the unwillingness of the Senate to commit resources was typical. But the situation was transformed when Italian businessmen trapped in Cirta with Adherbal persuaded him to surrender, in the aftermath of which some of the Italians were killed. A tribune, Memmius, stoked feelings of outrage in Rome. The Senate had no choice now but to declare Numidia a province, which was assigned to the consul of 111, Calpurnius Bestia.

But the outrage continued. Enjoying some quick successes, Bestia reached a preliminary settlement with Jugurtha and returned to Rome. Rumors circulated that Bestia and Jugurtha had cut a deal. The ferocious tribune Memmius again stirred up citizens at *contiones*. Sallust includes in *The Jugurthine War* a fiery speech composed – like all speeches in the writings of ancient history – by the historian himself but probably reflecting the kinds of arguments Memmius actually made. In the speech, he criticizes citizens for letting the senators take their money and for failing to avenge the deaths of the Gracchi. Basically, nobles strut around Rome flaunting their priesthoods and consulships; a foreign enemy has bought them.

Bypassing the Senate, Memmius enacted legislation requiring Jugurtha to come to Rome to testify. Once there, the king was summoned to a *contio* and was just on the point of answering Memmius' questions when another tribune stopped the meeting with his veto – he was bribed by Jugurtha, according to Sallust. Jugurtha, who had been promised safe conduct, soon slipped away.

A far worse disgrace followed. Another consul went to Africa but had no luck in pinning down Jugurtha, and the consul returned to Rome for elections. The army that he left behind was trapped and then forced to surrender and walk under a yoke of spears – a humiliation that rankled with the increasingly irritated Roman public. A new tribune, Mamilius, passed a law establishing an investigation into those Romans alleged to have abetted Jugurtha in exchange for bribes. The jurors condemned at least five distinguished men, most if not all enemies of the Gracchi, including Opimius, destroyer of Gaius Gracchus. The scandal of Numidia allowed old scores to be settled.

MARIUS' MOMENT

The tide of the Jugurthine War shifted in 109, with the arrival of Q. Caecilius Metellus, member of another branch of the powerful dynasty. He first restored discipline to the army, which had been going on raiding expeditions to pay for imported wine. He then proceeded cautiously from Roman Africa into Numidia and settled on a slow scorched-earth strategy that would eventually bring victory. A sign of Metellus' competence was his decision to include on his staff the talented Marius.

But when Marius asked about returning to Rome to stand for a consulship, Metellus scoffed at the new man. At this time, as Sallust writes, "the nobility passed the consulship from hand to hand among themselves." Marius made promises to impatient Roman and Italian businessmen in Africa that he would have Jugurtha in chains. They, in turn, wrote back to their associates criticizing Metellus. So did some of the other officers. Cleverly linking failures in Numidia to the haughtiness of an entrenched nobility, Marius turned his newness into an asset and was elected to the consulship for 107 on his return to Rome. The plebeian assembly passed a law taking the Numidian command from Metellus and reassigning it to Marius. All the Senate could do was reward Metellus on his return with a triumph and the honorary name Numidicus (meaning "victor in Numidia").

Marius held a fresh muster of troops, even allowing those without any property to serve – a waiver that had been issued before at moments of crisis. With this enthusiastic army, Marius captured Jugurtha's strongholds and pressed westward. Jugurtha's ally, King Bocchus of Mauretania, claimed he was now ready to help the Romans. Marius' officer, a fame-seeking patrician named Sulla, carried out the dangerous negotiations and with Bocchus' help laid a successful trap for Jugurtha. Whether Marius or Sulla should get more credit would later bring these two ambitious men to blows, but for now the war was over. Marius returned to Rome, with Jugurtha in chains.

Adding to the panic of this time were alarming events in northern Europe. The Cimbri, a Germanic people, were on the move, and a Roman army suffered a defeat at their hands in the Rhône valley in Gaul in 109. The Cimbri then moved north, but Celtic allies they had picked up on their migration moved west, precipitating a revolt of Roman allies in Tolosa, a trading hub on the Garonne River. The Roman garrison stationed there was captured. The consul of 106, Servilius Caepio, managed to take back Tolosa and in the process carried off a vast trove of gold, which then mysteriously disappeared. He was forced to stay on and fight the Cimbri when they returned.

What followed was Rome's worst military defeat since the Second Punic War. As the Cimbri came back down the Rhône valley, Caepio and Mallius Maximus (a consul of 105 and a new man like Marius) moved to meet them. But the patrician Caepio haughtily refused to cooperate with Mallius, leading to a disastrous loss of Roman lives in the ensuing battle at Arausio (modern Orange). Emergency measures were undertaken to defend Italy. Marius was elected to a second consulship in absentia, and despite the legal requirement of a 10-year interval between consulships. The People also granted him Gaul as his province. On the first of January 104, the new man reentered Rome, embarking on his second consulship and celebrating a triumph. It was Marius' moment.

CRISIS AND HISTORY

It is no accident that in the generally poor sources for the later second century BCE the tribunates of Tiberius and Gaius Gracchus loom large. The tribunes' actions, and also the massacres of 133 and 121, were shocking and divisive. In 121 the consul Opimius rebuilt the Temple of Concord at the western end of the Forum, to suggest that harmony had been restored. According to Plutarch, graffiti soon marred it: "A work of mad Discord makes a Temple of Concord." The Gracchi had no tombs, but offerings were made at the places where they had fallen. Images of the brothers went up around the city, and they were worshipped as if they were gods.

The Gracchi divided citizens – and senatorial politicians in particular. In the future, some would champion the authority of the Senate, while others would argue for the rights of the People as a whole. As later writers, including Sallust, put it, there were now two "parties" (*partes* in Latin, the source of the English word). Cicero frequently called those who spoke for the Senate the "good men" (*boni*), or "men of the best sort" (*optimates*), and in an especially famous passage he divided all politicians into two groups – the *optimates* and the *populares*. According to Cicero, the *populares* tried to please "the masses." Modern scholars have, accordingly, sometimes analyzed politics after the Gracchi in terms of an "optimate party" and "a *popularis* party," but because modern political parties are such well-organized and enduring institutions (whereas *partes* were really just shifting "groups"), the terminology is misleading. Language like "Senate champion" or "popular champion" is more helpful. A Senate champion would tend to criticize the actions of the Gracchi themselves, and a popular champion might condemn the murder of the brothers. In speeches to the citizens, however, virtually all would claim to be the true friends of the People.

A new fashion for senators writing history in Latin (as opposed to Greek), started by Cato the Elder, offered a way to stake out a position. The Gaius Fannius known to have written an anti-Gracchan history was almost certainly the consul of 122 who blocked the proposal to extend citizenship to Italians. Sempronius Asellio, who served as military tribune at Numantia alongside Gaius Gracchus, later wrote up the history of his times. He dismissed childish chroniclers and promised to show the logic of events, in the manner of Polybius. Virtually nothing of the work survives, but two quotations give a sympathetic account of Tiberius Gracchus' last days.

There was not just interest in recent events. According to Plutarch, Tiberius himself cited the overthrow of Rome's kings to defend his actions against Octavius. Other episodes from Rome's distant past were refashioned to provide precedents for the attacks on Tiberius and his brother. Two figures from the fifth century who were alleged to have aspired to kingship and were put to death for it were assimilated into the Gracchi. In the new version, one gained support by land distribution, the other by supplying grain to the people.

In many ways, the Gracchi themselves soon passed out of history and into mythology. While proponents of senatorial authority turned them into tyrants, angry tribunes like Memmius made them into heroic martyrs, absolved of any responsibility for the introduction of violence into public life. A later textbook of rhetoric shows the student how to describe Tiberius' last moments: "That man [Nasica], overflowing with wicked and criminal intentions, comes flying out of the Temple of Jupiter. In a sweat, with eyes blazing and hair bristling, his toga twisted up, he starts to quicken his pace, several others joining him." Vivid words like these could quickly catch a crowd's attention – and could also inflame situations such as mounting dissatisfaction with the Senate's progress in a foreign war.

A more balanced verdict on this period might be that reforms had been achieved, but at a price. Citizens enjoyed greater rights, such as the use of the secret ballot. Public land had been distributed to Romans in need. The taxes of Asia flowed to Rome, providing subsidized grain for the urban *plebs*. Those subject to Roman power had some recourse against thieving officials. Yet a tradition of harmony had been shattered. Far from being able to resolve disputes, the political institutions of Senate, People, and magistrates were now at the very heart of them. The use of violence set a dangerous precedent and invited revenge. In the years after 104, anger over what had happened to the Gracchi would boil over into more violence. Force replaced politics as a way to resolve controversial issues.

FURTHER READING

All of the political works referred to in Chapter 3 are relevant here. In addition, refer to three classic books of the late 1960s: A. E. Astin, *Scipio Aemilianus* (Oxford, 1967); A. W. Lintott, *Violence in Republican Rome* (Oxford, 1968); E. S. Gruen, *Roman Politics and the Criminal Courts, 149–78 B.C.* (Cambridge, MA, 1968). F. Santangelo, *Marius* (London, 2016), is brief and informative, while P. Kay gives Gaius Gracchus a key place in the transformation of the Roman economy and state finances in *Rome's Economic Revolution* (Oxford, 2014).

Important insights are found in more-focused essays, including these: E. Badian, "Tiberius Gracchus and the Beginning of the Roman Revolution," *Aufstieg und Niedergang der römischen Welt* 1.1 (1972), 668–731; A. N. Sherwin-White, "The lex repetundarum and the Political Ideas of Gaius Gracchus," *Journal of Roman Studies* 72 (1982), 18–31; N. Rosenstein, "Imperatores victi: The Case of C. Hostilius Mancinus," *Classical Antiquity* 5 (1986), 230–52; J. Linderski, "The Pontiff and the Tribune: The Death of Tiberius Gracchus," *Athenaeum* 90 (2002), 339–66; C. P. Jones, "Events Surrounding the Bequest of Pergamon to Rome and the Revolt of Aristonicos: New Inscriptions from Metropolis," *Journal of Roman Archaeology* 17 (2004), 469–85; H. I. Flower, "Beyond the *contio*: Political Communication in the Tribunate of Tiberius Gracchus," in C. Steel and H. van der Blom (eds.), *Community and Communication: Oratory and Politics in Republican Rome* (Oxford, 2013), 85–100; M. Stone, "Tiberius Gracchus and the Nations of Italy," in K. Welch, *Appian's Roman History: Empire and Civil War* (Swansea, 2015), 221–34.

Works on the Italian allies and demography of the city of Rome and Italy are mentioned more fully in Chapters 5 and 6, respectively. Especially pertinent for understanding Tiberius Gracchus are the overviews by L. de Ligt, "The Economy: Agrarian Change during the Second Century," in N. Rosenstein and R. Morstein-Marx (eds.), *A Companion to the Roman Republic* (Oxford, 2006), 590–605, and J. W. Rich, "Tiberius Gracchus, Land, and Manpower," in O. Hekster, G. de Kleijn, and D. Slootjes (eds.), *Crises and the Roman Empire* (Leiden, 2007), 155–66.

T. P. Wiseman's *The Myths of Rome* (Exeter, 2004) comprehensively shows how Roman historical events became mythical, with a good discussion of the Gracchi. On history writing in Latin, a classic is E. Badian, "The Early Historians," in T. A. Dorey (ed.), *Latin Historians* (London, 1966), 1–38, while individual authors can be pursued in T. Cornell (ed.), *The Fragments of the Roman Historians* (3 vols.; Oxford, 2013). For two different discussions of political "parties" after the Gracchi, see T. P. Wiseman, *Remembering the Roman People* (Oxford, 2009), and the highly skeptical M. A. Robb, *Beyond* populares *and* optimates*: Political Language in the Late Republic* (Stuttgart, 2010).

5

THE SPIRAL OF VIOLENCE (104–80 BCE)

In 102 a Roman citizen named Lucius Equitius appeared before the censors and as part of his declaration made the surprising claim that he was actually the son of Tiberius Gracchus. The censor, Metellus Numidicus, the proud noble from whom Marius had snatched the war against Jugurtha, refused to continue with the registration. Tiberius had had three sons, insisted Metellus, and all were now dead; "unknowns of low origin" should not be thrust into the distinguished family. A furious crowd, supporting Equitius' dubious assertion, soon tried to stone the censor. A tribune summoned Tiberius' surviving sister, Sempronia, to a public meeting where the audience demanded that she kiss Equitius. Staring them all down, she refused.

Equitius almost certainly was not Tiberius' son, and what his claim actually shows is how much the Gracchus brothers lived on in memory as a new generation of politicians questioned how the profits and prestige of empire were shared. Up and down the Rostra these politicians strode, grieving, mocking, attacking, gesturing dramatically. Chief among them was L. Appuleius Saturninus, a tribune who supported Equitius (and probably came up with the idea of the false Gracchus in the first place) and was determined to push through legislation, even by force, to help ordinary citizens. He used gangs to drive off other voters with stones and wooden clubs. When he sought a second term as tribune, some of his supporters ended up killing a rival candidate in a voting-place tussle. The following year, he ordered the assassination of a consular candidate.

"Every year some foul crime occurred in or around the Forum," wrote the historian Appian. His *Civil War* is the only extant history for the period from Saturninus' stormy entry into politics in 104 down through the far-worse crisis that erupted in 91. But he is all too brief on events of most of the 90s, a critical decade for the future of the Republic. Modern historians must piece together a narrative from small fragments of evidence, almost like forensic scientists. What emerges is growing dissatisfaction among key constituencies, including the Italian allies who had bled so often in Rome's wars. While some senators realized that reforms were needed, mutual jealousies, combined with voters' prejudices, proved an insurmountable obstacle – and so in 91 the Italians rebelled.

Roman citizens put aside their differences to meet the threat and ultimately gave the Italians citizenship. Yet specific plans to enfranchise the Italians divided leaders, and in 88 a new and deadlier cycle of violence began. Gangs armed with daggers were unleashed in the Forum; an attack was made on the two consuls; and, worst of all, one of them, Sulla, then marched on Rome with an army. That year marked a total breakdown of civic institutions. It was a bigger turning point than the more famous assassination of Julius Caesar in 44.

After Sulla's march on Rome, power now lay in armed force. Armies helped legitimize leaders, and leaders in turn lavishly rewarded soldiers. Leaders also claimed that they had the unique support of the gods. Marius insisted that he should have a seventh consulship because of a prophecy he had received in childhood after catching a falling eagle's nest with seven young ones in it. Sulla, whose blond hair and piercing blue eyes stood out in Rome, spoke even more awesomely. When he set out to fight the Italian allies, he said, a great chasm in the earth opened, out of which came much fire and one bright flame that reached the sky. According to his soothsayers it meant that a man of great qualities and striking appearance "would take the government in hand and free Rome from her present troubles."

Sulla's final victory seemed to bring civil war to an end, but his legacy proved an awful one. His lack of reconciliation inspired fresh outbreaks of violence in Italy after his death. The new constitution that he wrote for Rome failed to prevent new Sullas. Sulla, in the end, proved too wedded to using the old institutions of SPQR – especially the Senate – to bring stable government to the much-enlarged Roman state. A different framework would be needed to stop the killing.

THE DIN OF WARFARE AND THE VOICE OF LAW

Like Tiberius Gracchus, Saturninus rose to power against a backdrop of imperial crisis. In 105, at Arausio, the Romans were disastrously defeated by the Cimbri. Not since the battle of Cannae in the Second Punic War had so many citizens died in one battle. Afterward, the proud patrician commander, Servilius Caepio, was stripped of his command by the People. Marius, elected to his second consulship for 104, was to take over.

Rome's problems were not limited to the north. As he prepared to fight the Germans, Marius summoned aid from Roman allies, including King

Nicomedes III of Bithynia. Nicomedes replied that he had nobody to send because the majority of his subjects had been seized and sold into slavery, by Roman tax-collecting companies no less. The companies had grown far more powerful than Gaius Gracchus had intended when he turned Asia over to them. At the same time, thanks to Rome's weakening of Rhodes, pirates had infested the craggy coast of Cilicia and were enjoying a brisk sale in captives. Rome had done nothing to police the area (though it would finally, in 102, send a praetor there with naval forces). In 104, the Senate instructed provincial governors to free all those illegally enslaved. The praetor in Sicily began his investigation, and in the process stirred up a massive slave rebellion. Grain prices rose in Rome, and supplies began to run short.

Marius made his way from Rome to Gaul, and by a stroke of luck the Germans had left for Spain, allowing him to train his freshly recruited army intensively. He drove his soldiers so hard that they came to be called "Marius' mules." He also introduced a uniform battle standard for each legion, a silver eagle, the loss of which would bring disgrace. The reforms paid off. In 102, Marius destroyed many of the Germans at two battles near Aquae Sextiae (modern Aix-en-Provence in France). Coming to the aid of his fellow consul Catulus the next year, he defeated the Cimbri at the battle of Vercellae in northern Italy. Meanwhile, Marius racked up reelections to the consulship, winning his sixth for the year 100. He felt powerful enough to reward with Roman citizenship the Italians who had fought bravely under him. Called to account for this back in Rome, he replied that "the din of warfare had prevented him from hearing the voice of law." However worthy those Italians were, comments like this undermined republican government.

By the end of 100, imperial stability was basically restored. The Germans had been defeated and the slaves in Sicily put down. The pirate war was more or less over too. Cilicia became a regularly assigned province, and assurances were made throughout the eastern world that Rome would guarantee freedom on the seas. Rome's friends and allies were ordered to shut their ports to all pirates.

Back in Rome, tribunes had been apportioning blame for the losses to the Germans. By a tribunician law of 104, Caepio, the loser at Arausio, was expelled from the Senate, and as further embarrassment, an inquiry was held into the mysterious disappearance of the trove of gold he had carried off from the Gallic sanctuary at Tolosa. Junius Silanus, who had been defeated by the Cimbri back in 109, was also now put on trial before the People by the vigorous tribune Domitius Ahenobarbus. He was acquitted. Domitius did succeed in transferring to a special assembly made up of 17 voting tribes chosen by lot the election of members of the four great priestly colleges. Previously selection had lain with the priests themselves.

It was later in this year that Saturninus won election to his first tribunate. A strong speaker, he sought to champion popular interests at nearly any price.

Probably in 103 he proposed a new grain law, apparently increasing the subsidy offered. This was a clear effort to win over city dwellers on edge from recent shortages. The son of the disgraced Caepio, serving as quaestor, protested that the treasury could not afford it, and the Senate passed a decree trying to block it. Saturninus persisted anyway and, despite vetoes by other tribunes, initiated voting. Caepio then disrupted the assembly, pulling down the gangways that voters crossed on and toppling the voting urns. It was the tribunate of Tiberius Gracchus all over again.

Saturninus ultimately got the bill passed, along with other controversial laws. One of them granted allotments of land in Africa to Marius' veterans from the Jugurthine War. This was in the spirit of Gaius Gracchus' colonization of Carthage and the colonization of Narbo Martius in Gaul in 118. Again, one of Saturninus' fellow tribunes tried to interpose his veto but was driven off with stones by Saturninus' supporters. Another law established a new court to try those accused of "diminishing the majesty of the Roman People" – an impressive-sounding crime that could embrace corruption or the disrupting of voting assemblies. Over time, this court replaced the assembly for the hearing of treason charges.

In 103, though, it was in the assembly that Saturninus continued hounding the elder Caepio. For his actions at Arausio, Caepio was charged with treason by a fellow tribune and ally of Saturninus named Norbanus. Two tribunes tried to interpose their vetoes, and they too were driven off in a hail of stones, one of which struck the *princeps senatus*, the formidable M. Aemilius Scaurus. Caepio was forced into exile, but Norbanus' actions were not to be forgotten. The other loser of Arausio, the new man Mallius, was also prosecuted, this time by Saturninus himself, and he too went into exile.

Both Saturninus and his opponents clearly were willing to use violence to circumvent the political process. Like the tribunes during the Jugurthine War, he was putting on the mantle of the Gracchi. But he showed fiercer opposition to the Senate and its top leaders than the Gracchi themselves had. How much the memory of the Gracchi mattered in his and his supporters' eyes is shown by his support of the false Gracchus in 102. Not only did the censor Metellus Numidicus refuse to register the imposter, but Numidicus also tried to remove Saturninus from the Senate, along with Servilius Glaucia, a key ally of Saturninus who won popular support with his jokes. Glaucia's enemies dished it back by calling him "the Senate house shit."

Numidicus only succeeded in strengthening the resolve of Saturninus and of Glaucia. Glaucia held a tribunate (probably in 101) and passed an extortion law that restored the panels of juries entirely to the Equestrians. This was another jab at the Senate. The elder Caepio, before his disgrace, had managed to pass a law stipulating that all courts were to have juries that included senators as well as Equestrians. By reversing it, Glaucia was putting senators on watch – while also gaining the support of the Equestrians who hated Caepio's reform. Saturninus did not let up either. Later in 101, he stood for a second tribunate. Marius was back in Rome, eager to secure land in Gaul for his soldiers in the northern war, and lent his and his veterans' support to Saturninus. Saturninus' chances only increased when his supporters killed a rival candidate.

So with Marius' help and by murder, Saturninus was reelected for 100. Then with the help of the veterans, who drove off the opposition with clubs, he passed the legislation on their behalf. Saturninus simultaneously settled his score with Numidicus, to the delight of Marius, who was not one to forget a grudge quickly. As a safeguard, Saturninus' land bill required senators to swear to uphold it, and after Numidicus refused, he left Rome and a law was passed forbidding his return.

Marius benefitted too from a further provision of Saturninus' agrarian legislation, which ultimately embraced more than Gaul. Settlements were to take place in Sicily, Greece, and Macedonia also; and in each of the new colonies, Marius was empowered to create new citizens, thereby rewarding the Italians who had served with him on campaign. Saturninus and Marius were thus winning the support of poor citizens in the countryside, as well as Italian allies.

Through his own actions, in addition to his alliances with Marius and Servilius Glaucia, Saturninus had a formidable power base – strong enough to take on the Senate majority on such matters as land distribution. Later in 100, Saturninus gained election to yet another tribunate, and the false Gracchus was elected with him. It was reasonable now to see him as subverting republican government, the heart of which was a smooth turnover of annually elected magistrates.

Even Marius began to have reservations. When Glaucia sought permission to stand for a consulship, Marius, as presider over the elections, refused. To delay the voting, Saturninus ordered the assassination of one of the recognized consular candidates. He then seized the Capitol, planning to pass a law there to allow Glaucia's candidacy. Aemilius Scaurus shrewdly challenged Marius to defend the Romans' liberty and take action against Saturninus, and Marius agreed. The Senate passed the same "ultimate" decree it had against Gaius Gracchus, an improvised force was raised, and after the water was cut to the Capitol, Saturninus and his forces capitulated on a promise of safety. But some of them were soon massacred by an angry crowd armed with shards of roof tiles, likely including supporters of Metellus Numidicus. Marius had failed to save his former allies.

Challenging the Senate on matters like the grain supply or the distribution of land, Saturninus above all relied on the plebeian assembly, as earlier tribunes had. Some of his techniques, though, were novel, including the use of veterans in assemblies and, even more disturbing, premeditated assassination. The Senate was forced to take up arms itself. In the aftermath, parts of Saturninus' agrarian legislation were invalidated. A few lingering supporters of his were eliminated. No doubt deterred by Saturninus' own fate, tribunes were less aggressive in the next few years. A kind of stability returned to the Republic, but the Senate took no immediate action to make debates over the profits of empire less acrimonious, and so it missed an opportunity to solidify its power. The forces Saturninus had roused – including soldiers fresh off campaigns – could be stirred to action again.

A LOST DECADE

The 90s is among the most poorly documented periods in all of Roman history, but a key to understanding it may be found in a growing sense among some senators that it was not just rabble-rousing tribunes who were their problem. The Senate needed to consider at least some reform, if only to preserve itself. Even the formidable Aemilius Scaurus, whose nod was said practically to rule the world, saw this. But the violent quarrels of recent years had led to bad blood. Even when the surface was calm, strong currents of hostility lurked beneath and sucked in politicians.

First on the agenda for Senate champions was a concerted effort to restore the martyred Metellus Numidicus. Naturally, Marius opposed it, and he was supported by the tribune Furius, a one-time supporter of Saturninus who had turned on him. Furius refused to budge even in the face of conspicuous appeals by Metellus' son, whose own persistence earned him the extra name Pius (the Latin adjective meaning "dutiful"). But eventually a bill on behalf of Numidicus was passed, probably in 99.

Criminal prosecutions were a tempting way to settle scores. After his tribunate ended, Furius was prosecuted by a relative of Saturninus, Decianus, who took the chance to go off topic at the trial and deplore the death of Saturninus. When Decianus failed to secure a conviction, a second trial was held, and Furius was lynched by an angry audience before the trial could finish. Clearly, Saturninus retained the love of his constituents. But the tide turned when Decianus was himself successfully prosecuted, as was the tribune Sex. Titius, who kept a bust of Saturninus in his house. For the next few years, there is no trace of aggressive tribunician activity.

Senatorial unity still proved elusive. A notable pair of trials probably took place in 95. Norbanus, Saturninus' ally from 103 who had helped destroy the elder Caepio, was prosecuted in Saturninus' own treason court for his use of violence. His skilled advocate saved him by dredging up memories of the horrific loss at Arausio and also Caepio's judiciary law. For his part in breaking up

Saturninus' assembly, the younger Caepio also was now prosecuted. His defense was entrusted to Licinius Crassus, the superb orator by then well known for his stirring vindications of the Senate. While Caepio was acquitted, his prosecution was a reminder that Saturninus had not been the only one to use violence. At least indirectly, it was an attack on Senate champions, including Aemilius Scaurus, who had passed the ultimate decree. Possibly Marius had supported the prosecution.

No longer in command, discredited by his association with Saturninus and his intransigence to Numidicus, Marius was on the outs with many in the Senate. The Italian allies were a bone of contention. Marius had been generous with citizenship grants during and immediately after his various campaigns. Far more than in the 120s, citizenship must have seemed desirable, because it offered the prospect of land grants. At the same time, increasing benefits for Roman citizens must have made Italians – who had helped save Rome from the Germans – feel discriminated against. Questions arose about whether some Italians were illegally usurping Roman citizenship, apparently with the help of Marius and his remaining allies.

In 95, two consuls, the eloquent Licinius Crassus and the gifted lawyer Q. Mucius Scaevola, passed a law setting up a tribunal to investigate disputed claims. One of those put on trial was Matrinius, an Umbrian granted citizenship by Marius in 100 through Saturninus' law. With a few words from Marius, he was acquitted. Still, the law alienated Italians even more.

Another growing tension in the 90s was relations between the Senate and the Equestrian order, members of which had the lucrative contract for tax collecting in Asia. Mounting unhappiness with the tax collectors there, coupled with concerns about security in the east (see discussion further on), led the Senate to action. After his consulship in 95, Quintus Scaevola was sent to overhaul the administration of Asia. This huge job was completed by his legate, Rutilius Rufus, an old military rival of Marius, whose study of law and Stoic philosophy disposed him to reform. Back in Rome, Rutilius was put on trial for extortion – the very problem he had tried to solve. He modeled his defense on Socrates, which did nothing to endear him to the Equestrian jurors, already furious at how their interests had been tampered with. Convicted, he chose as his place of exile Asia and was welcomed by the people he had allegedly wronged.

For many senators, Rutilius' conviction was a travesty of justice. Gaius Gracchus had not brought the Equestrians into public life to undermine the Senate – just to watch over it and protect provincials. The outrage intensified the growing sense that reform was necessary and is the immediate explanation for developments of the momentous year 91. Rutilius' nephew, the hard-driven Livius Drusus, was tribune. A son of the Drusus who challenged Gaius Gracchus and a protégé of Licinus Crassus, the new tribune was another champion of the Senate. His first aim was to restore membership of the juries to the Senate. The Senate would be doubled in size to ensure a sufficiency of jurors (and, presumably, to win over the 300 leading Equestrians who would be asked to join the Senate). To help win support, Drusus offered voters lower grain prices as well as land grants. To the Italians he promised citizenship.

The sources for Drusus' legislative plans are thin and at times contradictory. There is, however, general agreement that he said he was acting on behalf of the Senate, and at critical moments he had the open support of no less than the *princeps senatus*, Aemilius Scaurus. It is also clear that he aroused opposition, including some from his fellow senators. Quite likely his plan to expand the Senate never got off the ground, and instead a law sharing juries between senators and Equestrians was passed. A certain type of die-hard senator would resist any new measures on grain or land. A proposal for citizenship would also be controversial – even if, as some modern scholars argue, many Italians had little interest in it and simply wanted greater recognition by Rome.

By the fall of 91, the consul Marcius Philippus had turned on Drusus. Also opposing him was the younger Caepio, who had once been a close friend. Philippus denounced not only Drusus but the Senate as a whole at a public meeting. An ailing Licinius Crassus appeared before the Senate to make what would be his final appearance, accusing Philippus of cutting the authority of the Senate to ribbons. He then passed a motion that "the Roman People be satisfied that the Senate had never failed in its advice and loyalty to the state." But Crassus was soon dead, and Drusus' own supporters were melting away. Some Italians were frightened that they would lose territory because of Drusus' efforts to distribute land to citizens.

The ship of state had hit turbulent waters again and was splitting apart. Drusus threatened to execute Caepio, and he got into a violent fight with Philippus. Philippus, in turn, had all of Drusus' laws invalidated. There was to be no accommodation for the Italians, whose impatience – which clearly added to Drusus' own desperate situation – started to boil over. Poppaedius Silo, the chieftain of the Marsi, a mountain people of central Italy, even led an armed posse to Rome. Drusus, his friend, managed to turn him back and also warned the consul Philippus that his life was in danger. But it was Drusus who was stabbed to death, in his house, by an unknown assassin. Among those suspected was his old friend Caepio. The broken friendship symbolized a broken politics.

THE BULL GORES THE WOLF

Learning of Drusus' fate, the Italian peoples living in and around the central and southern Apennines, including the Marsi and the Samnites, now decided to break away from Rome entirely. For some time they had been engaged in secret negotiations involving an exchange of hostages as guarantees of good faith, and in the course of 91 the Senate had sent out magistrates to investigate. The threats one senator made at Asculum, a town set amid the mountains near the Adriatic, resulted in his assassination and a massacre of the other Romans there at the end of the year. The rebels now revealed their preparations. At a new capital city in Corfinium – renamed Italica – delegates would meet as a federal senate. The Italians appointed commanders, raised a massive army of perhaps 100,000, and even issued their own coins, on which the Italian bull replaced the Roman wolf.

The bloody war that followed – usually called the Social War (from the Latin word for "allies," *socii*) – has been compared to the American Civil War. The Italian confederates had excellent generals, such as the wily Poppaedius Silo, and fierce fighters, and they achieved some impressive early victories. But they were, in the end, no match for a richer and better-organized opponent.

Two main theaters opened up. In the north, from their base in Corfinium, the confederates would try to head across the Via Valeria to Rome. In the south, they successfully captured the strategically located Latin colony of Aesernia, won over part of Campania (including Pompeii), and also began to penetrate Apulia and Lucania. The consul commanding the north was killed in battle, and command was reassigned to two of his officers, Drusus' opponent Caepio and Marius. Caepio and his army were led into an ambush by Poppaedius Silo, leaving Marius to rally Rome's forces, scoring a major victory over the Marsi. Still, as the rebellion threatened to spread, the Senate in Rome decided in late 90 that the consul Lucius Caesar should have a bill

Figure 5.1 The Italian bull gores the Roman wolf on this silver coin issued by the Italian confederation. Beneath the mauling the name of 'Italy' is written right to left in the alphabet of Oscan, a southern Italian language. (Photo © The Trustees of the British Museum.)

passed granting citizenship to those Italians who had stayed loyal. It was probably by further legislation that citizenship was granted also to those rebels who would surrender.

Many of the rebels, with long memories of struggles against Rome centuries earlier, held out. In 89, Sulla, who was now the principal commander in the southern theater, regained most of Campania and drove back the Samnites. In the north, the consul Pompeius Strabo recaptured Asculum, where the war had begun, after a long siege. The confederates moved their senate to Aesernia and made Poppaedius supreme commander. But he went down in battle, putting an end to major fighting. All the Italians, with the temporary exception of some Samnites and Lucanians, would now be Roman citizens thanks to the recent legislation. They would serve in armies on the same terms as Romans, receive the same rewards, and enjoy the same individual freedoms. They might even vote.

In hindsight, the Social War seemed to have all the tragedy of a great civil war. Yet contemporaries could see that despite the casualties and destruction, which left some bitter memories, war had reversed Roman policy. Roman legions putting out the last embers of Italian resistance would soon be called upon to settle another dispute.

THE EASTERN GAME OF THRONES

At just the same time as the Social War, and not by pure coincidence, Rome also faced a great challenge overseas. The establishment of a regular province in Asia in the 120s had destabilized the power dynamics of the wider region. Roman officials, along with tax collectors and moneylenders, were far less popular than the kings of Pergamum, and they provoked resentment. Neighboring kingdoms, especially Bithynia, grew increasingly worried about their own futures. Meanwhile, Cappadocia and Pontus, two kingdoms located farther away, although allied with Rome, increasingly pursued their own agenda.

Especially ambitious was King Mithridates VI of Pontus, a gigantic man made even bigger in legend. He could run as fast as a deer, outdrink anyone at a party, and even was said to have made his body resistant to poisons through his experiments in pharmacology. Around the age of 20, he killed his brother and coruler, along with his mother, and began an expansion in the manner of a Hellenistic monarch. He strengthened control of the southern coast of the Black Sea, the traditional heartland of his kingdom. And he championed the Greek cities on the north shore against Scythian barbarians. When he and King Nicomedes III of Bithynia partitioned the kingdom of Paphlagonia (c. 108), Rome did nothing more than send an embassy to protest. And then – at the height of the German war – Mithridates schemed to take over Cappadocia and place his eight-year-old son on the throne. Once more, the Senate did little.

Figure 5.2 Rome's most effective challenger in the first century BCE, Mithridates of Pontus. Artists depicted Mithridates as the reincarnation of Alexander the Great. Here, like the Macedonian conqueror, he wears the lion-skin cap of the hero Hercules. Louvre Museum, Paris, France. (Photo Wikimedia Commons, Sting.)

Several years later, probably in 99, Marius travelled east, ostensibly to make sacrifices to Cybele, the great mother-goddess who had predicted a Roman victory during the German war. He also probably wanted to see what Mithridates was up to. The two did meet, and Marius is said, tactlessly, to have told the king either to be greater than the Romans or to obey them.

More intrigue ensued over the Cappadocian throne, and this time the Senate acted more vigorously. It declared Cappadocia and also Paphlagonia free. When the Cappadocians then requested that the Senate name a king, they chose the Cappadocian noble Ariobarzanes, who was in Rome at the time. As governor of Cilicia, the new province set up to combat piracy, Sulla was to escort the king back and install him. He did so, and in the process of shoring up regional allies, Sulla agreed to meet on the Euphrates an envoy from the great Parthian empire. A shrewd astrologer in the Parthian entourage impressed Sulla with a prophecy of future greatness – and surprise that he had not yet taken first place among men. Sulla could play the game of thrones too.

The outbreak of the Social War in 91 gave Mithridates a new opening. He tossed Ariobarzanes back out of Cappadocia, acting in league with another up-and-coming ruler, Tigranes of Armenia, who had recently married Mithridates' daughter. Mithridates also contrived to drive out

Nicomedes IV, the new king of Bithynia – where Roman interests, including business, were stronger. The Senate sent a commission to restore the two deposed kings, headed by Manius Aquillius, son of the man who had organized the province of Asia in the 120s. With military help from the current governor of Asia and native allies, Aquillius fulfilled his assignment. Nicomedes then proceeded to invade Mithridates' own territories, allegedly at the insistence of Aquillius and other Romans, to whom he owed money. Mithridates appeared to retreat. In fact, he was preparing for war. He sent his son to toss out Ariobarzanes yet again and prepared to retake Bithynia in 89.

Now came the disaster for Rome. Nicomedes' army was roundly defeated in western Pontus, his infantry panicking at Mithridates' scythed chariots. Mithridates pressed on into Bithynia and then overran much of western Asia Minor. He promised freedom to the Greeks, tax remission, and cancellation of debts. Aquillius was caught and made to parade around bound on an ass, before molten gold was poured down his throat – a grisly jest at Roman greed. The Roman Senate and People declared war, but as we shall see shortly, the army was delayed for the worst of reasons. A few cities, including Rhodes, heroically held out for the Romans. Mithridates, meanwhile, sent out secret instructions to murder all the Romans and Italians in the Asian cities at the same time. A reported figure of 80,000 undoubtedly is too high, but the massacre of 88 – which bound the cities to Mithridates in blood – showed that Roman rule in Asia Minor had collapsed.

88 BCE: THE REPUBLIC STOPS

Fighting in Italy was largely over in 88, but there was a new poison pill in Roman politics: the question of how to enroll the newly enfranchised Italians. A tribune, Publius Sulpicius, introduced legislation that the Italians should be distributed in all of the 35 tribes, rather than in a limited number of them as had been proposed. Sulpicius' measure would ensure that the Italian vote was not diluted. He further proposed that freedmen should also be distributed across all 35 tribes rather than just the four urban ones.

Sulpicius, at least initially, was trying to finish the work of Drusus. Like Drusus, he had studied with Licinius Crassus, from whom he acquired an interest in reform and also an ability to speak exuberantly. He was a close friend of one of the consuls of 88, Pompeius Rufus, and apparently thought he would have the support of Rufus and the other consul, Sulla. But once again some senators were nervous about how Sulpicius' reforms would affect elections; even stronger was the resistance of longstanding Roman citizens, fearful of their votes being swamped. Armed gangs formed, to prevent Sulpicius passing his law, and fighting broke out.

Figure 5.3 A silver coin issued by Sulla's son Faustus in the 50s BCE. The reverse depicts Bocchus (on the left) surrendering Jugurtha (kneeling with hands tied, on the right) to a seated Sulla. Sulla had this glorious moment engraved on his signet ring. (Photo © The Trustees of the British Museum.)

A new cycle of violence was underway. The consuls now voted to suspend public business, but Sulpicius pressed on, equipping his own supporters with daggers and bringing them into the Forum to protest the consuls' suspension. In the fighting that broke out, Consul Pompeius Rufus' son was killed, and the consuls soon left Rome, seemingly backing down. Marius, perhaps already cooperating with Sulpicius, now helped him pass the enfranchisement bill – at a price.

Sulpicius had the plebeian assembly transfer command in the war against Mithridates from the Senate's appointee, Sulla, to Marius. The quarrel over who had really ended the Jugurthine War had been reignited in 91, when the Senate allowed King Bocchus of Mauretania to dedicate on the Capitol a monument that included figures representing Jugurtha being surrendered by Bocchus to Sulla. "Marius," Plutarch writes, "nearly lost it, he was so angry and jealous at the idea of Sulla stealing the glory of his achievements." Now in 88, he could settle the score.

Sulla still had his army from the Social War in Campania, which he was preparing to take east. On hearing of Sulpicius' measure, which also transferred this army to Marius, Sulla decided to challenge it. He would march on Rome with his troops. While virtually all of Sulla's officers refused to take this unprecedented step, the ordinary soldiers, after hearing Sulla out, did so. They were anticipating a profitable eastern war, and Sulla insinuated that Marius would replace them. Why should armed gangs in Rome get to decide *their* fate?

Joined by his consular colleague Pompeius, Sulla proceeded to Rome and entered with force, brandishing a lighted torch and threatening to burn the houses of any who resisted. There was fighting, but Sulpicius' gangs were no match for experienced legions, and Sulpicius and Marius fled. They and their other most prominent supporters were soon declared public enemies, and Sulpicius' legislation was rescinded. While Marius escaped to Africa, Sulpicius was caught and killed.

So began what afterward would be called Rome's first civil war (in Latin, *bellum civile*, meaning literally "citizens' war"). Although the Social War, with its fielding of large armies in Italy, added fuel, the fire had been lit earlier. The sparks included the violence that politicians had relied on to settle disputes, going back to the tribunate of Tiberius Gracchus in 133; an associated loss of respect for the institutions of SPQR and the growth of bitter personal rivalries; the inability of SPQR to resolve disputes about the allocation of resources and status; and unresolved debates about the balance of power between the Senate and the People. Before he left Rome, Sulla and his colleague Pompeius attempted to address this last issue by introducing legislation that all future laws must be approved by the Senate and should be voted on in the centuriate assembly, controlled by consuls and praetors, not tribunes. But that did not address the real problem now: a state of civil war had replaced republican government.

HEADHUNTING COMES TO ROME

The historian Appian writes that after Sulla's march on Rome, nothing – "neither law, nor political institutions, nor a sense of patriotism" – could deter men from violence. Another way to think about the situation is that with competing claims about who really represented Rome, armed force became a way of establishing power. Appeals to a leader's individual achievements or his connection to the gods could be important too.

Having made it to Africa, Marius was joined by his son and made plans to take back Rome. He was ready to use force, exactly as Sulla had. His allies back in Italy helped prepare the way by reminding all the new citizens of Marius' intention to distribute them across all the voting tribes. The new consul of 87, Cinna – whom Sulla had made swear an oath to uphold Sulla's acts – took up the new citizens' cause too. His colleague, Octavius, allied himself with the old citizens. An armed confrontation took place in the Forum, with many murdered. Cinna fled Rome and recruited troops in the towns of the newly enfranchised. He also won over a Roman army left by Sulla against Italian holdouts. Despite the Senate depriving Cinna of his consulship and the election of a replacement, this army declared that he was still consul, and he put his consular insignia back on. So an army was used to cobble together political legitimacy.

Marius sailed back to Etruria, boasting of his earlier victories over the Germans and insisting that he would see to the Italians' rights. He joined

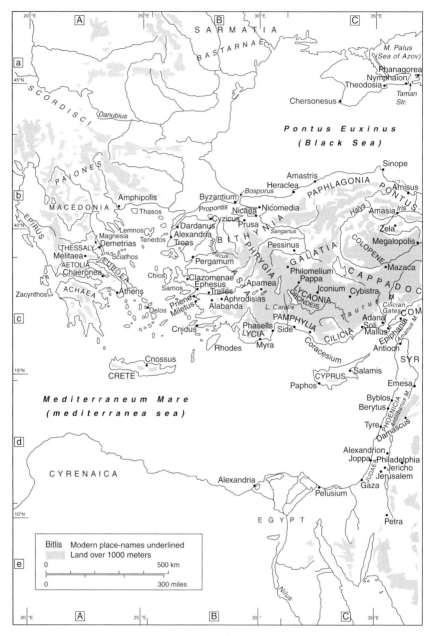

Map 5 The East

Cinna, and together they blockaded Rome to try to undermine Octavius and
his allies. The Samnites, in exchange for a very generous amnesty for themselves
and all who had deserted to them in the Social War, agreed to serve under
Marius. Octavius, meanwhile, had the dubious support of Pompeius Strabo,

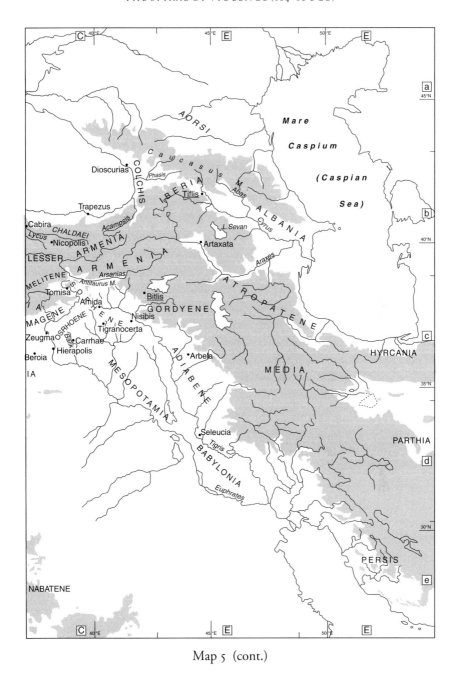

Map 5 (cont.)

a commander of Roman forces in the northern theater of the Social War. Camped outside Rome, Strabo refused to offer full use of his army until he secured election to a second consulship. But then he and his army succumbed to plague, probably aggravated by the Marian blockade.

Fearful of the anarchy that a food shortage might unleash, the Senate accepted the return of Marius and Cinna. Supporters of Marius found Octavius, decapitated him, and hung his head on the Rostra in the Forum. Other heads joined his there – in keeping with the new strategy of legitimation by terror. Cinna, however, like many of his fellow senators, was eager to rein in the violence in Rome, and he curtailed Marius' armed gangs. Sulla's laws were annulled, and Sulla himself was declared a public enemy.

For the next year (86), Cinna and Marius were elected consuls – Marius for the seventh time – in accord with the prophecy of the eaglets he had clung to for so many years. He died within a month, leaving Cinna dominant in Rome. Assessing Cinna's tenure in office is extremely difficult, so much did Sulla, after his final victory, come to control the historical record. Cicero, who lived in Rome at the time, would later recall that "for three years the city was free from fighting," which is probably a fair verdict. Cinna was eager to restore order (which was not necessarily the same thing as republican government) and enjoyed some success in doing so. Because the censors elected in 89 had failed to complete the census, a new attempt was made in 86 – apparently successful, although the recorded number of citizens is problematic (Table 1). There were also measures to stabilize the economy, badly damaged by the recent violence.

As for Sulla, officially he remained an enemy; and Marius' replacement as consul, Valerius Flaccus, was sent out to supersede Sulla, apparently through peaceful negotiation. Sulla made no move against Flaccus, and the two never met. Flaccus was assassinated in 85 by his own quaestor, Fimbria, who assumed command of the army. Many senators, meanwhile, were pressing for reconciliation, all the more so as it became clear that Sulla, having reached his own peace with Mithridates (also in 85) was planning to return to Italy. Those back in Rome had little taste left for fighting. Not so Cinna and his ally Carbo, who shared the consulship in 85. They felt they had no choice but to make military preparations, stoking fears among the recently enfranchised.

Sulla wrote to the Senate boasting of all of his military achievements, from the capture of Jugurtha – another jab at the now-dead Marius – to the defeat of Mithridates. Sulla also emphasized that he had taken in men driven from Rome and would soon be back to defend the interests of these men, and of Rome as a whole. Sulla was practically asserting that he *was* Rome.

The Senate continued to try to mediate, but in vain. Cinna and Carbo arranged for themselves to be consuls again, for 84, and they kept recruiting. After only part of their army crossed the Adriatic, other troops resisted, and Cinna was stabbed to death in a mutiny. Upon learning of it, Sulla immediately sailed to Italy with 40,000 troops. So the civil war would continue.

THE LION AND THE FOX

Sulla's war in the east and the civil war that followed in Italy were crucially intertwined. By the end of 88, Mithridates was master of Asia, holding court at Pergamum. But his ambitions did not stop here. Mithridates had sent his admiral, Archelaus, with a fleet to take control of the Aegean. Athens was won over to Mithridates' side, enticed by promises about the restoration of their democracy and debt relief. And a son of Mithridates swept through Thrace and harassed the Roman governor of Macedonia. Mithridates might soon control all of Macedonia and Greece.

Arriving in 87, Sulla put Athens and its harbor under an inexorable siege. Several Athenians came to Sulla in desperation and reminded him of their glorious past. "I was not sent to Athens by the Romans to study ancient history," he replied coldly, and the city soon fell to him. Moving into the plains of Boeotia, Sulla scored a major victory over the Mithridatic army at Chaeronea. When a second army landed, Sulla camped nearby and defeated it too. Mithridates' short-lived European empire was finished.

Ready to think about returning to Italy after these successes, Sulla began peace negotiations with Mithridates and made his way to Asia through Macedonia. Fimbria, with the army he had stolen from Flaccus, captured Pergamum in the meantime and narrowly failed to capture Mithridates. The king was ready to make a deal. At Dardanus, near Troy, he met Sulla and agreed to Sulla's terms: restoration of Bithynia and Cappadocia to their former kings, surrender of Asia and the Aegean fleet, and an indemnity.

Fimbria's army soon deserted to Sulla, leaving Sulla free to deal with Asia. Communities that had shown loyalty to Rome were generously rewarded, while the rebellious were punished. A massive indemnity was placed on the whole province, and Sulla's soldiers enjoyed a luxurious winter at the locals' expense. To some it seemed outrageous that despite the massacre of 88, Mithridates had sailed back home while Asia suffered. But as an opponent of his once said, Sulla was both a lion and a fox: he thought you won by force, but you had to be crafty in how you used it – he needed his troops to fight Romans.

In 83, Sulla's army landed at Brundisium in Italy. Several key allies soon joined him. From Africa came Metellus Pius, the son of Marius' great enemy Numidicus, and from Spain, Marcus Crassus, a refugee from Marius and Cinna. Pompeius Strabo's son (later Pompey the Great), only in his early twenties, had taken the even-bolder step of raising a legion, scored some victories over the Marians, and then presented himself to a clearly impressed Sulla. Although Cinna's ally Carbo had raised a massive army in Italy, Sulla encountered no resistance until reaching Campania, and it was fairly feeble at that. Sulla the fox won over one whole army by having his men fraternize with it. Carbo then rallied the Samnites – whom Sulla had crushed in the

Social War – while his fellow consul for 82, Marius' young son, chosen for the power of his name, recruited among his father's veterans. Both sides were relying on personal allegiances.

Young Marius was driven into the hilltop citadel at Praeneste, and Sulla briefly came to Rome, where the great Temple of Jupiter on the Capitoline had (probably accidentally) burnt down, aptly symbolizing the breakdown of the Republic. Carbo and his forces were worn down, Carbo fled to Africa, and it was left to the Samnites to try to relieve Marius. Failing in this, they made a dash to Rome – the wolf might still gore the bull – but Sulla quickly caught up with them. After a ferocious battle outside the city's Colline Gate (November 1, 82), the Samnite survivors were killed. The slain leaders' heads were sent to Praeneste, precipitating surrender of the Marians there. The main opposition was now in the provinces.

Sulla reinforced his victory with more violence. Long lists were issued of citizens who were named outlaws. Anyone thus "proscribed" could be killed for a large reward and their property confiscated. Some managed to escape Italy. The heads of those caught were displayed in the Forum. The sons and grandsons of the proscribed were legally banned from ever holding office, and at least some of the property confiscated went to Sulla's supporters, ensuring that the ban would not be lifted. Italian communities that had supported Carbo and Marius were also severely punished. Some, like Pompeii, were turned over for colonization by Sulla's veterans, who were given confiscated land in inalienable grants.

Sulla's final victory seemingly meant the end of civil war, at least in Italy (some high-profile opponents had escaped overseas). But even more than the events of 88, it also showed how the personal loyalty of a commander's soldiers allowed him to outmaneuver and defeat the Senate and the People of Rome – and make a mockery of Roman ideas of justice. What was to stop that from happening again? Could law replace force?

SULLA'S NEW CONSTITUTION

For Sulla, the gods were all-important. He was constantly on watch for messages from them, whether in dreams, prophecies, or portents. His accumulated victories proved that he had their special blessing – what the Romans called *felicitas*. After the Battle of the Colline Gate, the Senate and the People gave Sulla the new name Felix ("Blessed") to underscore his unique greatness. Sulla himself used it unhesitatingly after he celebrated a two-day triumph over Mithridates in January 81. A gilded statue of Sulla Felix was placed in front of the Rostra in the Forum. It clearly showed that civil war had fostered a more charismatic type of authority at Rome.

Part of Sulla's divine calling was to reestablish Rome: it would be the final victory in the life of greatness he had been promised by the eastern astrologer. Plans were made to rebuild the burnt Capitol. And Sulla had himself appointed to a dictatorship – the extraordinary office meant to cope with military crises and last used in the Second Punic War. Sulla's dictatorship was different. It had an unlimited term, and he was given a new, specific duty: "to write laws and put the state back in order." This would allow him effectively to create for Rome a new constitution (something he had just done in Athens). And so he did, with a series of laws that aimed to reform the Senate and make its members dominant overall, yet also more regulated.

Echoing his reforms of 88, Sulla reduced the power of tribunes. They could not introduce legislation without Senate approval, their power of veto was limited, and once elected they were debarred from holding any other political office. Nobody with any ambition would want the job now, and the plebeian assembly would not be able to override the Senate legislatively.

Meanwhile, the Senate itself was remade. Through the addition of as many as 300 new members, many of them Equestrian, its size was increased to around 450 members and would gradually rise even higher. This was because membership now was to be given automatically to former quaestors – it would not be up to censors to choose. The number of quaestors was increased to 20, and praetors to eight. As before, both offices had to be held prior to the consulship, minimum age limits were set, and the consulship could only be repeated after 10 years. To prevent long military commands – clearly a threat to republican government – it was planned that praetors and consuls alike would serve their magistracy fully in Rome and then hold a province for a single year following that, through an extension of *imperium*. There were now 10 provinces (Sicily, Sardinia with Corsica, the two Spains, Africa, Transalpine Gaul, Cisalpine Gaul, Macedonia, Asia, and Cilicia) – exactly the number of praetors and consuls.

Sulla also enacted a major overhaul of the criminal courts, the source of so much dissension in the 90s. Jurors would be drawn exclusively from the enlarged Senate to serve in seven different courts, each presided over by a praetor. The criminal laws were all rewritten, including the treason law, which attempted to rein in governors in command of armies. Governors were forbidden to leave the boundaries of their provinces or start wars without senatorial permission.

With the new constitution in place, Sulla gradually diminished his formal power, holding a regular consulship in 80 with Metellus Pius. He then left Rome for good, taking up residence in Campania, where he could cavort with the dancers, musicians, and actors and actresses whose company he had always enjoyed. He also was working on his lengthy, now lost memoirs, which gave the "definitive" presentation of Sulla Felix, the favorite of the gods, enjoying victory after victory.

THE END OF CIVIL WAR?

It was in Sulla's second consulship of 80 that an impressive speaker made his debut in the new criminal courts. Marcus Tullius Cicero was born in 106 in the small town of Arpinum, which happened also to be Marius' birthplace. Cicero's ambition was every bit as strong as the great general's. His wealthy father sent him to Rome to be educated by the best orators of the time, above all Licinius Crassus, staunch defender of the Senate and senatorial power. Cicero's education was interrupted by the Social War, in which he saw service under Pompeius Strabo, along with Strabo's son. Cicero returned to Rome, picking up the study of civil law and also philosophy, thanks to the arrival in Rome of the head of Plato's Academy in Athens, a refugee from Mithridates. Despite the troubles of 88 and 87 and then later in the decade, Cicero went on studying. He also made time for the theater, learning a trick or two from the actors' delivery.

Cicero's first jury trial saw him defending Sextus Roscius, accused of killing his father. Listeners would have been shocked when in his opening remarks Cicero mentioned an unpopular but powerful Greek freedman of Sulla's named Chrysogonus. He claimed that after the death of the elder Roscius, Chrysogonus had added the dead man's name to the list of the proscribed, in order to obtain valuable real estate in the Tiber valley. When Cicero's client made a protest, Chrysogonus hoped to remove him by accusing him of his father's murder. Chrysogonus must have assumed that his relationship with Sulla would protect him. What he did not count on was the young orator's nerve. While studiously exonerating Sulla, Cicero lambastes the freedman, with his Palatine mansion crammed full of art stolen during the proscriptions.

Cicero won his case, and with it his reputation was made. His published speech *For Roscius* survives and is a fine introduction to the man whose writings more than any other light up the last years of the Roman Republic. We see in Cicero's defense all the lawyer's tricks, many still used today. There is also a sincere denunciation of all the atrocities of his era. "Remove this cruelty from our state," Cicero urged the jurors. "Do not allow it to go on any longer . . . When every hour we are witnessing or hearing some terrible event . . . we lose all sense of humanity." Defending his client, Cicero was also imploring his contemporaries to stop the spiral of violence.

But it was in vain. In 82 Strabo's son Pompey had managed to regain Sicily from the Marians and put to death the former consul Carbo, who had gone there. Pompey then defeated the Marians in Africa under Domitius Ahenobarbus. Not yet a member of the Senate, Pompey refused in 80 to dismiss his army and demanded a triumph from Sulla. Another Marian, Sertorius, had been expelled from Spain in 81. The next year he returned and began building his own army, recruiting among the native Iberians. In time he even had his own senate, in Spain. The civil war was not over. Sulla's new constitution may have muffled the *plebs* in Rome and removed the Equestrians from the courts, but it was unable to restrain charismatic men like Sertorius and Pompey and their soldiers.

FURTHER READING

The Cambridge Ancient History (2nd ed.) Vol. 9 provides a sound narrative of political and military affairs (especially chap. 3 by A. Lintott, chap. 4 by E. Gabba, chap. 5 by J. G. F. Hind, and chap. 6 by R. Seager). E. Badian has written some particularly important essays on this period, including "Waiting for Sulla," *Journal of Roman Studies* 52 (1962), 47–61; *Lucius Sulla the Deadly Reformer* (Sydney, 1970); "The Death of Saturninus: Studies in Chronology and Prosopography," *Chiron* 14 (1984), 101–47. Kit Morrell, "Appian and the Judiciary Law of M. Livius Drusus," in K. Welch (ed.), *Appian's Roman History: Empire and Civil War* (Swansea, 2015), 235–55, reassesses the tribune.

Other valuable work on Sulla is A. Keaveney, *Sulla: The Last Republican* (2nd ed.; London, 2005); F. Santangelo, *Sulla, the Elites, and the Empire* (Leiden, 2007); C. Steel, "Rethinking Sulla: The Case of the Roman Senate," *Classical Quarterly* 64 (2014), 657–68. H. Flower, *Roman Republics* (Princeton, 2010), has a particularly strong reinterpretation of Sulla, and helpful for Sulla's memoirs is C. Smith and A. Powell (eds.), *The Lost Memoirs of Augustus and the Development of Roman Biography* (Swansea, 2009).

A challenging reinterpretation of the Italian question (not entirely accepted here) is given by H. Mouritsen, *Italian Unification: A Study in Ancient and Modern Historiography* (London, 1998); less radical and informative is C. J. Dart's *The Social War, 91 to 89 BCE* (Farnham, 2014). Older but still valuable discussions can be found in E. Badian, *Foreign Clientelae* (Oxford, 1958); E. Gabba, *Republican Rome, the Army, and the Allies* (Berkeley, 1976); P. A. Brunt, *The Fall of the Roman Republic and Related Essays* (Oxford, 1988).

The (initially hesitant) growth of Roman administration in the east is well analyzed in R. Kallet-Marx, *Hegemony to Empire: The Development of the Roman Imperium in the East from 148 to 62 B.C.* (Berkeley, 1995). A. N. Sherwin-White, *Roman Foreign Policy in the East, 168 B.C. to A.D. 1* (London, 1984), is good on military affairs. On the great enemy, see also B. C. McGing, *The Foreign Policy of Mithridates VI Eupator, King of Pontus* (Leiden, 1986), and J. M. Højte (ed.), *Mithridates VI and the Pontic Kingdom* (Aarhus, 2009), which includes a paper by J. M. Madsen with a less aggressive Mithridates than the one here.

Works on Cicero and Pompey are mentioned in subsequent chapters. On the ragged endings of civil war, see J. Osgood, "Ending Civil War at Rome: Rhetoric and Reality, 88 B.C.E.–197 C.E.," *American Historical Review* 120 (2015), 1683–95.

6

―

ITALY AND THE REINVENTION OF ROME

(150–50 BCE)

Sometime in the later second century BCE, Maras Atinius, a magistrate in the Italian city of Pompeii, had a marble sundial erected in one of the city's major baths. Built perhaps as early as the fifth century, these Stabian Baths originally consisted of a Greek-style exercise court and a few tubs. In the second century they became far more luxurious. Water now flowed copiously from Pompeii's aqueduct, heated air circulated beneath the floors and warmed the rooms above, and there were separate suites, with beautiful stucco decorations, for men and women to undress and bathe in. Atinius' sundial was just one part of the refurbishment.

On the sundial itself he had inscribed these words: "Maras Atinius, son of Maras, quaestor, with the money raised from fines, by decree of the assembly, saw to this being set up." The name he shared with his father, Maras, instantly reveals that he was not Roman. In the second century, Pompeii, while allied with Rome, was an independent town, controlled by local families who descended from earlier Samnite settlers. They spoke Oscan, not Latin, and the inscription on Atinius' sundial is in fact in Oscan, with letters written from right to left.

Yet Atinius' official title, "quaestor," shows that despite its political independence, Pompeii's government had borrowed at least some of its political terminology from Rome. As the city grew richer, it developed a more specialized administration, and new offices were given Roman names. The practice of using fines to fund public works was also probably a borrowing from Rome. The sundial suggests, then, how leading members of the elegant town on the Bay of Naples distinguished themselves by appeals to Roman politics and power as well as to Greek culture and sophistication. Pompeii was part of a larger world.

Thanks to its burial by Mt. Vesuvius in 79 CE, Pompeii is by far the most fully known city of Roman Italy, archeologically speaking. Not just baths, but

Figure 6.1 The undressing room of the Stabian Baths in Pompeii. The well-preserved stucco decorations on the ceiling give a sense of the baths' increased opulence after renovations in the second century BCE. (Photo Wikimedia Commons.)

also houses, bars, temples, political buildings, a theater, and an amphitheater have been recovered, along with furniture, dinnerware, cooking vessels, foodstuffs, mosaics, paintings, and even graffiti. To walk along its paved streets gives an unparalleled sense of day-to-day life in the Roman world.

Inevitably Pompeii is easiest to grasp in the years immediately preceding its final destruction, but its earlier history can be pieced together, including its flowering in the second century BCE. At that time leading families, enriched through their participation in the Mediterranean-wide economy that developed alongside Roman *imperium*, built houses comparable to those of Greek kings. We can also trace the consequences of Pompeii's decision to hold out against Rome in the Social War (91–88 BCE). Sulla besieged the city and late in the 80s sent some of his veterans there. For a time they dominated Pompeii, and they gave the city a new look – as well as a new language, Latin.

Pompeii will be a guide to us for tracing the hugely important history of Rome's relationship with Italy from about 150 BCE onward. Of course, Pompeii cannot stand for all Italian towns. The Italian Peninsula was made up of distinct regions, with varied landscapes, economies, languages, and customs. But like Pompeii, many communities were transformed by the growth of Roman *imperium*. They developed new, more intensive types of agriculture to supply the growing metropolis, and they made money through war and trade. They were embellished with amenities in the latest Greek fashion. It is this success that helps explain the resentment that led to the Social War.

While in one sense the Italians lost that war, in another they were victors. They gained Roman citizenship and the rights that came with it, and gradually their towns became incorporated into the Roman state. Their leading members had access to new economic opportunities and positions on military commanders' staffs; some would even penetrate the top political class at Rome. But as Italians started to feel more Roman, the limitations of the city-based SPQR became clearer: if you lived hundreds of miles from Rome and could never make it to the city, how meaningful was your vote? Meanwhile, Sulla's victory in civil war and colonization program left a legacy of instability, with gangs of struggling men roaming the countryside. Some were willing to join armed uprisings, including the rebellion of the now legendary gladiator Spartacus. In this way too Italians challenged SPQR.

The history of Italy after the Social War is a troubled one, but also vital. Rome's bold move of massively extending the citizenship – a unique event in ancient history – led to problems. But it also inspired men and women across the peninsula and beyond to devise new political institutions and new cultural forms that would help transform Rome from a city-state into the world state.

ITALIAN LANDSCAPES AND ROMAN MIGHT

The Italian Peninsula is naturally fragmented and quite varied in its landscapes. While the Alps create a barrier to the north, the Apennine Mountains, starting in the northwest, are a spine stretching down the country for more than 600 miles. Quite steep in places, and also broad, in antiquity they tended to block easy passage from one coast to the other and also cut off the flat Po valley, with its immensely fertile lands, from the rest of the peninsula. Mountainous areas, like Lucania and Bruttium in the southwest, are full of peaks and intricate valleys, which made them most suitable for pasturage. The volcanic landscapes of Campania, where Pompeii was located – and also Latium and Etruria to the north of Rome – enjoyed a rich soil that yielded excellent wines, olive oils, and cereals.

It is not surprising that many of Italy's earliest cities were in these last three regions, which also enjoyed access to the sea. Greeks arrived in the Bay of Naples in the eighth century BCE and established colonies along the Campanian coast, as well as in southwestern Italy and Sicily. In the second century, Greek culture – and the Greek language – still flourished in places like Neapolis (modern Naples). The Etruscans were influenced heavily by

Greek culture but maintained their own Etruscan language into the second century.

The Oscan-speaking Samnites dominated the southern Apennines. Divided into four main tribal states, each of which was administered by a chief magistrate, they were linked together in a federal structure that made them a powerful military force. From the mid-fifth century they extended their control into Campania and Lucania, taking over Pompeii during this time. But when they came up against Latium, Rome drove them back in a series of bitter wars. The Samnites fought with all their traditional ferocity against Rome one last time in the Social War. Although based in a mountainous part of Italy and less urbanized, they did build impressive religious sanctuaries where they could come together.

Difficult terrain, linguistic diversity, local traditions, and warriors' pride: all of these were obstacles to the Romans as they tried to impose a basic order on the Italian Peninsula that would allow greater exploitation of natural and human resources. By 150, successful strategies had been developed, worth looking at here because they would later be used throughout the empire, especially in the west.

Perhaps most important was the alliance system. Put most simply, other than slaves, those living in Italy were either Roman citizens, Latins, or *socii* ("allies"). Citizens lived in the city of Rome itself, of course, but also in towns granted Roman citizenship as a privilege or in specially founded citizen colonies, often located on the coast, which were part of the Roman state. Latins originally were the Romans' neighbors in Latium, but later the term came to refer to those communities given a package of rights such as the permission to marry Romans. Latin colonies were established too; typically they were settled with Romans who gave up their citizenship, in exchange for a grant of land as well as the Latin rights. Unlike Roman colonies, they were self-governing. Obliged to participate in Rome's wars, the Latins were a core part of the military machine. The third group, the *socii*, were simply bound by treaty to Rome; in exchange for protection, they were required to offer military service. Many Etruscan communities, along with communities in far southern Italy, were *socii*. The beauty of the alliance system was that it required minimal direct administration, brought stability to Italy, and allowed Rome access to vast reservoirs of soldiers, who were eager to share in the profits won on campaigns.

Colonies were integral to the success of the alliance system and helped transform the landscapes of Italy. Citizen colonies were usually founded from scratch rather than on major preexisting settlements and were strategically located. Residents were typically excused from regular military levies since their settlements acted as garrisons. Colonies on the coast – the most popular location – protected vital ports and policed against pirate ships. Eighteen were founded in southwestern Italy after the Second Punic War, when piracy had flourished.

Latin colonies, located in territory seized in war, also acted as Roman strongholds. In the 260s BCE, for example, Beneventum and Aesernia were established on old Samnite settlements as Latin colonies to keep a watch on the Samnites. The Via Appia, the great road leading from Rome to Capua, was extended so as to pass through Beneventum and also the Latin colony at Venusia, ultimately going all the way to the key port of Brundisium. Roads that sped up and regularized connections between settlements helped the Romans overcome the difficulties in controlling vast and fragmented territories.

The Roman transformation of Cisalpine Gaul in what is now northern Italy was profound and provides a good preview of the developments to come later in the provinces. The story begins all the way back in the 280s, when, after war with the Celtic Senones, the Romans seized their territory and founded a Roman maritime colony, Sena Gallica. A Latin colony, Ariminum (modern Rimini), was founded in 268 as a reinforcement. An ambitious scheme by the tribune Gaius Flaminius to distribute the territory to needy Roman citizens in the 230s helped unify the Celts in war against Rome. Crossing into Etruria through the Apennines, they were defeated by the Romans, who then counter-invaded northern Italy. Large Latin colonies were founded at Cremona and Placentia (modern Piacenza), key crossings on the Po River. As censor in 220, Gaius Flaminius built a great highway from Rome to Rimini across the Apennines, about 200 miles in length. After the war with Hannibal, Rome resumed war against the Celts, and more colonies and roads followed. The provincial landscape became a great network of roads.

Moreover, in conjunction with the new colonies and roads, annexed territory underwent centuriation – the division of land into exact squares, which were then subdivided among settlers. Like roads, centuriation imposed Roman ideas on the landscape itself. Hand in hand with it came great hydraulic engineering projects to manage the tremendous amounts of water and silt unleashed each spring by the melting of mountain snow. Through these efforts, the land of Cisalpine Gaul became some of the most agriculturally productive in Italy. It supported herds of pigs that fed Rome and sheep whose wool clothed the households of Italy. There were bumper crops of cereals and, according to an ancient geographer, wine was stored in wooden jars bigger than houses.

By 150, then, the Romans had what seemed to be a firm grasp on Italy up to the Alps. The alliance system had allowed domination of the peninsula and manned armies for wars overseas. Colonies and roads helped overcome the difficulties imposed by geography. The end of fighting in Italy, though, meant that no new colonies were being created in Italy, removing a safety valve for struggling Romans. At the same time, many Italians were benefitting economically from their involvement in the empire, and from the opportunities empire created in Italy.

A NEW HARVEST OF PROFITS

Agriculture was the most important sector of the Italian economy. Along with cereals and legumes, olive oil and wine were staples of the diet. Fruits, vegetables, fish, and meat – including the Roman favorite, pork – supplemented them. Ancient sources, including accounts of the tribune Tiberius Gracchus, once led scholars to assume that over the second century the smaller farms that produced such crops or raised livestock, including sheep for wool, were replaced with huge estates. Slaves poured in from overseas to work them, the argument went, while military service took peasants away from their farms. The spoils of war and empire allowed wealthy landowners, whether Roman citizens or Italian allies, to buy up more and more. Grain increasingly was imported from Sicily, Sardinia, and beyond, allowing these investors to intensify production of more lucrative crops, such as grapes for wine.

More recent research has called some of this picture into doubt. Slaves were arriving before the second century, and soldiers underwent extended tours of military service long before Tiberius Gracchus came on the scene. What did change in the second century was the end of colonization within Italy. Moreover, warfare on the whole after 168 became less lucrative. Opportunities for less well-off Romans were shrinking. Meanwhile, population probably was increasing, heightening competition over the land. As survey archeology also suggests, small farms survived, but there were not enough to go around. Almost certainly some peasants migrated to Rome.

All of that said, there was a growth of estate-based agriculture in certain regions of Italy in the second century, affecting Romans and Italians alike. Some areas did enjoy unusual natural resources, for example Campania, whose volcanic soil allowed the hills to be covered with olives and grape vines. Along with access to the sea, rivers, or even good roads, these resources, when exploited more fully, allowed landowners to produce larger crops that could be transported to markets farther away. The growing city of Rome was the most obvious of these. Estates in Campania, Latium, and Etruria over time started producing more olives and wine to feed city dwellers and quench their thirst. There also increasing opportunities to supply Rome with perishable products such as fruits, vegetables, fresh meat, fish, and flowers.

Estates did not really become mammoth in size, nor would they specialize entirely in one crop. Rather, they would engage in a range of activities, including growing vines, growing fruit, raising animals, and cultivating fish in artificial ponds. Much like modern investors with stocks and bonds, wealthy landowners were more inclined to build a portfolio of smaller estates rather than one huge compound. All this diversification was a hedge against the risk of agricultural failure. While slaves certainly did provide labor, there also were roles for the growing number of struggling peasants – as extra help during the busy harvest time, for example, or as full-time tenants.

Cato the Elder's book *On Agriculture* gives a sense of how estates were being run in the second century. To be sure, Cato at times waxed nostalgic for a more rustic past – as Tiberius Gracchus did too – and included a long celebration of the humble cabbage: among other virtues, it promotes digestion, is a laxative, and if you eat enough of it before drinking you can avoid a hangover. But alongside such homely advice, a ruthless system of management is outlined. When you visit your estate, Cato warned the absentee owner, first inspect it yourself and then check in with the slave overseer. Don't accept any excuses for failure to get work done. If it was rainy, the slaves should have cleaned the farm buildings "or mended their patchwork clothes and hoods." If the slaves said they were sick, their food rations should have been cut. The overall goal was to sell whatever was surplus or no longer needed: "sell the oil, if the price is satisfactory, sell the wine and the surplus grain; sell the old work oxen, the blemished cattle . . . the old tools, the aged slave."

The expansion of Roman power overseas clearly was intertwined with the new estates. Successful wars yielded slaves to work them. The profits of empire flowed into the city of Rome and fueled the growth of a huge market there for agricultural products, including wool. Also, there were increasing opportunities overseas. As the Celtic peoples of Transalpine Gaul developed a taste for wine – still flourishing two millennia later in France – Italians catered to it by shipping larger and larger quantities of their inventory to them. Using the clay of riverbeds, estate-owners created huge jars in which to ship the wine – and other products too, including olive oil, fish sauce, and preserved fruits. Smaller pieces of pottery themselves became a popular export. Wrecked ships have been recovered with a holding capacity of thousands of large wine jars.

One shipwreck likely points to the growing fortunes being made in Pompeii in the second century thanks to agriculture. Found off the French Riviera near Cannes, it held wine jars with seals labeled in the Oscan script with the name Lassius. People with this name are only otherwise known in Pompeii and nearby Surrentum (modern Sorrento). Another indication of the success of Pompeian wine was that a grape called *Pompeiana* became well known beyond Pompeii. So too did the "Pompeian onion" and "Pompeian cabbage." Roman *imperium* helped make Pompeian landowners rich: exploiting their fertile land, they found markets in the city of Rome and even farther away, in Gaul, Spain, and Africa.

LIVING LIKE A KING

Rome's growing power enriched Pompeians and other Italians in other ways too, with profound cultural and political consequences. Warfare could be hugely profitable. The Italian allies shared in plunder on campaign, with their leaders probably getting significant shares. After Mummius sacked Corinth and stripped it of its treasures, he donated to Italian communities artistic masterpieces in recognition of their contributions to Rome. A statue base inscribed in Oscan found in Pompeii's sanctuary for Apollo reveals that the town received one. Supplying armies with food and equipment, including ships, also created opportunities for enterprising Italian communities.

Trade with the eastern Mediterranean – along with the financing of it – was another benefit Italians enjoyed. Greek-speakers from the Bay of Naples, including those based at the key port of Puteoli, made money by importing fine eastern wines, spices, silks, works of art, and other luxuries, as well as more basic items.

The now-abandoned island of Delos in the Aegean has yielded numerous inscriptions that give vivid glimpses of this economic network. One man who turns up several times is Philostratus, son of Philostratus, a Syrian-born emigrant to Naples who took citizenship there but maintained an active role in Delos' trade and finance. There are plenty of Oscan names in Delos' inscriptions as well, belonging to men from Campania or Samnite territory. In the early first century, "the merchants and those who do business in the square marketplace dedicated to Apollo, Artemis and Leto" set up a statue to Maraeus Gerillanus, the son of Maraeus, "banker at Delos." Despite his clearly Oscan name, they call him "Roman," a term Greeks typically used for Italians. Romans depended on Italian trade and the financiers who supported it, like Maraeus. When problems arose with piracy in the late second century, a law passed in Rome insisted that "citizens of Rome and Latin allies from Italy" be able to conduct "without peril whatever business they require" and safely sail the seas.

Excavations at Pompeii have produced evidence of just how well some Campanians were doing economically. Leading Pompeians built houses on a staggering scale. Most famous is the House of the Faun, named for a delightful bronze statue of a dancing Dionysian reveler found in its

Figure 6.2 Pompeii's grandest mansion, the House of the Faun, built in the second century BCE. The dancing reveler seen here welcomed visitors to the intoxicating parties that would take place in the house's entertaining spaces. (Photo Gianni Dagli Orti/The Art Archive at Art Resource, NY.)

atrium. The house occupied 31,000 square feet (although a little more than half of this was open courtyards). It boasted splendid multicolor mosaics. A variety of marine creatures are depicted with great accuracy on one – delicacies no doubt enjoyed at banquets in the house. There were mosaics showing theatrical masks and life on the River Nile. Most impressive was a huge mosaic, made up of one and a half million tiny colored cubes, illustrating Alexander the Great on a rearing horse facing off against the Persian king Darius in his chariot. It was probably based on a painting, perhaps one made for one of the kings who succeeded Alexander. The opulence and hedonism of Hellenistic royal courts was a clear inspiration for the owner of this house, and others like him in Pompeii.

Pompeii's public buildings also reveal the embrace of contemporary Greek culture. Not only was there the refurbishment of the Stabian Baths with Atinius' sundial. Nearby a whole theater quarter developed, with a theater of course, built in the Greek style, but also associated facilities, including Greek-style exercise grounds. Sacred precincts in the town were renovated. An entirely new sanctuary went up outside the city, honoring the favorite god, Dionysus. Civic space was upgraded too. Pride of place was the

Figure 6.3 The showstopper of the House of the Faun's many mosaics, depicting Alexander the Great on the verge of a great victory over the King of Persia. Alexander's conquest held a mirror up to the success Italians like the owners of the house enjoyed on the Mediterranean stage. Museo Archeologico Nazionale, Naples, Italy. (Photo Alfredo Dagli Orti/The Art Archive at Art Resource, NY.)

basilica, a building covering 16,000 square feet that was used for financial and commercial exchange as well as legal business.

Pompeii is unique for the extensiveness of what is preserved, but other Italian communities show impressive building campaigns around the year 100. In Latium, the allied city of Praeneste thoroughly renovated its great sanctuary for Fortune, an appropriate goddess to honor in a period of enrichment. Inspired by Greek sanctuaries that were laid out theatrically on a series of terraces, the complex at Praeneste exploited the emerging new technology of concrete, which not only allowed huge platforms to be built but also was much cheaper than cut stone. Also in Latium, the town of Aletrium was overhauled, as an inscription for its benefactor Betilienus Varus reveals. He oversaw construction of new pavements, an exercise area, a sundial, a basilica, a bathing pool, an aqueduct, and more. Even in the less urbanized Samnite heartland, the major sanctuary at Pietrabbondante was redeveloped along Hellenistic lines, with a Greek-style theater positioned on axis below a temple. It too is a testimony to the growing wealth of Italians, and to commercial voyages east.

Figure 6.4 The elegant theater of the Samnite sanctuary at Pietrabbondante. A fancy architect – who possibly worked at Pompeii too – designed the handsome curved steps and brackets with griffins and the figure of Atlas. (Photo © DeA Picture Library/Art Resource, NY.)

By standing at Pietrabbondante, or in the House of the Faun at Pompeii, we more fully understand the buildup to the Social War. Italians made numerous contributions to the success of Roman *imperium*. They benefitted in turn. But they as much as Romans would have had concerns during difficult periods, such as the Spanish Wars of the 140s and 130s or the crisis of the last decade of the last century BCE. Moreover, while Romans had been exempted from direct taxation on their land since 167, Italians still had to pay for the contingents they sent to fight in Roman wars. Add to this the tales of abusive Roman magistrates – such as the consul who flogged the Campanian magistrate because he failed to clear the men's baths quickly enough for his wife (Chapter 4) – and it is easy to see why Italians leaders sought to renegotiate their relationship with Rome.

THE PARADOXICAL AFTERMATH OF THE SOCIAL WAR

While the Romans prevailed militarily in the Social War, they did so by conceding almost from the start that Italians would gain political recognition. The 50-year resistance to extension of citizenship was over. There were, it is true, efforts to limit Italians to only some of the voting tribes, in order to discount their votes, but Cinna finally distributed them throughout all

35 tribes (Chapter 5). Even the status of Cisalpine Gaul changed: a measure passed by Pompeius Strabo gave Latin rights to those north of the Po, full Roman citizenship to those south.

The end result was a huge increase in the number of citizens. The recorded figure for the census of 70/69 is 910,000, dramatically higher than second-century figures. Yet the political organs that governed the much-increased Roman People would continue to be based totally in the city itself. Since many of the newly enfranchised would have found it hard, if not impossible, to appear in Rome for legislative or even electoral assemblies, the assemblies could hardly be thought to reflect the views of the People as a whole. Similarly, the Senate was not instantly filled with new Italians. In fact, quite the opposite was true. To be sure, on some occasions towns sent decrees to the Senate in Rome expressing their views. But there was no effort to reimagine the Senate as a federal council, an institution perfectly well known to the Romans. Thus one result of the enfranchisement was to increase, and advertise, the unsuitability of Roman political institutions.

Yet paradoxically, at exactly the same time, Roman-style institutions would spread through all the towns of what was now Roman Italy. All the Latin colonies and formerly independent allies had to be incorporated, and they would become *municipia*. In much earlier times, *municipia* were communities inhabited by Roman citizens who explicitly lacked the right to vote. Most, though, had later received the vote, and so this seemed the most pertinent model.

In the new *municipia*, at least in principle, there would be an assembly and a town council as well as magistrates, with a great deal of power going to this last group. One would hardly expect the Romans to spread radical democracy! To make a *municipium*, envoys familiar with the territory might come from Rome and would arrange for the drafting of a charter, on bronze tablets. Fragments of such tablets (mostly of later provenance) survive and show a preoccupation with the magistrates and the councilors – including property and residency requirements for office holders. Some allowances were made for local circumstances, and there probably was a great deal of variety, in practice at least, until the time of Augustus.

As part of the organization of the new *municipia*, the Romans had to determine which land belonged to which community. Like earlier colonizations, the rulings made could have a profound impact on the landscape. This would be especially true in areas not previously organized around towns, including parts of Cisalpine Gaul. Landscapes would be surveyed and divided and towns created to host the council and magistrates who were now to govern. Since towns were the key to the new system, the reorganization led to a wave of urbanization.

Meanwhile, to reward his own veterans, punish his opponents, and maintain control of Italy as civil war wound down, Sulla carried out his own colonization scheme. Unlike in earlier colonization, which often created settlements from scratch, Sulla sent his soldiers to live in existing communities or even to take them over. A full list does not exist, but colonies are attested for Campania, Latium, Etruria, and Umbria – areas that had sided with the Marians.

Pompeii, which had been besieged by Sulla during the Social War, probably was little inclined to support him afterward. It was one of the sites he had marked out for colonization, and there is uniquely rich evidence from here to show the impact of Sulla's policy. Perhaps around 3,000 of the dictator's soldiers arrived, led by a younger relative, Publius Sulla. Publius established a new constitution for the town, which was given a new name: *colonia Cornelia Veneria Pompeianorum. Cornelia* referred to Sulla's family name and *Veneria* to Venus, his patron goddess, who would also now guard Pompeii. Roman-style magistracies were established, held by Sulla's veterans, and Latin took over as the official language.

The new settlers oversaw large building projects that demonstrated that their interests were not entirely the same as those of the affluent Samnite families. A new temple to the patron goddess Venus was erected. A new covered theater was built, with construction directed by the two chief magistrates, Quinctius Valgus and Marcus Porcius. (Quinctius Valgus almost certainly was a close associate of Sulla and a man who built up a portfolio of Italian real estate during Sulla's proscriptions). Smaller than the old theater, the new structure might primarily have been desired as a political meeting place for the colonists. It closely resembles the theater at Pietrabbondante, showing that Greek-style architecture was appreciated by the new settlers.

By far, though, the most important new building – supervised *and* paid for by the same Quinctius Valgus and Marcus Porcius – was an enormous amphitheater, which could seat 20,000. It was partly built on the old city walls. Since walls were a source of tremendous pride for ancient cities, their incorporation into the new structure helped efface Pompeii's former civic identity. In this new structure, quintessentially Roman gladiatorial contests were staged, and they became quite popular, drawing spectators from neighboring towns.

On another section of the city wall, new houses went up, boasting terraces with remarkable views out to the sea – echoing the much bigger villas that leading Romans were now building along the Campanian coast. The colonists also built ostentatious tombs for themselves on the roads leading out of the city, just as Romans did back in Rome.

Figure 6.5 Pompeii's giant of an amphitheater, built around 70 BCE. The lower tiers of seating were reserved for the leading members of the recently colonized town, reinforcing the social hierarchy. In the background, steam billows out of Mt. Vesuvius. (HIP/Art Resource, NY.)

Pompeii was becoming more focused on Rome than it had been before. While it can hardly speak for all Italian communities, this was a general trend, whether in colonies, old Italian towns that became new *municipia*, or newly created towns. This does not mean that towns gave up the well-established taste for Greek-style amenities. After all, Rome itself had already embraced Greek architecture with its grand basilicas and marble temples, and in the 50s BCE it would finally get a stone theater too (Chapter 7). Italy was becoming more Roman, but Rome was also becoming more Italian.

Leading members of the old Italian towns, while continuing to invest in their villas and fishponds, increasingly integrated themselves into Roman life. Some would join the Equestrian order, with the opportunities that status brought for obtaining lucrative state contracts. Others – especially those whose families enjoyed the franchise before the Social War – would even try to break their way into the political class, following in the footsteps of earlier new men like Cato the Elder and Marius. Key to their success was networking with well-established Roman senators. Some rhetorical ability was essential, and a particular gift for it could be a real asset. So too was military ability. Prime examples of men with these abilities are the fluent speaker M. Lollius Palicanus and the soldier L. Afranius, two supporters of Pompey (son of Strabo) from Picenum, east of the Apennines – where Pompey had large estates and many clients.

Overall, relatively few of the new or newish Romans made it into the Senate, and certainly not all the way to the consulship, in the years immediately following the Social War. Competition for office was ferocious, and there were plenty of members of old Roman families, who reinforced ideas of hereditary distinction through ever more splendid funerals, monuments, and even scholarship they commissioned about their families' histories. The real opportunity for the Italians came when full civil war resumed in the 40s BCE and the victorious Julius Caesar was able to reward the talented men who had helped him. By then, traditional government by SPQR had broken down, and Italians would have a greater role in the new political system that followed.

CHAOS IN THE COUNTRYSIDE

Further contributing to that final breakdown of republican government was ongoing instability in many parts of the Italian countryside – in part a legacy of the Social and civil wars. Whole regions had been devastated, none more than Samnium. Old Latin colonies like Aesernia were sacked, as were sanctuaries like Pietrabbondante. The Samnite countryside was ravaged. While many Samnites died in battle, several thousand more were put to death on Sulla's orders following the battle of the Colline Gate. This resulted in countless refugees, in this part of Italy and elsewhere too, for instance Etruria, which received a number of colonies.

One consequence was an increase in banditry. Mountainous regions of Italy, such as Lucania and Bruttium, had long been turned over to sheep grazing, as had also the dry southeastern part of the peninsula. To protect the valuable flocks, whether from wolves or thieves, shepherds were armed. In fact, it was not always easy to tell a shepherd from a bandit, since the skill set involved for each was nearly identical. In difficult times, some shepherds became predators, and others joined their ranks. Gangs roamed the hills and sprang attacks on those travelling the highways.

The unsettled countryside is the context for a great slave war that broke out in 73 BCE, bringing still more instability. The uprising began in a prisonlike gladiatorial school in Capua, in northern Campania. As the taste for gladiatorial entertainment grew – evidenced by Pompeii's massive new amphitheater – entrepreneurs bought up male slaves with imposing physiques and trained them for competition.

One of these unwilling gladiators was Spartacus, a Thracian who probably served for a time as an auxiliary in the Roman army. He and about 70 others broke out, armed initially only with kitchen knives, and fled to Mount Vesuvius, which was not yet known to be a volcano. When put under siege by a Roman force of a couple of thousand, they wove a ladder from vines and escaped by lowering themselves down a steep precipice. They took the Roman force by surprise and then drew hundreds, and ultimately thousands, of supporters, as agricultural slaves, shepherds, and even poor free men joined them. Spartacus' army defeated further Roman armies and then marched up and down Italy – exploiting Roman roads – with some nearly making it over the Alps.

Both consuls of 72 were dispatched against the rebels, who had now split up. Some took refuge in the massive limestone promontory called Gargano and were defeated, but Spartacus still eluded capture. Later in 72, the Senate awarded supreme command to M. Licinius Crassus, an ally of Sulla notorious for the fortune he had acquired in real estate in Rome and craving military distinction. Spartacus hoped to cross to Sicily with the aid of pirate ships, but Crassus managed to trap him on the peninsula at Rhegium, the toe of the Italian boot. Spartacus and his troops broke through Crassus' barricade but they were then defeated in a series of engagements. Six thousand captives were crucified along the Appian Way, a gory sight for travelers between Rome and the far south of Italy. Meanwhile, some additional fugitives in the north were captured by Pompey, returning now from a war in Spain (Chapter 7).

The story of Spartacus does not end with his death. He haunted the imaginations of later Roman writers and in modern times was turned into a powerful symbol of opposition to oppression – perhaps most famously in Stanley Kubrick's 1960 film, *Spartacus*. His more immediate legacy was his destabilization of Italy, especially its south. The rebels had devastated swathes of countryside. Farm buildings were destroyed, equipment seized, fields ravaged, flocks lost. Stray followers of Spartacus who had not been captured continued to roam the hills and woods. Pirates, meanwhile, who had grown in number during the Mediterranean-wide instability of the 80s BCE, took the opportunity to raid Italy's coasts during Spartacus' war, and they continued to do so afterward (Chapter 7).

Small farmers struggled throughout this period. Even if not driven from their lands by Sullan colonists, slave armies, or bandits, they would still find it hard to make a living in such chaotic times. Sulla's veterans, in particular, seem to have struggled on their new farms. Some in the countryside flocked to Rome, attracted by the hope of work there and by grain handouts, further swelling the metropolis. Others volunteered for military service, hoping for a generous cut of plunder, or even a grant of land, the difficulties of making a go of farming notwithstanding.

Others still – including those dispossessed by Sulla – rallied under politicians demanding reform, to the point of taking up arms. In 63 BCE, a financially desperate senator, L. Sergius Catilina ("Catiline"), joined forces with struggling peasants to put pressure on the government in Rome (Chapter 8). From a speech of Cicero we know that Sulla's relative Publius, even though it was he who established the new colony at Pompeii, was accused of trying to rally the old native Pompeians – along with some gladiators – to the side of Catiline. Whatever the truth of that allegation, Cicero's speech reveals that there were tensions in Pompeii – tensions that also existed in other towns of Italy, where memories of the civil war did not die easily.

The history of Italy outside Rome is at the heart of Roman history from 150 BCE onward. Italian successes and resentment fueled demand for more respect from Rome, leading to the Social War. Political recognition was conceded, forcing the Roman state to reorganize in part. Now the state would be made up of Rome itself but also several hundred Roman towns, from the Po valley to southern Italy. The reforms created a system that would allow the Roman state to stretch even farther, ultimately to become, in the age of Augustus, a stable world state. But the imperfect integration of leading Italians into the top political class in the late Republic fueled resentment. Many more ordinary Italians were not integrated at all and would not stand up to defend SPQR when it came under heavy attack in the 40s. The political framework required further adjustment, and new ideas of what it meant to be Roman had to be worked out. Pompeii, we shall see, like other Italian communities, was to have another makeover.

FURTHER READING

M. Beard, *Pompeii: The Life of a Roman Town* (London, 2008) is a vivid introduction to the buried city. For its tangled history with Rome, especially valuable are P. Zanker, *Pompeii: Public and Private Life* (Cambridge, MA, 1998) and A. E. Cooley and M. G. L. Cooley, *Pompeii and Herculaneum: A Sourcebook* (2nd ed.; Abingdon, 2014).

T. W. Potter, *Roman Italy* (London, 1987), is a useful, though now somewhat dated, introduction focused on archeological evidence. A new approach to landscape was suggested by N. Purcell, "The Creation of the Provincial Landscape: The Roman Impact on Cisalpine Gaul," in T. Blagg and M. Millett (eds.), *The Early Roman Empire in the West* (Oxford, 1990), 7–29. For more recent scholarship on the economy, see the works mentioned in Chapter 1 and also P. Kay, *Rome's Economic Revolution* (Oxford, 2014), especially chaps. 7–9. There has been intense debate in recent years on the demographic profile of Italy, including N. S. Rosenstein, *Rome at War: Farms, Families, and Death in the Middle Republic* (Chapel Hill, 2004); A. Launaro, *Peasants and Slaves: The Rural Population of Roman Italy (200 BC to AD 100)* (Cambridge, 2011); L. de Ligt, *Citizens and Soldiers: Studies in the Demographic History of Roman Italy 225 BC–AD 100* (Cambridge, 2012); S. Hin, *The Demography of Roman Italy: Population Dynamics in an Ancient Conquest Society (201 BCE–14 CE)* (Cambridge, 2013). Foundational, especially for its collection of data, is P. A. Brunt, *Italian Manpower, 225*

B.C.–A.D. 14 (Oxford, 1971). K. Lomas, *Roman Italy, 338 BC–AD 200: A Sourcebook* (London, 1996) is a useful collection of texts with helpful introductory essays; a good overview is also provided by J. R. Patterson, "Rome and Italy," in N. Rosenstein and R. Morstein-Marx (eds.), *A Companion to the Roman Republic* (Oxford, 2010), 606–24.

On Italy's history after the Social War, the major study is E. Bispham, *From Asculum to Actium: The Municipalization of Italy from the Social War to Augustus* (Oxford, 2007). Briefer, and full of insight, are E. Gabba's "Rome and Italy: The Social War" and M. Crawford's "Italy and Rome from Sulla to Augustus" in *The Cambridge Ancient History*, Vols. 9 and 10, respectively. Violence in the countryside is discussed by S. Dyson, *Community and Society in Roman Italy* (Baltimore, 1992). T. Urbainczyk, *Spartacus* (Bristol, 2004), and A. Schiavone, *Spartacus* (Cambridge, MA, 2013), are brief (and different) introductions; students can make up their own minds with B. D. Shaw, *Spartacus and the Slave Wars: A Brief History with Documents* (Boston, 2001).

For the integration of Italians into the Roman political class – and much else besides – read T. P. Wiseman, *New Men in the Roman Senate, 139 B.C.–A.D. 14* (Oxford, 1971). A wide-ranging study of ideas about being Roman is E. Dench, *Romulus' Asylum: Roman Identities from the Age of Alexander to the Age of Hadrian* (Oxford, 2005).

7

***

ROME BETWEEN REPUBLIC AND EMPIRE:

THE STUCK ELEPHANT (80–60 BCE)

It was March of 81 BCE, Pompey had just returned to Rome, and to make a splash, he decided that he would enter into the city in a chariot drawn by four elephants. Back in 83 he had raised troops on his father's estates and appointed himself general. Sulla sent him to Sicily to chase down supporters of Marius, and when most of them fled to Africa to join fellow Marians, he followed in pursuit. Defeating them, Pompey then spent a few days hunting lions and elephants in Numidia. "The wild animals who live in Africa," he said, smirking, "should have some experience of Roman strength and daring."

A letter soon arrived from Sulla ordering Pompey to discharge his troops and await a successor. Instead, he brought back the whole army and demanded a triumph. Pompey was only 24, had not held any magistracy, and was not even a senator. He was too young. Sulla and the senators were shocked at his request, but Sulla felt compelled to give in and even started calling him Magnus (meaning "the Great"), as Pompey's soldiers did. The handsome young man, who bore a physical resemblance to Alexander the Great, was only too eager to add substance to the comparison. This is why he went on the Alexander-like hunt in Africa and brought the elephants back to Rome. Unfortunately for him, the city gate proved too narrow to accommodate the giant animals, and he had to switch to the conventional team of horses.

The impasse perfectly symbolized not just Pompey's own difficulties in fitting in back at Rome but also the growing divide between the type of government the larger Roman world now required and the traditional institutions of city-based SPQR. The terrible wars of the 80s had left the whole Mediterranean destabilized. Pirates were laying waste to islands and cities on the mainland coast. Political refugees from Rome challenged Sulla's Senate. One of them, Sertorius, virtually created an alternative Roman state in Spain. In 75, the Senate began to take concerted action to deal with the widespread crisis, designing a comprehensive strategy against the pirates. But its success was limited.

Figure 7.1 A heavily restored head of Pompey now in Venice, Italy. The thick cap of hair and the turn of the head recall the portraiture of Alexander the Great, a likeness Pompey was keen to emphasize. Museo Archeologico Nazionale, Venice, Italy. (Photo Wikimedia Commons.)

In sharp contrast, Pompey was repeatedly granted extraordinary power, first by a sometimes-desperate Senate and then by tribunes after all their powers were restored in 70, and he racked up a string of victories. With his officers and soldiers, he restored stability to the Mediterranean and also massively expanded Rome's empire and its revenues. The terms of his extended commands in the 60s, against first the pirates and then a resurgent Mithridates, were creative, as were Pompey's own strategies, and both provided crucial precedents for the government of Augustus and later emperors. Upon returning to Rome in 61, Pompey, the most powerful man in the Roman world, brought back not just heaps of treasure and plans for Rome's first permanent theater, but also a new vision of the Roman empire as a worthy successor to Alexander's.

In and of itself, this vision might have been compatible with SPQR. Indeed, citizens living in Rome supported it. The problem lay more with the *S* in SPQR. Some senators remained determined to thwart Pompey and to try to prevent anybody else from achieving the supremacy he had, however much it had helped Rome. If a chariot with four elephants could not fit through the city gate, it was just fine with them. But other senators saw the immense power the swaggering Pompey had gained overseas and wanted it themselves.

GOING ROGUE: PIRATES, SLAVES, AND POLITICAL REFUGEES

Sulla's resignation from his dictatorship and retirement in 79 might have suggested that the civil war was over; however, it was anything but. A couple of towns in Italy were still holding out against him and his senatorial government, with Volaterrae in Etruria only falling in 79. Far more serious was Sertorius, a tough officer who had fought under Marius against the Germans and later commanded in the Social War. His insistence on leading his men from the front cost him an eye – a source of pride to him forever after. Late in 83 he had been sent from Italy to Spain, to prevent it from falling into Sullan hands. But when a commander sent by Sulla with a large army arrived in 81, Sertorius was forced to join up with a pirate fleet and, after a voyage out into the Atlantic, ended up in North Africa, hiring out himself and his soldiers as mercenaries. In 80, the Lusitanians of western Iberia invited him to be their leader, and once he was back in Spain, he was joined by exiles of Sulla, including proscribed men. Another army was sent against him, and this time he crushed it. Clearly, Sertorius did not accept the legitimacy of the government in Rome.

Events in the west were just one example of the widespread instability fostered by Rome's destructive wars of the 80s. By 78, the year of Sulla's death, his enlarged Senate had far more on its plate. There was serious trouble on the Macedonian border and also in Dalmatia, just across the Adriatic. Cilicia, the province established to fight piracy, required attention too. Indeed, piracy was flourishing everywhere. During Mithridates' war with Rome, pirate fleets had grown in size and sophistication throughout the east. Rome's civil dissension encouraged them to spread their sails further. Shipping, ports, and whole cities were ravaged. Romans fumed that the pirates were enjoying drunken revels on every coast of the Mediterranean. Despite successes in southern Asia Minor by the proconsul Servilius over the years 77–75, which would earn him the extra name Isauricus from the hilly region he subdued, the year 75 witnessed a terrible grain shortage in the city of Rome. And by that time, Mithridates was planning for another war against Rome. Many around the Mediterranean found appealing his claim that the Romans were "the common enemy of all."

Just as the Mediterranean connected Rome with its empire, in this unstable period it was connector of *enemies* of Rome, or of the Roman Senate in particular, allowing them to communicate, make alliances, or learn quickly of and exploit one another's victories. Sertorius and Mithridates each cooperated with so-called pirates. Between 76 and 75, Sertorius and Mithridates themselves made an alliance, with Mithridates sending money and ships to Sertorius, and Sertorius sending back military advisors. Spartacus, leader of the terrible revolt that broke out in Italy in 73 (Chapter 6), had contacts with some "pirates" and perhaps Mithridates too. The better-organized pirate fleets of this time were also of course fully exploiting the sea – as well as the recent plunge in Roman prestige and power.

WHOSE REPUBLIC? COUNTERINSURGENCY IN NORTH ITALY

Sulla's death in 78 brought renewed trouble to an Italy full of malcontents. In Rome, the two consuls, M. Aemilius Lepidus and Q. Lutatius Catulus, quarreled over whether the late dictator should get a public funeral. Over the protests of Lepidus, Catulus, who was to be a stalwart Senate champion over the next two decades, prevailed. Sulla's body was carried to Rome in a grand procession, with plenty of his former soldiers on hand to make sure everything went off smoothly. But hardly had the funeral pyre been lit when the consuls resumed their fighting. Lepidus – despite having personally benefitted from Sulla's proscriptions – was in favor of undoing some of the dictator's harshest measures, restoring lands to the dispossessed, and reinstating political exiles. While later sources claim that Lepidus was seeking power for himself, he might actually have been seeking to bring about reconciliation with Sulla's victims – something badly needed, as Sertorius' success had made all too clear.

While the Senate as a body did not support Lepidus' program, he still had their trust. When Sullan colonists in Etruria were attacked by evicted landowners, Lepidus was sent, along with Catulus, to quell the uprising. But in Lepidus the insurgents soon found a champion. Summoned back to Rome to hold elections, he marched there with his army and demanded a second consulship for himself. The Senate passed its "ultimate" decree and empowered Catulus to bring down Lepidus. The Senate also empowered Pompey, although he was still not a senator, to help Catulus by going to Cisalpine Gaul, where there were more insurgents, these under the command of another senator, M. Junius Brutus, father of the famous assassin of Caesar.

The Senate's counterinsurgency achieved quick results. Pompey drove Brutus' forces into Mutina, an old Roman colony located at an important crossroads; and after a siege, Brutus surrendered on the promise that he would be spared. Pompey had him killed anyway. Meanwhile, after being defeated outside Rome, Lepidus returned to Etruria and was then driven by the joint forces of Pompey and Catulus to Sardinia, where he died. His supporters, led by M. Perperna, fled to Spain.

To the Senate, Lepidus was and would after death remain a rebel, and later historians largely concurred. But to say so was to treat Sulla's restored Republic as totally legitimate – which is exactly what the insurgents were challenging. To them, Lepidus remained their consul, and he needed more time in office. Civil war was not over.

ALTERNATIVE STATE: SERTORIUS' SPAIN

The arrival of Roman troops led by Perperna would be an immense help to Sertorius. Since 80, Sertorius had been winning over native Spaniards with his bravery and fairness – a welcome change from the typical behavior of Roman governors there. He travelled around with a snow-white doe, saying that she was a gift from the gods and had prophetic powers. By guerilla warfare – and with help from "pirates" – the charismatic leader gained control of much of Iberia, several times defeating the Senate's star general Q. Metellus Pius.

Yet as much as he relied on provincials, Sertorius always kept his eye on Rome. He formed the high-ranking refugees who came to him into a senate. His army was organized along Roman lines, with Roman decorations handed out for valor. Sons of leading Spaniards were dressed in togas and educated in Latin at a school he set up at the base of the Pyrenees – which was really a clever way of making them hostages, a standard Roman practice. Sertorius' ambition was not to empower native Spaniards but rather to put enough pressure on the Sullan Senate to win major concessions for himself and the other refugees, and perhaps undo other features of the Sullan settlement – by restoring more power to the People, for example.

In 77 Sertorius was able to go on the offensive, but he also faced a new challenge: Pompey. Ordered by the consul Catulus to disband his troops after the defeat of Lepidus, Pompey – in a replay of his post-Africa showdown with Sulla – refused outright and remained with them on the outskirts of Rome until he was given a command in Spain, with *imperium* equal to that of Metellus Pius. This was a mistake on the Senate's part. It should have begun negotiations with Sertorius to bring civil war to an end. Instead, by elevating Pompey's power, it created a bigger threat to itself. While Sertorius enjoyed several victories over Pompey and Pius, his fortunes ultimately deteriorated. He reverted to guerilla warfare and also made his desperate alliance with Mithridates. One of Sertorius' senators travelled to help Mithridates train armies and also announced tax breaks in Asia given "by grace of Sertorius," even though Sertorius had no control over Asia.

As part of a concerted effort to restore security around the Mediterranean, the Senate sent Pompey fresh troops and money as well as a better fleet. Driven to the high plateau of Celtiberia in central Iberia, Sertorius was worn down and lost support. Spaniards and Romans alike turned on him, and, finally, in 73 he was assassinated at a banquet, in a conspiracy organized by Perperna. Perperna promised to turn over to Pompey Sertorius' correspondence, including letters from secret high-ranking allies back in Rome. Pompey had the treacherous Perperna killed, but he also destroyed the correspondence – a calculated display of amnesty, which did much to bring to an end this last chapter of the long war of Roman against Roman.

Pompey remained in Spain for some time afterward to reach settlements with local populations, and as he had in Sicily and Africa earlier, he took the opportunity to build up a network of clients. Even though Sertorius had lost, his alternative state in Spain had a great impact. Not only did it lead the Senate to build Pompey up into a more formidable military leader, but it also showed how the resources of the massive Iberian Peninsula could be used to fight civil war. In an ironic reversal, years later in the 40s, Pompey and his sons would themselves fight fellow Romans by using Spain as their base.

REMATCH WITH MITHRIDATES: THE SENATE TAKES ACTION

In 75, the Mediterranean crisis bore down directly on the city of Rome. A food shortage led inhabitants to attack the two consuls as they were escorting a candidate for the praetorship to the Forum. When the consuls fled, the infuriated crowd tried to demolish one of the consul's houses. Adding to the popular fury was Sulla's decision to end, or at least reduce, the grain subsidy back in 81. Short-term measures were now taken to alleviate the situation: for example, the aedile Hortensius, a Senate champion like Catulus (his brother-in-law), distributed grain voluntarily.

The Senate also took a page out of Gaius Gracchus' book and found a way to fund a more permanent solution. Cyrenaica, a fertile territory in North Africa that was part of the Ptolemaic Empire but often ruled separately, was bequeathed to Rome by its last king, in 96. In keeping with its traditional preference for minimal overseas commitment, the Senate made no attempt to administer it directly, even though the region was particularly famous for a lucrative export in silphium, an ancient wonder drug now unfortunately extinct. Cyrenaica slipped into a state of anarchy that persisted until 75, when a quaestor was sent to restore order and raise money. With the profits realized, legislation was passed providing for purchase of extra grain in Sicily, to be sold at a subsidized price.

The consul of 75, Gaius Cotta, who was a friend of the martyred tribune of 91, Livius Drusus, was behind this scheme, as was perhaps Lucullus, an old officer of Sulla's who was a key figure in the Senate in the 70s. Lucullus and

Gaius Cotta's brother Marcus held the consulship in 74, and they contrived to have major eastern provinces allocated to themselves while still in office. It was clear to them that another war with Mithridates was inevitable. Not only had the Pontic king made his alliance with Sertorius. In 74, King Nicomedes of Bithynia died, leaving his kingdom to Rome, and the Senate intended to accept the lucrative bequest, a sure provocation to Mithridates.

Despite the victories of Servilius Isauricus in southern Asia Minor, pirates had bases across the Mediterranean now, and on this front too the Senate resolved in 74 to take concerted action. The ex-praetor M. Antonius was granted *imperium* across the whole Mediterranean Sea, including the right to requisition ships. He proceeded west first and provided critical help to Pompey against Sertorius. But before fully clearing all the seas there, he went to Crete, where he was defeated and then died. So his command, while bold in scope, was not a success.

In the meantime, Mithridates had overrun virtually all of Bithynia. Marcus Cotta, who had been given command of a fleet, was trapped in Chalcedon on the Bosporus. It was now up to Lucullus, in charge of Asia and Cilicia, to stop the king. Lucullus turned him back at Cyzicus in Asia and then invaded Pontus, ultimately forcing Mithridates to flee to his old ally Tigranes in Armenia. Lucullus' army proceeded systematically to reduce the strongholds of Pontus, while Lucullus himself was forced to return to Asia, to cope with a financial crisis. Already saddled with a huge indemnity by Sulla, and now suffering from the disruptions of renewed war, the cities were going bankrupt. Lucullus cut back the money owed by two-thirds, earning the lasting hostility of Roman financiers, to whom much of the debt was owed. In due course they would have their revenge.

POMPEY'S TRIUMPH: THE SENATE LOSES CONTROL

The Senate's more ambitious policy thus had mixed results. While Antonius had failed through incompetence, Sertorius was defeated, Lucullus had driven Mithridates from his homeland, and increased revenues had ameliorated the plight of city dwellers. An unexpected complication, though, was the outbreak of the Spartacus war in 73, which threw the whole Italian Peninsula into a state of terror (Chapter 6). Only through yet another special command awarded to the ambitious M. Licinius Crassus was the rebellion crushed. Returning from Spain with his army, Pompey joined in the pursuit of the last fugitives and so claimed, along with Crassus, credit for ending the threat.

Although they had used Pompey to defeat Sertorius, senators were deeply distrustful of the general, who was *still* not a member of the Senate. As was the case in 81, 10 years later he was on the outskirts of the city with an army – again demanding a triumph and a consulship. Crassus was there too, eager for maximum recognition of his victory over Spartacus and also for a consulship. Pompey was ineligible because of Sulla's strict reform of the magisterial career path, but Crassus was willing to support him, in exchange for Pompey's help. New currents in domestic politics played into their hands.

As the 70s wore on, demands had been mounting to undo some of Sulla's major reforms. Of most importance to the People was the full restoration of the tribunate. In 75, the reform-minded consul C. Cotta passed a law once again allowing former tribunes to hold higher office. But tribunes still could not independently propose legislation to the People.

Another source of controversy was the composition of jury panels. Allegations had arisen that Sulla's exclusively senatorial juries were being corrupted by bribes, allowing provincial governors to enrich themselves and ruthlessly exploit provincials. C. Verres, who governed Sicily for three years (73–71), was particularly rapacious. In 72, one of Pompey's Sicilian friends came to Rome to seek help and by the end of the year had the tribune Lollius Palicanus making public demands for restoration of the tribunes' full power and removal of the senators' monopoly on juries.

So the way was paved for Pompey – and Crassus – in 71. In the face of the two generals' troops and the overwhelming support of the People, the Senate passed a decree exempting Pompey from the Sullan requirements. Pompey won the consulship and also a second triumph, Crassus the consulship and a military ovation. On the last day of 71, Pompey entered Rome in the victor's chariot and the next day embarked on his consulship, his first political office. For Pompey, it might have been even more exquisite than being pulled by a team of elephants – and it certainly would mark the end of the Sullan Senate's exclusive control over imperial affairs.

During their year in office, Pompey and Crassus passed a law restoring to the tribunes their legislative powers. The People again would have a say in the running of empire and much else. Marcus Cotta, brother of the consul of 75, passed a law that reconstituted jury panels in three equals groups: senators, Equestrians, and the wealthiest class below them. And just before this, Cicero unleashed all of his talents on Verres, who went into exile before the trial was even concluded. In a further reversal of the Sullan reforms, Pompey and Crassus saw to it that a pair of censors was elected, the first since 86. The censors purged, altogether, 64 members of the Senate; Verres was not the only of Sulla's associates to be punished.

What Sertorius failed to achieve, to a large degree Pompey did. Key parts of Sulla's new constitution were in tatters. Those who had fought for change with Lepidus in 77 were granted amnesty and allowed to return to Rome. But none of this meant the old Republic, with balanced equilibrium between Senate, People, and magistrates, was back. If Pompey had not quite marched on Rome in 71 as Sulla brazenly had in 88, he had attained an extraordinary amount of power through his prolonged series of commands. Asked by the censors whether he had participated in all required military campaigns, Pompey replied in a loud voice that he had, "and all under myself as commander." People standing nearby cheered and, along with the censors, escorted Pompey home.

SEA POWER AND SOLE POWER: THE PIRATE WAR

After the failure of M. Antonius in his war against the pirates, the Senate appointed no successor for his Mediterranean-wide command. Following his consulship in 69, Q. Caecilius Metellus proceeded to Crete and through hard campaigning asserted Roman control over the island, but this was insufficient to stop the larger problem. Piracy flared up, seemingly worse than ever. Delos, the small Aegean trade hub, was sacked and never recovered. The coastline of Italy was ravaged, and a pirate fleet even had the nerve to sail into the harbor of Ostia at the mouth of the Tiber. Prominent Romans, including magistrates, were kidnapped and ransomed. Once again the grain supply was in jeopardy, putting further pressure on politicians.

Meanwhile the eastern war bogged down. Lucullus demanded that Tigranes of Armenia surrender Mithridates. When Tigranes refused, Lucullus took it upon himself to invade Armenia, an area of difficult terrain with steep mountain ranges. By a brilliant stratagem, Tigranes' fortress at Tigranocerta was captured. But the subsequent pursuit of the Armenians was far more difficult, and Lucullus' troops, further demoralized by harsh winter weather, finally refused to go further. Lucullus successfully backtracked to Mesopotamia. In Rome, there was some unhappiness over his unanticipated attack on Tigranes, while financiers remained furious over their losses through his debt settlement in Asia and were eager to see the war end, since the fiscal settlement afterward would provide them with new opportunities.

Tribunes were back on hand now to rake up allegations of senatorial greed and incompetency. Lucullus was alleged to be prolonging the eastern war for his own enrichment. One tribune, Gabinius, went so far as to display a painting of Lucullus' luxurious villa on the Bay of Naples to suggest where the money was going. Gabinius saw to it that Lucullus was stripped of his command, the area of which had already been reduced. In 67, to deal with piracy, Gabinius also proposed legislation that would appoint a single commander for three years over the whole Mediterranean and 50 miles inland. This commander would have a large fleet, the right to appoint his own officers with *imperium*, and also the right to levy troops and draw on the public treasury. At least in its preliminary form, the bill did not actually name who the commander would be, but there was no doubt in anyone's mind. It would have to be Pompey.

Senators such as Catulus and Hortensius were furious. As they saw it, this command was a virtual monarchy. A scheme to block the bill by a tribune's veto came to nothing. At a *contio*, Catulus, while carefully commending Pompey, pleaded with citizens that to empower one man so much would undermine the Republic. But again it was to no avail. The legislation passed, and what was almost worse from the senators' point of view, Pompey delivered astonishingly quick results.

Dividing the Mediterranean and its coastland into 13 parts, each of which was under its own officer, he systematically cleared the seas from west to east, cornering its last pirates in Cilicia. His victory was won in just three months. Much of the credit for this lay in Pompey's humane treatment of those who surrendered and even those he captured. He settled them in underpopulated towns such as Soli, in Cilicia, which was renamed after him as "Pompeiopolis." This confirms that many had taken up piratical activity only recently, in desperation, as part of the crisis that overwhelmed the Mediterranean because of Rome's civil wars and the wars with Mithridates and Tigranes. But that did nothing to belittle Pompey in the eyes of most Romans. It was inevitable now that their handsome general, the new Alexander, should go east and finally defeat Mithridates.

POMPEY SETTLES THE EAST

In the summer of 66, the tribune Manilius proposed legislation that would transfer to Pompey the provinces of Bithynia, Cilicia, and Pontus and the war against Mithridates. The bill was welcomed by large numbers of Romans, including wealthy Equestrians who felt that Lucullus had sold them out in Asia. Catulus again tried to rally opposition in the Senate, but a number of senators supported Manilius' proposal. Cicero recommended passage of the legislation in a speech in the Forum that he later published and that still survives. It was the People, he claimed, who had restored Roman self-respect by empowering Pompey against the pirates; it was the People's business to run the empire; the People's money was at stake. Cicero also more or less revealed that Equestrians involved with tax collecting had been in touch with him about their investments; "their business and property ought to be a concern of yours," he told the People. With overwhelming support, the bill passed.

Once again Pompey would demonstrate what a sole, extraordinary commander, untethered from the Senate, could achieve. He began by securing new allies, including the Parthian king, who invaded Armenia to keep Tigranes occupied. Pompey then advanced into Lesser Armenia, where Mithridates had

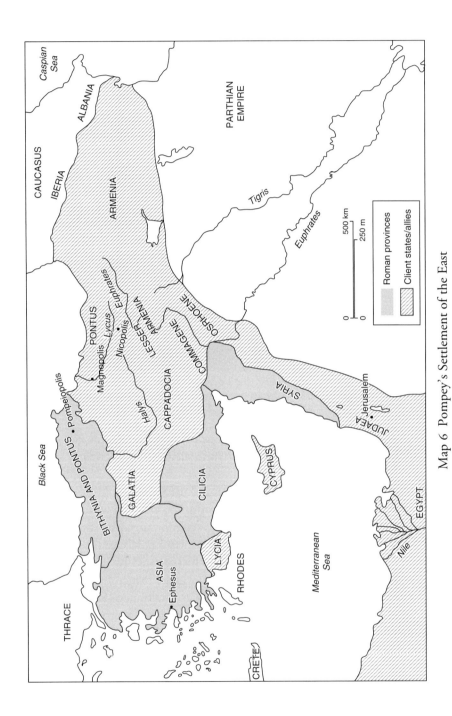

Map 6 Pompey's Settlement of the East

Caspian
Sea

CAUCASUS

IBERIA

ALBANIA

ARMENIA

PARTHIAN
EMPIRE

Tigris

Euphrates

THRACE

Black Sea

PONTUS

Euphrates

Lycus

Nicopolis

Magnopolis

LESSER
ARMENIA

OSRHOENE

COMMAGENE

Pompeiopolis

BITHYNIA AND PONTUS

Halys

CAPPADOCIA

GALATIA

CILICIA

SYRIA

Jerusalem

JUDAEA

ASIA

Ephesus

LYCIA

RHODES

CYPRUS

Mediterranean
Sea

Nile

EGYPT

CRETE

500 km

250 m

0

0

Roman provinces

Client states/allies

fled, and destroyed a large part of the king's army. Near the battle site, Pompey established a victory city of "Nicopolis," emulating Alexander the Great. Mithridates, avoiding Pompey's patrol boats in the Black Sea, made it by land to the Greek cities of the Crimea.

Old King Tigranes, meanwhile, decided to make peace overtures to Pompey and went to Pompey's camp. There he dramatically threw his tiara to the ground, only for Pompey to place it back on Tigranes' head. Rome did not want to rule the whole of the east directly, yet it also did not want any one ruler – like Tigranes' rival, the Parthian king – to grow too powerful. So Tigranes was saved.

Pompey fought peoples just south of the Caucasus Mountains and made their rulers allies of Rome, and then began to organize Pontus. The eastern portion was again assigned to kings friendly to Rome, while the west, the core of Mithridates' kingdom, was boldly transformed into a province, to be joined with Bithynia. The territory here was divided among self-governing cities with councils made up of ex-magistrates, echoing Roman practice.

For several decades, Seleucid Syria had been gripped by civil war, and Pompey went there in 64 to sort out the mess. Much of this territory, with its rich fields and proximity to the coast, would become a regular province. Jewish kings had benefitted from Seleucid weakness and expanded the size of the kingdom, but here too there was civil war in the 60s. Pompey chose one of the contenders to rule – but only as high priest, not king – and he also transferred part of the kingdom to the new Syrian province. It was in Judea that Pompey received word that Mithridates had died. Mithridates' son Pharnaces had turned on him with an army, and the old king had taken his life, defiant to the end.

Like his erstwhile ally Sertorius, Mithridates had had a huge impact on Roman history, above all through the empowering of Sulla and then Pompey. Pompey, not bothering to wait for the traditional commission of 10 senators, was able to reorganize the entire east on his own. Along most of the Mediterranean and some of the southern Black Sea coasts there would be direct Roman rule in provinces. Cilicia was expanded and left with a permanent garrison. Inland, facing Parthia, a band of client states would have more internal autonomy but had to defer to Rome on foreign policy. This was traditional practice, and some old allies of Rome, such as Cappadocia, were awarded with territory for loyalty shown during the Mithridatic Wars. But at least some of the client states were now also required to pay taxes, making them more truly a part of the empire. Provinces would pay taxes too. To secure local order and collect revenues, Pompey founded or refounded Pontic cities with names like Magnopolis and Pompeiopolis (the latter distinct from Pompey's Cilician city). The scale of the reorganization was unprecedented.

In all but name Pompey was the king of kings in the east, and he raised staggering sums of money. By the end of the campaigns, he was able to distribute nearly 400 million sesterces to his army and staff. This worked out to 6,000 sesterces for an ordinary soldier, more than five times the regular yearly salary, and to tens of thousands for the officers who fought and administered for Pompey throughout the east. Pompey acquired spoils for himself, including a large portfolio of loans to kings and communities.

In addition to all that, upon returning to Rome, Pompey deposited perhaps as much as 480 million sesterces in the treasury and claimed to have raised yearly imperial revenues from 200 to 340 million, an increase of 70 percent. This was the old Gracchan idea that the empire should exist for the benefit of the People multiplied several times over. The obvious difference between now and the 120s was that the riches were pouring in thanks to Pompey's long years of untrammeled military power.

THREE CONTINENTS: A NEW VISION OF EMPIRE

Pompey's first two triumphs had been galling enough to many senators, and now he came back to a far more splendid celebration, the most lavish Rome had ever seen. Over two days in September of 61 – the second of which, not coincidentally, was Pompey's birthday (his 45th) – he paraded through the streets of Rome with the choicest spoils, including the throne of Mithridates and the king's golden scepter. There were dozens of captives representing all the nations Pompey had pacified, and they were not made to march in chains but were proudly dressed in their native costumes. Some of them were celebrities: the children of Mithridates and Tigranes, a one-time king of the Jews, even a few pirate chiefs. Presiding over this diverse entourage, Pompey now truly lived up to his name "the Great," and he is even said to have worn a cloak that once belonged to Alexander himself.

Paintings depicted highlights of the campaigns: great scenes of battles, the flight of Mithridates, the moment of his death. Placards proclaimed awesome statistics: the number of ships Pompey had captured, the number of cities he founded, the sums of money added to the treasury. There was a huge and costly trophy representing the whole world. After all, this third triumph of Pompey was over the third and by far the richest continent of the Mediterranean basin, Asia. As Plutarch later wrote, "In his three triumphs, Pompey seemed in a way to have brought the whole world under his power." From Spain, through Africa, to the east – and across the waters – he had brought order, Roman order.

To perpetuate the glory of his victories, Pompey began work on a vast theater complex on the Field of Mars, covering more than 11 acres of land.

Figure 7.2 Global conquest celebrated on a silver coin of the mid-50s BCE. The globe on the reverse may specifically recall the trophy of the world carried at Pompey's triumph in 61, and the three smaller laurel wreaths his grand total of three triumphs. (Photo © The Trustees of the British Museum.)

Finally Rome would get a permanent stone theater, and a massive one, perhaps seating 40,000. Brightly colored awnings shielded spectators from the sun, while water flowed through the theater for cooling. Behind the theater stretched the colonnaded Portico of Pompey. It was filled with trees, fountains, and precious works of art, no doubt many of them souvenirs of the recent campaign. There were also sculpted personifications of the 14 peoples defeated by Pompey. A famous painting of Alexander yet again reminded Romans of Pompey's likeness to the great king and conqueror of the east.

Theater and triumph together embodied Pompey's vision of Rome as head of a world empire, which entailed spreading peace and stability to the edges of the earth, and in return collecting tribute from subject nations. The contrast with the *imperium* of a century earlier is sharp. Provinces were not just military assignments but permanent administrative districts, not developed piecemeal but created at a stroke. Taxation too could be planned from the start. *Imperium* really was coming to mean territorial empire. Most Romans were happy to embrace this: inhabitants of the city of Rome, Italian soldiers who grew rich with Pompey, businessmen, even many senators. The Senate's own policy in the 70s helps show this.

But if the senators could accept world empire à la Alexander, they could not abide a Roman Alexander. Upon his return to Italy from the east, Pompey immediately dismissed his troops, who perhaps were quite eager to go home. There was no doubt that if he needed them again, they would rejoin him, especially as he was planning legislation to grant them land in Italy. Pompey expected senators to support this, just as he felt sure they would ratify

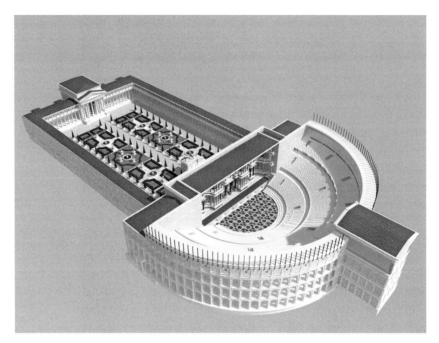

Figure 7.3 A restored view of Pompey's Theater and the Portico that stretched behind it. According to Rome's love poets, the art-filled portico with its gardens was a favorite spot to meet women. (Image from Virtual Rome, a digital model © 2016 University of Reading. Virtual Rome was developed by Dr. Matthew Nicholls.)

his whole eastern settlement. Here he was badly mistaken: senators were far more prone to jealousy of Pompey than ordinary Romans and had concerns about super-commanders acting unilaterally. Lucullus and several others demanded that the Senate review Pompey's arrangements one by one, and they had enough of their colleagues' support to prevail. Despite Pompey's success, almost by instinct they could not accept that the traditional institutions and practices of SPQR were insufficient to rule the world well.

In irritation, Pompey reunited with the more experienced political operator Crassus, who had jealously looked on at Pompey's successes since the Spartacus War. But the true mastermind of their reconciliation was a rising politician, Julius Caesar. As consul in 59, Caesar was able to obtain for Pompey's soldiers their farms and to ratify the eastern settlement by taking both to the People. Afterward he tried to emulate Pompey's military success, as did Crassus. While Crassus would lose disastrously to the Parthians, Caesar built up what was practically his own alternative state in Gaul. And when the Senate tried to thwart him, unlike Pompey, he did turn his army on them. With Caesar, the elephants would make it into Rome, a new type of government with them.

FURTHER READING

Roman politics after Sulla until the advent of civil war, covered in this and the next chapter, is a major field that has seen constant reinterpretation. Highlights include L. R. Taylor, *Party Politics in the Age of Caesar* (Berkeley, 1949); E. S. Gruen, *The Last Generation of the Roman Republic* (Berkeley, 1974); P. A. Brunt, *The Fall of the Roman Republic and Related Essays* (Oxford, 1988); F. Millar, *The Crowd in Rome in the Late Republic* (Ann Arbor, 1998). See also the general works referred to in Chapter 1, such as C. Steel's *The End of the Roman Republic* and H. I. Flower's *Roman Republics*. The wider Mediterranean setting and its importance are well brought out by P. O. Spann, *Quintus Sertorius and the Legacy of Sulla* (Fayetteville, 1987), and M. H. Crawford, "States Waiting in the Wings: Population Distribution and the End of the Roman Republic," in L. de Ligt and S. Northwood (eds.), *People, Land and Politics: Demographic Developments and the Transformation of Roman Italy, 300 BC–AD 14* (Leiden, 2008), 631–43.

For general accounts of the pivotal period covered in this chapter, see *The Cambridge Ancient History* (2nd ed.) Vol. 9 (chap. 7 by R. Seager, chap. 8a by A. N. Sherwin-White, and chap. 9 by T. P. Wiseman). R. Seager, *Pompey: A Political Biography* (Oxford, 1979), and P. A. L. Greenhalgh, *Pompey, the Roman Alexander* (London, 1980), complement each other well as introductions. F. Vervaet, "Pompeius' Career from 79 to 70 BCE: Constitutional, Political, and Historical Considerations," *Klio* 91 (2009), 406–34, is an important reexamination. Three articles focus on politics in Rome in the 70s, with less attention on Pompey than is traditional: F. Santangelo, "Roman Politics in the 70s B.C.," *Journal of Roman Studies* 104 (2014), 1–27; A. Rosenblitt, "The Turning Tide: The Politics of the Year 79 B.C.E.," *Transactions of the American Philological Association* 144 (2014), 415–44; P. Burton, "The Revolt of Lepidus (cos. 78 BC) Revisited," *Historia* 63 (2014), 404–21.

The pirates are dealt with by P. De Souza, *Piracy in the Graeco-Roman World* (Cambridge, 1999), and M. Tröster, "Roman Hegemony and Non-State Violence," *Greece & Rome* 56 (2009), 14–33. On Pompey's arrangements in the east and Rome's "imperial" turn, see R. Kallet-Marx, *Hegemony to Empire: The Development of the Roman Imperium in the East from 148 to 62 B.C.* (Berkeley, 1996), and J. Richardson, *The Language of Empire: Rome and the Idea of Empire from the Third Century BC to the Second Century AD* (Cambridge, 2008). Pompey's celebrations back in Rome and their impact are discussed in three works of broader importance: R. C. Beacham, *Spectacle Entertainments of Early Imperial Rome* (New Haven, 1999); M. Beard, *The Roman Triumph* (Cambridge, MA, 2007), I. Östenberg, *Staging the World: Spoils, Captives, and Representations in the Roman Triumphal Procession* (Oxford, 2009).

8

RIVAL LEADERS AND THE SEARCH FOR

POWER BASES (66–50 BCE)

As aedile in the year 58 BCE, M. Aemilius Scaurus put on games that set a new standard for extravagance. At his exotic beast hunts, it was recalled even centuries later, 150 female leopards were unleashed at once. His "temporary" theater constructed in the Forum was sheathed in marble, glass, and gold; its stage was three stories tall and adorned with 360 columns and hundreds of bronze statues. So fine was the stage equipment, including costumes woven with gold, that much of it was put to use later in Scaurus' villa in the hills outside of Rome.

In between his games, Scaurus found other ways to grab attention. He exhibited a set of beautiful old master paintings, recently sold by the Greek town of Sicyon to pay off community debts. In a temporary water channel he staged Rome's first exhibition of a hippopotamus and also five crocodiles. The animals, and probably their handlers, came from Egypt. Another novel attraction was a massive skeleton. Scaurus claimed that it was the remains of the monster to which Andromeda was offered up, naked, by her father, only to be rescued by Perseus with Medusa's head.

The bones were perhaps really those of a whale and had been found in Judea, where Scaurus served on Pompey's staff in the late 60s. When Pompey learned that Mithridates was dead, he left Scaurus to carry out without him a planned expedition into Nabatean Arabia. The Roman force soon got bogged down, and for a relatively small bribe of 300 talents, the Nabatean king was able to persuade Scaurus to leave. You wouldn't have guessed this from the coins that Scaurus issued as aedile. They showed the king kneeling in surrender, in front of a suitably exotic camel.

Scaurus' splashy aedileship helped launch him into a praetorship two years later. By now, he had spent far more than 300 talents winning recognition and support. Assigned to govern Sardinia in 55, he did everything he could while there to raise money to pay off his debts. So it

Figure 8.1 One of the silver coins issued by Scaurus as aedile in 58, showing the Arabian king meekly extending an olive branch. (Photo © The Trustees of the British Museum.)

was no surprise that when Scaurus returned to Rome in 54 to campaign for the consulship, an ambitious young senator with Sardinian connections spearheaded a prosecution for extortion against him. Despite his almost-certain guilt, Scaurus' all-star defense team, including Cicero, managed to secure an acquittal.

The campaign continued, but the elections of 54 were a fiasco. Allegations of bribery and threats of violence hung over Rome. Scaurus was supported by his stepbrother, Faustus Sulla, the dictator's son, who went around the city announcing that he had 300 armed men ready to swing into action. The elections were pushed back until the year 53, fully 12 months behind schedule. Scaurus lost – and was then convicted of bribery. This time Cicero could not save him, nor could his supporters who tried to interrupt the prosecution. Pompey, serving as consul, had posted soldiers in the Forum to make sure the trial proceeded. Scaurus went into exile.

Scaurus' story highlights the increasingly dysfunctional politics of the 60s and 50s. Competition for the top office was cutthroat, in part because Sulla's reforms had increased the number of all magistrates except the consuls. Far larger numbers of men could vote now, and reaching this expanded electorate was crucial. Lavish spectacles drawing in out-of-towners to Rome was one strategy, and bribery another. While by custom a candidate could make gifts to members of his own voting tribe, the officials in charge increasingly were distributing handouts offered by others. Accusations of bribery were rife, often lobbed to knock out competitors rather than uphold the public interest.

The key question was where to get money, and Scaurus shows the answer: the provinces. The growing empire fueled the struggle for power in Rome. Candidates took out massive loans, in anticipation of lucrative governorships, where there were practically countless ways to make money, including collusion with the Equestrian tax collectors (Chapter 9). Frontier wars brought profits, and prestige too, and so politicians cultivated military talent in themselves and others. Good soldiers and officers were recruited throughout the towns of Italy. Provincial leaders were useful allies too. Some would collaborate with Romans to rip off their own countrymen.

Thus the power bases for Rome's politicians were many: Roman voters, Italian peasants, financiers, prominent provincials, and of course fellow senators. A distinctive feature of these years, especially the 50s, was increased mobilization of city dwellers, like Faustus Sulla's streetfighters. The politician Clodius took this to a new level, and his murder in 52 spawned terrible violence. In other ways too calloused city dwellers exerted pressure on events, making sure to get *their* share in the spoils of empire, as did suffering peasants.

But the civil war that broke out in 49 was not a rebellion to overturn society launched by any one power base. Rather, as with the earlier Sullan war, it was a boiling over of violent competition within the ruling class. The Senate had difficulty brokering compromises, and the assemblies were incapable of it. Meanwhile, leaders could appeal to power bases left unsatisfied by SPQR and in doing so further undermined it. Yet for all the turbulence, leaders and bases together were building an alternative framework that would, in the long run, satisfy the aspirations of more men and women and so provide greater stability.

The political history of the 60s and 50s is uniquely well documented. A variety of sources sometimes allows a day-to-day narrative to be put together, with dramatic twists and turns. Most important are the manifold writings of Cicero, especially transcripts of his speeches and letters to his family and friends, including a splendid series to the Equestrian banker Atticus. There are letters written to Cicero as well, and also a handbook on electioneering allegedly by his brother. All of this is no accident. Cicero wanted his version of events to prevail, especially concerning his consulship in 63, when he, as the new man, claimed to have uncovered and then thwarted a massive conspiracy by the noble Catiline to topple the Republic.

After his violent murder in 43, there was a cult to Cicero's memory. Works of his were brought out posthumously. Later sources, such as biographies by Plutarch, often reflected his influence, but they also drew on other contemporary writers with different perspectives. Offsetting Cicero are the extant commentaries of Julius Caesar and the histories of Sallust, especially Sallust's *War with Catiline*, written around 40. In that work, Sallust interpreted the politics of the age as a clash between defenders of the People's rights and champions of the authority of the Senate, a view that has influenced many later historians. But the picture must be broadened to include the relationship between politicians and a variety of power bases, as well as the untethering of leaders from SPQR altogether.

CATILINE AND THE HEADLESS BODY

The debate over Pompey's command against Mithridates (Chapter 6) was not the only major political issue of 66: a bribery scandal rocked Rome. The consuls elected for the following year, P. Autronius Paetus and P. Cornelius Sulla (a relative of the dictator), were prosecuted by the losers and, despite violent protests on their behalf, were convicted. A new election was called, and one man now interested in running was Catiline, a reckless patrician who had used the Sullan proscriptions to repair his family's decayed fortunes.

Catiline had just returned to Rome in 66 from a governorship in Africa, accompanied by complaints that he had plundered the province. The consul presiding over the new elections refused to recognize his candidacy, and two rivals were elected. Later sources claim that an unsuccessful plot was hatched to murder the new consuls on January 1 of 65 BCE, with Catiline heavily involved. Almost certainly this is just an echo of false allegations made by Cicero, only in 64 and afterward – a lesson in how cautiously evidence must be read.

Others later tried to pin the alleged plot on Crassus and another young patrician who was accumulating enemies, Julius Caesar. The tall, handsome nephew of Marius, Caesar had used the funeral of Marius' widow in 69 to honor the great general, to popular acclaim. As aedile four years later, Caesar was cheered even louder. His games were lavish, and even more thrilling was his restoration of Marius' victory monuments on the Capitol that had been torn down by Sulla. Senate champion Catulus was furious at how Caesar was undermining the Sullan settlement. Demands were growing to punish those who had profited in Sulla's proscriptions and to restore full citizen rights to the sons of the proscribed. The old civil war was still not entirely over.

While Caesar and Crassus were almost certainly innocent of the alleged New Year's plot, they were political partners. After his election to the censorship in 65, Crassus tried to grant full citizenship to communities north of the Po that had only Latin rights. Since these areas were filled with Marian supporters, Caesar had supported this too. Crassus' colleague as censor, Catulus, stopped the plan, and after further quarreling, both abdicated before the census could be completed. Another scheme involved passing a bill that would make Egypt tributary to Rome. The kingdom had been left to Rome in an earlier royal will, but nothing so far had been done about it. Caesar was to serve as agent of the fiscal takeover, giving him a large personal share in the windfall. Cicero ingratiated himself with outraged senators by crushing the whole plan with his oratory.

Catiline, meanwhile, was growing frustrated. After he was tried for maladministration of Africa and acquitted, he was finally able to run for consul in 64, along with C. Antonius and Cicero. Badly handicapped by his status as a new man who lacked distinguished ancestors, Cicero savagely attacked Catiline. Catiline, he claimed, had personally killed a relative of Marius and brought the man's head "still alive and breathing" to Sulla. Cicero asked, who would want you as consul? Not the leading men, not the Senate, not the Equestrians, not the urban populace.

In defeating Catiline, Cicero was helped by his own verbal dexterity and by a mounting debt crisis and partially overlapping problems in the countryside. By the mid-60s debt levels in Italy were high. With Pompey's suppression of the pirates and the prospect of greater stability in the east, financiers were likely to call in loans made in Italy and reinvest their capital overseas more profitably. This would spell ruin for the indebted, including politicians like Catiline as well as struggling farmers, especially the Sullan colonists. Cicero, it was clear, would take a hard line with debtors, winning him support from the financial interests across Italy he had helped so often in the courts.

Calls for debt cancellation grew. A tribunician proposal at the start of Cicero's consulship called for using Pompey's contributions to the treasury to buy up land at a good price, thus helping struggling farmers, and then redistributing it to the most deserving in the colonies. Appealing to the interests of urban voters, Cicero managed to quash the legislation. Later in the year, Catiline stood again for the consulship, this time explicitly on a platform of debt remission. By now, something like a full financial crisis was on, fueled in part by Catiline's demands. Loans were called in, debtors had to sell land, and the glut of properties drove prices down. Italy threatened to slide off a cliff.

Catiline's own debts had swollen so much that he no longer tried to hide them. Instead, he boasted of them, in empathy with others. Cicero, fearing that he would be murdered by Catiline's supporters, postponed elections and called out Catiline in the Senate. Catiline was defiant: "There are two bodies in the state," he said, "one feeble with a weak head, the other strong, but headless." Catiline would be the head for this strong body. Horrified, Cicero put on a breastplate and made sure to let a bit of it show beneath his toga. When elections were finally held, financial interests prevailed: Catiline lost.

In October, Crassus went to Cicero with some anonymous letters implicating Catiline in a plot to overthrow the Roman government. Meanwhile, the indebted farmers and the dispossessed Marians were gathering and arming themselves across Italy. A retired army officer headed one group at the struggling Sullan colony at Faesulae, in the hills outside modern Florence. They sent a deputation to the Senate, begging for help with their loans, but were told to lay down their arms and come to Rome. They refused. Cicero insisted that Catiline was behind all these uprisings. Whether that was true or not, Catiline was – like the Italians – being backed into a corner.

On November 8, Cicero denounced Catiline in one of his most famous speeches. "How long, I ask you, Catiline, will you abuse our patience?" he began. Cicero laid out the conspiracy – as he saw it – and called on Catiline to leave Rome. The patrician haughtily responded that nobody should trust the new man consul, "an immigrant citizen in the city of Rome." But Catiline fled that night, and a week later was at the camp at Faesulae.

Through a clever trap, Cicero obtained evidence against several men, including two senators, who remained in Rome trying to collaborate with Catiline. It suggested that they were going to torch the city of Rome during the chaotic year-end festival of the Saturnalia. The Senate debated these men's fate. A forceful speech by Cato, great-grandson of Cato the Censor, swayed them to vote for execution. A practicing Stoic who studied scrolls of philosophy in the Senate house before meetings began, Cato was unrelenting in his efforts to stamp out corruption and prevent too-powerful men from usurping the government of the Senate and the People. After his intervention, he immediately became the favorite of a small but powerful group of conservative senators – men like Catulus.

Cicero carried out the punishment, ignoring the conspirators' right to appeal capital judgments to the People. For Cicero, they were no longer citizens. Catiline and the army in Etruria were put down early the next year. Cicero was exultant: not only had he saved Rome, but he had also shown the strength of the Republic. Catiline's claim of a divided state was false. When threatened, all good citizens could come together, Cicero insisted.

In the next few years Cicero would promote this idea as the *concordia ordinum* ("harmony among society's orders"). While the Republic had survived the threat of Catiline, consensus was largely a figment of Cicero's imagination. The episode was really another example of the ruthless competition in Rome, which escalated into a minor civil war. Most of the power bases did rally behind Cicero – except Italy's struggling peasants – but they remained to be exploited by others.

THE GANG OF THREE

At the end of 62, Rome was engrossed with a scandal centering on P. Clodius Pulcher. A patrician like Caesar and Catiline, Clodius was equally good at striking defiant poses. He and his friends proudly sported goatees, a protest against their clean-shaven elders. In December of 62, Clodius dressed up as a woman and snuck into the house of the *pontifex maximus*, Caesar, during the women's-only festival of the Good Goddess. The rumor was that Clodius was interested in seducing Caesar's wife, whom Caesar promptly divorced, famously insisting that a wife of his must be above suspicion. But Clodius' action could also be considered sacrilege, and so he was put on trial at the insistence of Cato and other senators. Despite testimony from Cicero breaking Clodius' alibi, Clodius was exonerated, allegedly in exchange for bribes of cash and sexual favors to the jurors. Cicero thus acquired a dangerous enemy, and Clodius and his "little beards," in frustrating the conservative senators, increased in popularity – or at least notoriety.

Pompey, returning now to Rome from his victory over Mithridates, supported the Senate's handling of the Good Goddess affair. But influential senators remained determined to frustrate his effort to ratify his eastern settlement and to move forward with grants of land for his veterans. The Senate was also taking a hard line with the corporation in charge of tax collection for Asia, which had asked for its contract to be modified. Crassus, who probably had a financial interest in the matter, supported the businessmen. So did Cicero, preaching at length the *concordia ordinum*, but Cato would not hear of it. So much for harmony among the orders; even the Senate was bitterly divided.

Crassus could soon commiserate with his old associate Caesar, who had his own quarrel with the Senate. Caesar had gone as governor to Farther Spain in 61 and fomented a profitable war in Lusitania. Campaigning in the northwest corner of Iberia, he was even able to boast, Pompey-style, of extending Roman power to the ends of the earth. When he returned to Rome in 60, he planned on celebrating a triumph and standing for the consulship. Before the triumph could take place, however, the deadline came for candidates to make their declaration. This required crossing into Rome and so forfeiting *imperium* – and with it, the opportunity to triumph. Caesar asked the Senate for an exemption, but Cato filibustered until Caesar decided to enter Rome and forgo the victory parade. He would not soon forget the insult to his pride.

Winning the consulship, Caesar persuaded Crassus and Pompey to put aside their differences and cooperate with him in advancing their goals in the years ahead. Modern historians have called this pact the "first triumvirate," thinking of the board of three who officially gained power over Rome in

43 BCE, but the term is misleading. This was a private alliance. Still, in later years, Romans saw it as a turning point. As Plutarch argued, "it was not the quarrel between Caesar and Pompey [in the late 50s] that brought about the civil wars, it was rather their friendship." There is truth to this view: by collaborating, Caesar and Pompey strengthened one another (and Crassus) such that they became practically the heads of rival states that could wage war on one another. Money, soldiers, and supporters flowed to them.

After Caesar entered the consulship at the start of 59, the most pressing task was securing land for Pompey's veterans. Caesar prepared the legislation, gave senators an opportunity to modify it (which they declined), took it to the People, and finally, over the objections of his dull-witted fellow consul Bibulus, pushed it through with violence. Pompey had summoned some of his soldiers to Rome to ensure that voting went their way. Bibulus soon retreated to his house for the rest of the year, claiming that he was watching for bad omens. Normally this was sufficient to stop voting on legislation, but no magistrate before had watched night after night as Bibulus did. All subsequent business, the joke went, was transacted "in the consulship of Julius and Caesar" (rather than "Caesar and Bibulus"). But as a consequence, there was a serious question about the legality of Caesar's measures. Over the rest of his term, he bought up additional land for distribution to veterans and other needy citizens, had Pompey's eastern settlement ratified, and reduced the amount the Asian tax collectors owed. The Gang of Three achieved its immediate ends.

Their methods, though, cost them public support, and for Pompey, who was used to being the people's hero, this was painful. In the absence of opinion polls, the behavior of audiences at games was the most useful gauge. In July of 59, Cicero wrote to Atticus of how, at the Games of Apollo, a famous actor recited with particular emphasis a line from the play's script: "it is through our misery that you are great." The crowd acknowledged this as a reference to the great man Pompey himself, and clamored so much that the actor repeated the line 12 times. As Cicero wrote, Pompey was "a fallen star." To try to keep an exasperated Pompey from joining the opposition, Caesar gave his only daughter Julia to him in marriage.

A final development of the year was legislation passed by the tribune Vatinius that granted Caesar an extraordinary command. It was on the model of those held earlier by Pompey, with the difference that there was no major crisis at the moment. Immediately following his consulship, Caesar would have for five years Cisalpine Gaul and Illyricum, with three legions. When the governor of Transalpine Gaul died, an acquiescent Senate quickly added that province too.

The advantages of this huge frontier province were numerous. Cisalpine Gaul was a superb recruiting ground for soldiers and close enough to Rome to allow Caesar to receive visitors there. After the census of 70, many Roman citizens were registered there, spread across a number of voting tribes and willing to travel to Rome for electoral assemblies; Caesar could canvass among them for his allies. Beyond northern Italy, there were multiple opportunities for campaigning. While initially Caesar's thoughts probably lay with the Dacians threatening Illyricum, he would in fact spend eight years in the add-on province of Transalpine Gaul.

CAESAR CONQUERS GAUL
(AND THE LATIN CLASSROOM)

The Gallic wars were the making of the Caesar posterity knows. Like Cicero, Caesar sought to control the record and so produced "commentaries" about his campaigns. Written in a straightforward Latin that has endeared them to schoolteachers to the present day, ostensibly these "commentaries" were meant only to be a "source" for later historians. But with their fast-paced narrative, they are – like their hero – impossible to beat. The author's famous use of the third person ("Caesar marched with top speed . . .") lulls the reader into thinking that these writings are objective too.

Before Caesar, the "province" of Transalpine Gaul was little more than a path from Italy to Spain along the southern coast of modern France (Chapter 2). But exposure to the Romans and to earlier Greek settlers, especially at Massilia (modern-day Marseilles), had transformed Celtic societies farther beyond. Not only were they intoxicated by Mediterranean wines; larger states were forming, ruled not by warrior kings with swarms of retainers but by annually elected magistrates. One of the strongest states was that of the Aedui (occupying modern Burgundy). The Roman Senate had recognized it with a treaty of friendship and, more unusually, referred to the Aedui as Rome's "brothers," probably because the Aedui were thought to share descent from the Trojans. In forging such alliances, natives who learned Latin were critical intermediaries.

Caesar was still at Rome in early 58 when he learned that the Helvetii, a Celtic people who had recently been driven by an expansionist German state into the area of modern Switzerland, were on the move again. According to his commentaries, their leader Orgetorix, an old-style king, had begun planning the migration several years earlier, lining up alliances with leading Gauls. Despite the king's death, the plan continued. Recalling an earlier Roman loss to the Helvetii, Caesar did not want them passing through or settling anywhere near his province, and the Aedui were also opposed. Caesar

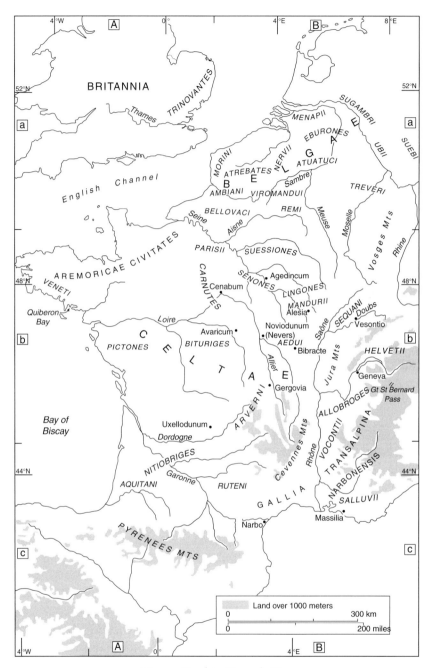

Map 7 Gaul in Caesar's Day

travelled to Transalpine Gaul and blocked them by fortifying the west bank of the Rhône River, forcing the Helvetii north. He then marched back to Cisalpine Gaul "at top speed," recruited two legions (to add to his existing four), and "hastened back" with his troops through the Alps. The migrants persisted in their plan, Caesar met them in battle, and the few survivors were forced back to where they had begun.

The Aedui, along with other Gallic states, now asked Caesar for help against Ariovistus, one of the "uncivilized" Germans from across the Rhine. Invited in by some of the Gauls for help in an earlier war, Ariovistus had never left. Unsuccessful negotiations with the Romans culminated in Ariovistus kidnapping one of Caesar's envoys, C. Valerius Procillus. A young Gaul from the old Gallic province whose father had been granted Roman citizenship, Procillus had enjoyed a good Roman education and was typical of a whole class of men who helped Caesar. After several skirmishes, Caesar marched his army up to the enemy camp, precipitated battle, and was victorious, thanks to some quick thinking by one of his officers, Publius Crassus, son of Caesar's ally. Ariovistus barely made it back across the Rhine.

Procillus was rescued just in time from the Germans, and this pleased Caesar as much as the victory itself. Procillus was (according to Caesar) "the worthiest man in the Province" and – even more important – "Caesar's own close friend." Back in the Roman camp, Procillus recounted how the Germans had three times cast lots to decide whether to burn him to death at once or wait until later. Tales like this one would have delighted Roman readers, and it may be that Caesar released his commentaries book by book over the 50s to influence public opinion as well as to shape the later record.

The Gauls might have turned out the Germans, but when Caesar left his army, they realized that they had a new occupier. Caesar himself returned to north Italy, where he raised two more legions in the winter of 58/57. Word reached him there that all of the Belgic tribes in the north were conspiring against the Romans. Only the Remi wished to help Caesar, and so Caesar crossed into their territory to stop the massive enemy coalition. Protected by the River Aisne, Caesar resisted battle, and the enemy, facing a lack of supplies, had to split up and make their way home.

Caesar then started picking off the Belgic tribes in a lightning campaign. Soon only the Atuatuci were left, gathered together in a well-fortified town. They laughed when they saw the Romans building a siege tower far away. By what means "could men, especially of so tiny a stature, hope to move it?" (All the Gauls, Caesar noted, made fun of the Romans for their short height.) When the tower started moving, the Atuatuci surrendered but then snuck out at night, hoping to surprise the Romans. The midgets made short work of the giants. The next day, Caesar smashed into the city and sold into slavery all residing there – 53,000 souls, he claimed.

Another detachment of Caesar's army under the command of young Publius Crassus subdued territory on the western coast of Gaul, from Normandy to the Garonne. This was a Pompey-style war with multiple theaters and multiple commanders. And just like Pompey in the east, Caesar was amassing great prestige and profit. Tales of Gallic gold recruited young Italians for the legions; coveted staff positions often went to the sons of leading Italian families, some fairly recently enfranchised. Ambitious politicians served as officers. Far removed from Rome and its tiresome squabbles, Caesar was building a formidable power base and developing a taste for sole command.

THE PATRICIAN TRIBUNE

Being a "little beard" was not enough to satisfy Clodius' ambitions. Since his acquittal in the Good Goddess trial, he had sought to shed his patrician status and run for the tribunate. His chance came in 59, when Cicero made the mistake of publicly badmouthing the violence of the Gang of Three. Within hours of Cicero's remarks, Caesar cleared the way for Clodius to be adopted by a plebeian three years Clodius' junior, who then immediately legally emancipated him. Election to the tribunate followed, and after entering office on December 10, Clodius announced a bold legislative package.

Among its highlights were measures concerning grain distribution and the occupational and neighborhood associations. The grain subsidy, abolished or reduced by Sulla, had been reinstated in the 70s and was augmented in 62 when none other than Cato persuaded the Senate that it needed to be more attentive to city dwellers' needs. Clodius now proposed to distribute grain for free, to perhaps as many as 300,000 men in Rome. He would also overhaul the whole supply system, from the grain fields overseas to the warehouses in Rome. To help pay for it all, Clodius passed separate legislation authorizing Cato to oversee the annexation of Cyprus, part of the Ptolemaic kingdom, and so, because of the old royal will, available for takeover. This conveniently removed Cato from Rome.

The popularity that free grain won Clodius can hardly be exaggerated, and nearly as important were his plans for the associations. Organized around professions, neighborhoods, religious cults, or a combination of the three, these were the bedrock of many city dwellers' lives, providing a safety net, entertainment, and prestige (this last not least for their elected officials, who got to wear special clothing on ceremonial occasions). A boisterous midwinter festival of the Crossroads was a yearly highlight, especially for the neighborhood associations. After disturbances in 66, the Senate had banned some of the associations and restricted celebration of the Crossroads festival. Now Clodius proposed to restore the festival, restore the associations, and allow new ones to be established. As part of this effort, a registration across the city would take place, giving Clodius an unrivaled knowledge of Rome and its local leaders.

The legislation was passed and quickly implemented, and the popularity that Clodius achieved soon became dramatically clear. At a trial of one of Caesar's associates in early 58, Clodius offered his aid to the accused and was backed up by crowds of city dwellers, who knocked over the praetor's bench and broke up the proceedings. These thugs were a far more powerful force than the "little beards."

Now was the time for Clodius to settle his score with Cicero from the Good Goddess trial and simultaneously affirm his commitment to the liberty of the Roman People, especially the traditional right of appeal. The patrician tribune proposed a law that would banish from Rome anyone who put to death a Roman citizen without trial. Its target was unmistakably Cicero. Cicero, of course, had his own power bases, especially the Senate. But Clodius rendered that body ineffective by winning to his side the consuls of 58 with legislation granting them special commands in the style of Pompey's. Resolutions passed by the towns of Italy on behalf of Cicero were also powerless to help him. In early 58 he fled Rome, and Clodius then formalized the exile and had Cicero's property confiscated. Cicero's house on the Palatine, which neighbored Clodius', was torn down, and a shrine to the goddess Liberty was consecrated there.

Clodius now turned his attention to Pompey, his greatest rival as the hero of the *plebs* of Rome. The tribune began by upsetting a few details of the eastern settlement. He also raised questions about the legality of Caesar's legislation. After a slave of Clodius' was caught with a dagger as Pompey was entering the Senate, Pompey remained at home, and his house was picketed by Clodius' gangs. Not surprisingly, Pompey was soon backing efforts to recall Cicero. When voting on a tribunician bill on behalf of Cicero was to take place in early 57, a bloody riot broke out in the Forum. One of the new tribunes, T. Annius Milo, had recruited gladiators to take on the Clodians, escalating violence.

In 57 Pompey found ways to mobilize further power bases on behalf of Cicero. Earlier in the year, he had travelled through the towns of Italy to speak with local notables. All were encouraged to attend the Games for Apollo in July, where they could demonstrate their support for Cicero. Despite attempts by Clodius to induce a riot, the plan went off, and the Senate voted 416 to 1 to call Cicero the "savior of Rome" and initiate legislation for his return (Clodius was the lone nay vote). Unusually, voting on the law took place in the centuriate assembly – to ensure that the wealthier Italians would prevail. Although they did, the whole episode underscores their lack of integration into the normal day-to-day politics of Rome, including its legislative assemblies.

DIVIDING THE WORLD

Despite (or perhaps because of) Clodius' recent legislation, Rome was experiencing grain shortages, and Pompey saw this as an opportunity to regain popular support. Cicero, now back in Rome, persuaded the Senate to authorize legislation giving Pompey a five-year command over the grain supply across the Roman world. With his knack for getting results, surely he would have the problem fixed in no time.

More controversial was the debate over King Ptolemy the Fluteplayer. On the throne of Egypt since 81, he constantly had to look over his shoulder at Rome. In 59, Caesar had the Senate recognize him as "Friend and Ally" – allegedly in exchange for a bribe of 6,000 talents to Caesar and Pompey. His subjects, who had no fondness for Rome, drove him out, just at the time his brother, the ruler of Cyprus, lost his island thanks to Clodius' legislation. One of the consuls of 57 arranged for a Senate decree authorizing him to restore the Fluteplayer the following year. While Pompey's own views were not explicit, friends of his were eager for him to have this plum assignment. Crassus, who had his own ambitions here, was none too pleased.

The Gang of Three was threatening to split apart, and its critics, especially Caesar's enemies, saw an opportunity. The Gang was unable to control the outcome of elections for high offices, since wealthy Italians, the type who supported Cicero, could prevail in the centuriate assembly. The consuls elected for 56 were certainly no friends of the Gang (one was Cato's father-in-law), and there was talk of striking down Caesar's legislation and ending his command. One of Caesar's most formidable foes, Domitius Ahenobarbus, was planning to run for a consulship in 55. Meanwhile, the grain shortage was stubbornly resisting even Pompey's efforts.

In early 56, a new deal among the Three was called for, and this time they would effectively divide the Roman world and all its resources between them. Still wintering in Cisalpine Gaul, Caesar first met with Crassus and then called for a meeting with Pompey at Luca. The agreement was that Pompey and Crassus would stand for the consulship in 55 – fending off Domitius – and, once in office, ensure renewal of Caesar's command while creating glorious super-commands for themselves in Syria and Spain. The task of restoring the Fluteplayer would be given to Pompey's old ally Gabinius.

Back in Rome everything went more or less as planned. It helped that Clodius, consumed in his nearly gladiatorial match with his rival Milo, was now ready to go along with the Gang. Pompey and Crassus contrived to postpone the consular elections to the start of 55, meaning that the unfriendly consuls of 56 would not preside. Cato did what he could to stiffen the resolve of his brother-in-law Domitius. The Three were now tyrants, Cato said, and this was a fight not just for political office but freedom. Domitius and Cato tried to secure the Campus Martius the night before elections. Caesar, however, had sent soldiers of his to Rome, under the command of Publius Crassus, to vote. Fighting broke out in which Cato was badly wounded. Pompey and Crassus were elected consuls.

If the collapse of republican principles was not clear enough already, what followed made it so. The new consuls passed a bill – with more violence – adding five years to Caesar's command. The tribune Trebonius, in turn, arranged for Crassus to have a five-year command in Syria and Pompey in Spain. While there was no crisis as there had been in the 60s, the legislation was in keeping with Pompeian ideas of world rule for Rome and all the profits it could bring. But it also helped lock up military resources for the Three. Pompey commanded his province through deputies while he stayed in Italy. He travelled around recruiting soldiers – and cultivating Italian notables. Crassus, desperate for trophies to match his colleagues', planned to launch a war against the Parthians.

Nobody needed reminding of Pompey's own glory in 55. It was the year his great marble theater was dedicated (Chapter 7). After the Luca conference, Pompey urged Cicero to drop his opposition to Caesar, and in the months that followed, he was to put his oratorical talent to use defending friends of the Gang of Three facing trial. In a letter written to a friend on the Bay of Naples, Cicero took grim delight in reporting how the last day of Pompey's dedicatory games for the theater, featuring an elephant fight, flopped. The beasts were brought out and, far from delighting the crowds, aroused a feeling of compassion. It was a reminder that military greatness alone could not solve all of Pompey's problems, or Rome's either. Elephants still could not fit through the city's gates.

CAMPAIGNING AT THE ENDS OF THE EARTH

The dispatches Caesar sent back to Rome at the end of 55 had their own thrills. The incursion of two German tribes into Gaul allowed him to cross (in retribution) the Rhine, where (he wrote) the men were as tall as giants and wore practically nothing despite the cold. Caesar spanned the river with a spectacular bridge – crossing by boat was "beneath his and the Romans' dignity." But later in the year he had no choice when he sailed to Britain, claiming that tribes there had been helping the rebels in western Gaul. Economic gain may have been Caesar's real motive, not to mention the glory of campaigning at the ends of the earth, where men still fought on chariots, dyed their bodies blue, and sported mustaches.

While Caesar spent a second year campaigning in Britain in 54, Gaul grew restless, especially in the north. Over the winter of 54/53, a legion and a half was massacred. Roman reprisals spawned further insurgencies, in a spiral of violence. Caesar increased the number of his legions to 10 (one was a loan from Pompey). The Gauls themselves formed a better-organized army under the leadership of a young noble of the Arverni, Vercingetorix. Losses by Caesar to this clever general led practically all the tribes to join the uprising, even the Aedui. Caesar nearly lost his grip on Gaul completely, until Vercingetorix made the mistake of occupying the hilltop settlement of Alesia. Caesar surrounded it with two rings of siege works, to prevent both escapes and reinforcements. The Gallic rescue operation failed, and with the capture of Vercingetorix, Gaul's fate was sealed.

With this war his from the start, narrated in his own brilliant commentaries (rather than those of paid writers), Caesar had outdone Pompey. He had added a vast tribute-paying territory to the Roman Empire. Caesar himself had grown wildly rich, and his officers and soldiers – along with friends and allies back in Italy and Rome – benefitted too. By the start of 50, Caesar had been away from Rome for seven years and in many respects had created his own state in Gaul. As general, he was its clear leader, and under him was a hierarchy of officers and soldiers. A mint issued coins; a secretarial staff handled logistics and diplomatic relations.

The contrast with Crassus and his Parthian war in the east could not have been sharper. Originating in the Asian steppe, the Parthians expanded westward in the second century BCE, encroaching on the Seleucid Empire all the way to the Euphrates River. While the Parthian rulers embraced some of the flamboyance of Hellenistic kings, they never abandoned their tradition of fighting on horseback. King and nobles would fight like medieval knights, with heavy armor and lances, while mounted archers would gallop alongside them and turn backward to fire the famous "Parthian shot." Relations between Rome and Parthia had been strained since Pompey's less-than-faithful dealings with the king during the Mithridatic Wars, but Crassus was entirely to blame for precipitating full war.

Refusing to wait for winter storms to pass, Crassus set out from Brundisium for Syria. He crossed the Euphrates, successfully raided Mesopotamia, and then returned to Syria, awaiting the arrival of his son Publius, who had a special force of 1,000 Gallic cavalry. These horsemen, not to mention Publius' own talents, were crucial to Crassus' plans for the following year, and the whole plan shows how much leaders were detached from SPQR and developing their own power bases.

In 53, on the dry plains near Carrhae, the Roman forces were encircled by a major Parthian force. The rain of arrows on the Romans was unceasing, as a special camel corps replenished the archers. Publius and his Gauls charged out heroically and were annihilated. Altogether 20,000 Romans are said to have been killed, and 10,000 captured, while the elder Crassus' head arrived at the Parthian capital just in time to be used as a prop in a gory Greek tragedy being staged for the king's amusement. Political distractions in Rome postponed any plan to recover the lost battle standards and restore Roman honor.

SPQR FAILS

The regular transmission of political office, even basic order, was breaking down in Rome. The year 54 witnessed the bribery scandals of which Aemilius Scaurus was a part; so much cash was sought for distribution that interest rates shot up. By year's end, there were no magistrates. In addition, the *interregnum* continued until the middle of 53, at which point consuls were elected but another scramble for office for the next year began. Milo was one of the candidates for the consulship of 52, Clodius for the praetorship, and each was determined to stop the other. There was continuous fighting on the streets.

Elections again were postponed, and as the year 52 opened there were no senior magistrates, and the violence persisted. On January 18, Milo set out from Rome for his hometown of Lanuvium and along the Appian Way ran into his old rival Clodius. After Milo's gladiators picked a fight with Clodius' entourage, Clodius was wounded and then later killed and left lying on the road. His body was brought back to Rome, and his widow, Fulvia, put it on display in the courtyard of his house, leaving all the wounds visible. An enraged crowd, devastated by the loss of their champion, took the body to the Forum, a riot broke out, and the Senate house was burnt to the ground. Popular demands grew for Pompey to assume dictatorial power and restore order.

The anarchy played into Pompey's hands, allowing him a chance to save the day, just as he had so many years before in the crisis of the pirates. The Senate, unwilling to have a dictator, decided instead to pass a decree arranging for Pompey to be elected as sole consul, without a colleague. Caesar's old foe Bibulus made the motion, and Cato supported it. Pompey then went to work with all his energy, passing strict laws against electoral bribery and violence. Streamlined trial procedures were introduced, and armed men posted in the Forum. This was when Scaurus was convicted and forced into exile. Milo was also, as were a number of Clodius' allies.

Throughout these events, Pompey (quite irregularly) retained his command in Spain and seized the opportunity to renew it for five years. He also had a law passed that would allow Caesar the right to run for the consulship without having to declare his candidacy in person. Avoiding a repeat of the humiliation he had faced after his return from Spain, Caesar could celebrate a triumph and pass straight into a consulship, just as Pompey had in 70. Thus retaining *imperium*, he would be immune from prosecution or any other obstruction his enemies were plotting. There was, however, a wrinkle, when Pompey passed a law instating a five-year interval between the holding of political office and a provincial governorship. A praiseworthy measure aimed at cutting down electoral bribery and sparing provincials, the law would, incidentally, allow the Senate to replace Caesar immediately in 50 and instruct him to return to Rome, potentially upsetting his neat plan to pass straight from his Gallic command into a second consulship. But, as Pompey presumably intended, a tribune could easily veto any move to replace Caesar.

As Pompey finally returned to preeminence in Rome, Caesar's enemies saw the chance to turn him to their side. Crassus was gone, and so was the wife Pompey adored, Caesar's daughter, Julia, who had died in childbirth. A fierce critic of Caesar, M. Claudius Marcellus, was elected consul for the year 51 and demanded that, with the Gallic war finished, Caesar should give up his army. Pompey, for his part, agreed to recall in due time the legion he had lent to Caesar in 53. But he refused to hear any discussion of a successor to Caesar until the next year (50), thereby honoring the law he had passed in 55 extending Caesar's command.

Securing allies in Rome was critical for Caesar. One of the consuls of 50, Aemilius Paullus, was won over by a massive bribe that would allow him to complete a refurbishment of the Basilica Aemilia, a monument to his family's glory on the north side of the Forum. A heavily indebted tribune, Scribonius Curio, might have been bribed too. Certainly he had gained fame for his earlier attacks on Caesar, yet in March of 50 he used his veto to prevent the Senate from reassigning Caesar's provinces.

Something other than bribery might have been at work. As tribune, Curio had embarked on a plan of becoming the new Clodius, to the extent that he had even married Clodius' widow, Fulvia. A military confrontation between Caesar, on the one hand, and his enemies in league with Pompey, on the other, was not in most Romans' interests and was a source of widespread anxiety. Toward the end of his year, Curio proved this, when he proposed to the Senate that Caesar should dismiss his troops, provided Pompey did the same. The proposal passed 370 to 22. After he exited the Senate, crowds of grateful Romans – his own growing power base – threw flowers at him and escorted him home.

But the consul C. Claudius Marcellus took matters into his own hands. The cousin of the previous year's consul and also deeply suspicious of Caesar, he refused to act on the Senate's vote. He instead went to Pompey and made the appeal that Pompey had heard so many times before – that he step forward to save the Republic. Pompey could not resist and assumed command of the two legions in Italy earmarked for a Parthian war. From his headquarters in Cisalpine Gaul, Caesar sent a letter to the Senate, read out on January 1, 49, agreeing to dismiss his troops if Pompey did his. The new consuls would not allow it, and within a week negotiations broke down completely. Caesar crossed out of his province into Italy with troops, and full civil war was on.

The rights and wrongs of the final descent into war were a major issue at the time and have been ever since. There is a temptation to blame, as Caesar himself did, Marcellus and the enemies of compromise. But one can equally blame Caesar and Pompey. Their use of soldiers to intimidate voters in 59 and 55 against their political opponents arguably was the start of the war. Others, too, had eroded the power of the Senate and the People and the rule of law – or tried to: Catiline and the Italian debtors; Clodius and Milo, with their gangs; Marcus Crassus and his son, with their Parthian schemes. In the mad dash for electoral success, politicians like Scaurus stretched rules to their breaking point. There were efforts to solve problems, such as laws trying to restrict bribery and improve provincial government, some of which would leave a lasting footprint on Roman ideas of government. But the repeated violence of the 60s and 50s showed the failure of Senate, People, and magistrates to maintain order, and the civil wars of the 40s would provide brutal confirmation.

FURTHER READING

Refer to the previous chapter for works on politics by Taylor, Gruen, Brunt, and Millar. T. P. Wiseman's two chapters on the 60s and 50s in *The Cambridge Ancient History* (2nd ed.) Vol. 9, give a splendid narrative. Essays on particular topics are abundant, including these classics useful for the interpretation suggested here: E. Badian, "M. Porcius Cato and the Annexation and Early Administration of Cyprus," *Journal of Roman Studies* 55 (1965), 110–21; A. W. Lintott, "P. Clodius Pulcher – *Felix Catilina?" Greece & Rome* 14 (1967), 157–69, and "Cicero and Milo," *Journal of Roman Studies* 64 (1974), 62–78; E. D. Rawson, "Crassorum funera," *Latomus* 41 (1982), 540–49.

Because so many of his writings survive, Cicero is an appealing subject for biographers. D. Stockton, *Cicero: A Political Biography* (Oxford, 1971), is complemented by the more cultural E. Rawson, *Cicero: A Portrait* (London, 1975). Most vivid is the work of an experienced political reporter, H. J. Haskell, *This Was Cicero: Modern Politics in a Roman Toga* (New York, 1942). For guidance on the writings, consult A. W. Lintott, *Cicero as Evidence: A Historian's Companion* (Oxford, 2008); J. Powell and J. Paterson (eds.), *Cicero the Advocate* (Oxford, 2004); C. E. W. Steel, *Reading Cicero* (London, 2005). On oratory more generally see C. Steel and H. van der Blom (eds.), *Community and Communication: Oratory and Politics in Republican Rome* (Oxford, 2013). Cicero's great enemies are well treated by B. Levick, *Catiline* (London, 2015), and W. J. Tatum, *The Patrician Tribune: Publius Clodius Pulcher* (Chapel Hill, 1999).

The classic biography of Caesar, still unmatched for its reporting of the evidence, is M. Gelzer, *Caesar: Politician and Statesman* (trans. P. Needham; Oxford, 1968). A. Goldsworthy, *Caesar: Life of a Colossus* (New Haven, 2006), is livelier. W. J. Tatum, *Always I Am Caesar* (Oxford, 2008), and T. Stevenson, *Julius Caesar and the Transformation of the Roman Republic* (Abingdon, 2015), relate Caesar's career to broader issues. On his writing, see the essays in K. Welch and A. Powell (eds.), *Julius Caesar as Artful Reporter: The War Commentaries as Political Instruments* (Swansea, 1998). M. Griffin (ed.), *A Companion to Julius Caesar* (Malden, MA, 2009), has many fine essays, including J. T. Ramsey's lucid account of "The Proconsular Years: Politics at a Distance."

Scaurus' career can be traced through A. R. Dyck, *Marcus Tullius Cicero: Speeches on behalf of Marcus Fonteius and Marcus Aemilius Scaurus* (Oxford, 2012), along with Kit Morrell, "Cato and the Courts in 54 BC," *Classical Quarterly* 64 (2014), 669–81. On the perils of electioneering see A. Yakobson, *Elections and Electioneering in Rome: A Study in the Political System of the Late Republic* (Stuttgart 1999), and R. Feig Vishnia, *Roman Elections in the Age of Cicero* (New York, 2012).

9

———

THE COURSE OF EMPIRE: PROVINCIAL

GOVERNMENT AND SOCIETY (90–50 BCE)

On July 31 of 51 BCE, Cicero began a one-year governorship of the overseas province of Cilicia in Asia Minor. Just four days into his term he wrote to his friend Atticus, complaining that he was bored. The legal hearings he had to preside over were tedious. And the chance of military campaigning? That held no interest either. "The Forum, Rome, my house": it was around these that Cicero's life normally revolved.

But by the end of the year, Cicero was writing rather more cheerfully, even reporting some martial exploits. In October, he had taken his small army to the Amanus, the mountain range separating Cilicia from Syria, "full of everlasting enemies of Rome." Plundering and destroying these settlements, Cicero camped near Issus – exactly where Alexander the Great had several centuries before, he noted with some mirth. Then began an eight-week siege of Pindenissum. "Pindenissum? What the heck is that? I've never heard the name!" Cicero imagines Atticus saying. It was, Cicero explains, a well-fortified town, "in arms for as long as anyone can remember; the people there were savages." Parodying the style of an official military dispatch, Cicero then continues: "We threw a rampart and moat around it, built a huge earthwork with sheds and a high tower, lots of siege artillery and a great number of archers." The town fell without any Romans killed. Cicero let his men plunder it, while the captives were sold into slavery.

Although inflating these minor victories for his friend brought some pleasure, Cicero had to handle far more sensitively an unpleasant discovery he made about Senator Marcus Brutus (the future assassin of Julius Caesar). Brutus and Atticus were close, and Atticus had requested that Cicero help Brutus with some business he had abroad. The king of Cappadocia was late in making loan payments to Brutus, and Cicero applied what pressure he could. Owing money to Pompey too, the king was totally broke, Cicero feared.

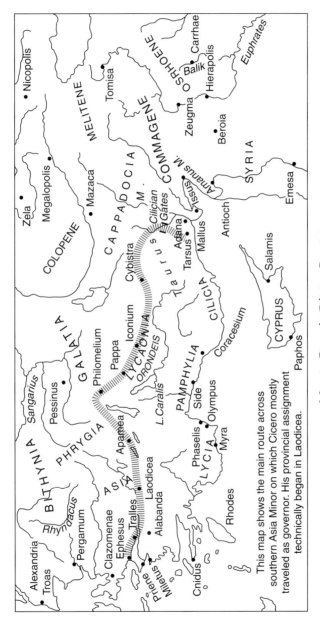

Map 8 Cicero's Cilician Province

This map shows the main route across southern Asia Minor on which Cicero mostly traveled as governor. His provincial assignment technically began in Laodicea.

Cicero also agreed to help two associates of Brutus who had lent money to the town of Salamis, on the island of Cyprus. Summoning the town's magistrates to Tarsus, Cicero ordered them to pay up, and they said they were willing to. Only when they began reckoning up what was due did Cicero learn that the interest rate on the loan was 48 percent per year, four times the maximum allowed. Brutus' friends had in their possession copies of Senate decrees, passed with Brutus' help, that legitimized the loan, and they refused to settle on any other terms.

Eventually, one of Brutus' two associates, Scaptius, produced a letter from Brutus revealing the shocking truth: the real lender was not Brutus' associates but Brutus himself. The letter also demanded that Cicero give a staff position to Scaptius – as had Cicero's predecessor as governor, who happened to be Brutus' father-in-law, the haughty patrician Appius Claudius. With troops assigned to him by Appius, Scaptius had shut up the senators of Salamis in their senate house. Five senators had died of starvation during this "siege," according to Cicero. Had Cicero not been sent to govern Cilicia, he never would have discovered that Brutus, nephew of the younger Cato and eager to uphold a similar reputation for rectitude, was really a usurer. Atticus apparently had been as much in the dark as Cicero.

In penetrating what really was happening in the provinces beyond Rome in the late republican period, Cicero is a uniquely important guide. His prosecution of Verres, the governor of Sicily, in 70 led him to launch major investigations in Rome and on Sicily itself, the results of which he shared in published speeches. Even more revealing is his correspondence from his yearlong governorship. While Cicero can be suspected of presenting himself in the best light possible even when writing to friends, his letters show better than any other source how provincial government worked, and the way events hundreds of miles from Rome were intertwined directly with plotting in the capital.

Cicero's writings, the works of Julius Caesar and other contemporaries, and government documents inscribed on bronze tablets or stone monuments supply material for investigating provincial history. The topic is crucial. The taxes collected in the provinces, year after year, provided most of the Roman state's regular revenue. A major job of the provincial governor, the main representative of the Roman state, was to oversee tax collection and maintain basic order. But because of their extraordinary powers, governors and their personal staff were able to exploit provincials for their own or their friends' gain. Even those less inclined to, like Cicero, felt pressure to do so.

While Rome's growing presence overseas was challenged, sometimes violently, and there was plenty of complaining about exploitation, a number of local leaders in the provinces came to embrace Rome. Just as Italians had been incorporated into Roman society, provincials were too, with the prestige of the world conqueror rubbing off onto them. In exchange for recognition by the Roman state or help from powerful Roman politicians, or both, they helped maintain order. They joined in, and helped shape, a more coherent vision of empire as a political structure that promised lasting peace, in exchange for submission to Rome and payment of taxes. Like the reinvention of Italy, transformations in provincial society prepared the way for the world state of Augustus and his successors – a state with greater administrative capability than SPQR had had in the mid-second century BCE.

THE FACE OF ROME: THE PROVINCIAL GOVERNOR

While "provinces" (*provinciae*) had originally been tasks assigned to magistrates, Sulla's reforms made them much more like permanent administrative districts. The dictator's scheme was that upon completing their year of office in Rome, consuls and praetors would each be assigned a province that they were not to leave unless given specific permission by the Senate or the People. Internally, the province was organized as a series of communities recognized by Rome with varying statuses. Those that had shown loyalty to Rome in times of war, for example, might be given particular privileges. These included "freedom," which in practice might mean immunity from certain taxes or from the requirement to quarter Roman troops. Just as was true in Italy, maintaining good roads or secure sea routes between communities was critical in the provinces.

Cicero's Cilician province, despite its vastness, in fact was little more than a glorified road, a highway running across southern Asia Minor, in part developed centuries earlier by the Persians. Aside from campaigning, which could take him further afield, the Cilician governor's job simply involved moving up and down the road, stopping at designated centers along the way to preside over legal hearings or sort out other problems. (When the island of Cyprus was added to Cilicia after Cyprus' annexation in 56, it was administered mainly from Tarsus.) Other provinces, even when their road networks were more elaborate, had a similar organization. As he made his way along the roads, the governor could be instantly recognized by the attendants carrying the bundle of rods (*fasces*) and the axe that represented his power. Word of the governor's arrival preceded him, and communities were well advised to prepare a generous welcome reception.

Accompanying the governor and the attendants was the rest of his small staff. Typically, he had a few legates who served as his deputies, especially in military affairs. No general himself, Cicero arranged for his brother Quintus, who had honed his military skills under Caesar in Gaul, to be one of his officers. The governor would also appoint prefects, men who commanded smaller military units or oversaw logistical tasks like disposing of war plunder. Each province also had a quaestor (except Sicily, which by custom had two), the junior magistrate who along with the governor prepared the financial accounts. A small number of professional secretaries assisted the governor and also helped the quaestor with the accounts.

This tiny staff was supplemented by the governor's personal entourage. His own slaves and former slaves would come along to take care of him and help him in his duties, including correspondence. Younger friends, relatives, or men seeking the governor's favor also joined the governor, offering advice or amusement during the long and dreary months away from Rome. The poet Catullus accompanied Memmius when he was governor of Bithynia in 56 and later groaned in his verses that he had not made the money he had hoped for: Memmius had "screwed" Catullus. According to his letters, Cicero's entourage made similar complaints to him. Caesar's generosity in Gaul – where staff members went to be "covered in gold" – had set stiff competition for other commanders.

The essential job of the governor was to maintain order in his province. One part of this was to prevent incursions from hostile neighbors. The Roman state often made shrewd alliances with rulers of territories beyond provincial boundaries. In exchange for recognition, the "friendly" king would report any threats and sometimes offer military assistance. As governor of Cilicia, Cicero had numerous dealings with such kings. It was from several of them that he learned of a westward movement of the Parthians, across the Euphrates, which he took measures to resist, with the support of the kings.

He also carried out the Senate's instructions to lend support to the young, new king of Cappadocia. Fearful after a massive conspiracy had been detected, the king asked Cicero for military protection. Cicero felt unable to spare any troops, only offering as help the Machiavellian tip that self-preservation is "the first lesson in the art of ruling." In the official dispatch reporting his actions to the Senate, Cicero nowhere mentioned his private commission to extract from the king the money he owed to Brutus and Pompey.

Maintaining order had an internal aspect as well. Because the governor's staff was so small, communities were largely left to supervise themselves and the territories that surrounded them, but the governor might have to adjudicate in disputes between communities. Inscribed documents reveal how governors could assign a third community as an arbiter (a practice earlier followed by the Senate). When two Spanish peoples got into a water-rights dispute in the 80s, for example, the governor assigned settlement of the matter to the town of Contrebia, applying the principles of Roman law. More violent altercations between neighboring communities, such as the cattle raids that were a traditional part of Iberian life, had to be dealt with by armed force. Periodic food shortages arising from crop failure were another challenge. Cicero tried to deal with one during his governorship by urging both natives and Roman citizens to release rather than hoard grain in the hope of higher profits.

Unless a community enjoyed officially recognized freedom from Rome, technically it was under the governor's jurisdiction. Since he would not have the time or inclination to deal with every minor squabble, he would leave local bodies to settle many disputes. Charges involving Roman citizens were much likelier to be heard by him, or one of his deputies, or by panels of judges he selected, usually by lot. Increasingly, communities were assigned to larger assize districts, each of which had a center where matters could be brought to the governor. The governor would travel to these centers, just as United States Supreme Court justices used to "ride circuit."

At the start of his term, a governor would issue an edict setting out the laws by which he would administer his province. Cicero, not surprisingly, was particularly proud of his. He had modeled much of it on the edict that Quintus Scaevola (the distinguished jurist with whom Cicero had studied as a young man) had created for Asia in the 90s. Included was a clause stating that cases between natives should be tried under their own laws. By his edict, Cicero limited interest to 12 percent per year, which is a major reason he came to blows with Brutus over Salamis. Ultimately, Cicero never settled Brutus' matter, leaving it for his successor to deal with.

While Cicero's letters illustrate, by his own exemplary actions, the role of a good governor, the orations against Verres do so by negative example. In both cases, one goal was to showcase Cicero's diligence. Accused by the Sicilians after his return to Rome in 71, Verres was defended by the leading lawyer of the day, Hortensius. Eager to advance his career, Cicero jumped at the chance to represent the Sicilians. He collected documentary evidence and witnesses on the island and then returned to Rome, rushing through his opening speech so he that could share what he found. Verres and Hortensius were caught off guard, and Verres went into exile before the trial even concluded. Cicero published the set of speeches he had planned to give after the review of evidence. They are stylistic masterpieces, exhibiting a full range of tones, from indignation to humor. There is a horrifying account of Verres' crucifixion of a Roman citizen without trial. But there is also an account of a dinner party that took place in Rome, during the course of the trial, at which the rapacious Verres could not stop himself from pawing the silver tableware, as the host's poor slaves nervously looked on.

Cicero devotes a large section of the published orations to Verres' corruption of justice. Men who inherited large estates would be accused falsely and secured acquittals only through bribes to Verres or an intermediary on his staff. To judge cases, Verres selected members of his own personal entourage, including doctors and soothsayers. His was not "the staff of Q. Scaevola," Cicero noted tartly, "though it was not Scaevola's custom to draw upon his staff for this activity." Not only did Verres arrange false charges, but he also had false testimony introduced and let trials proceed in the absence of the accused. In Cicero's telling, Verres' tour of the assize seats was a travesty. He travelled on a litter with cushions stuffed with rose petals and upon reaching a city would be carried, still on the litter, straight into his bedroom to sell a few verdicts before partying all night in scenes of tumult that degenerated into pitched battles. The Verrines should not always be taken at face value, but even if we sometimes doubt the prosecuting attorney, it can be revealing to see Cicero's own sense of justice. For example, Roman citizens living in Sicily, or prominent Sicilians with established relationships with leading politicians, deserved, in his view, special consideration.

SHEARING THE SHEEP: TAXATION

As provinces became less like military frontiers and more like administrative districts, the plunder of campaigning was replaced with more regular taxation, the main source of state revenue. The details are enormously complicated and varied from place to place, since the Romans often preserved what they found. Fundamentally, there were two main types of provincial tax: direct taxes (*stipendium*) and tithes. Direct taxes were based on the number of people in a community and the property they held, while tithes took a share of yearly agricultural output. There were other "percentage" taxes like tithes (such as taxes on grazing animals), and the collection of customs at harbors and toll stations also was an increasingly important revenue stream in the provinces.

Aside from *stipendium*, most taxes were not collected directly by the Roman state but rather by subcontractors. While the government set the tax rate, it would solicit bids for how much individual firms thought they could collect *and* hand over after taking a profit for themselves. Since most contracts were for five-year terms, this had the advantage of creating more predictable revenue streams even for percentage taxes and customs. Firms that won contracts were given special privileges, such as indemnification for losses during war and also the right to exist in perpetuity (i.e., beyond the lifetime of the firm's partners). Since the contracts dealt with public property (*publica*), the men who made up the companies were known as the *publicani*.

With the growth of overseas *imperium*, the fortunes of the *publicani* were transformed. In earlier days, their largest contracts typically were for supplying armies and building major public works. Later, mines, including the profitable silver mines of Spain, were turned over to them. A watershed was Gaius Gracchus' legislation in the late 120s selling the collection of tithes and customs in Asia to the highest bidders. Because the sums involved were colossal and the overhead costs of collecting taxes high – requiring investment of large amounts of capital – only the very wealthy could form partnerships. While they would run their businesses from Rome, they had huge staffs, including local managers, as well as scores of slaves and former slaves.

The sophisticated nature of these firms compensated for the minuscule resources the Roman government itself devoted to provincial administration. Governors like Cicero relied on the courier service of the *publicani* to get letters to and from Rome. The *publicani* also served as bankers. After taxes were collected, the profits were deposited locally and a credit note issued that the Treasury could use to meet other expenditures, thus obviating the need for coin to go back and forth to Rome. So in this way too the firms cut risk for the Roman government. Of course, the *publicani* could exploit the information they had to increase their own profits – lending money at high interest to communities in default on their tax payments, for example. Still, in the absence of a more robust central government, they deserve credit for the growth of the Roman Empire and its transformation into a stable fiscal entity.

There was a danger to the system of farming out taxes. A government that subcontracts must monitor the contractor carefully. The Senate tried to do so, but in practice much of the job fell to the provincial governor, and it was all too convenient for him to turn a blind eye to abuses by the collectors. Crossing the *publicani* could have a political cost back at Rome, as Lucullus discovered when he massively reduced the debt owed by Asian communities in late 71.

Some governors might even be tempted to collaborate with the *publicani* for mutual enrichment. In his Verrine orations, Cicero reports uncovering a devious scheme. Verres, he claims, initially snuck goods out of the harbor at Syracuse without paying customs. The local manager reported this back to the collecting company in Rome. But when Verres went into collusion with another of the company's managers, his new ally started filing reports of how helpful Verres was being to the company. The company managers greeted Verres warmly when he returned to Rome, and the chairman arranged to destroy the early, incriminating documents. Cicero managed to find copies of some of them, kept by a former chairman.

Cicero's Cilician letters offer a very different picture. Responding to an inquiry from Atticus about how he dealt with the tax farmers, Cicero replied that for those communities in arrears he offered settlement of their debts at a reduced rate of interest. He also kept his own impositions, such as requests for lodging, at a minimum. Many communities were soon entirely debt-free and up to date on their tax payments, and Cicero claims that the *publicani* were thrilled: "I am their darling." If this suggests less rapacity on their part than do other sources, still Cicero's desire to please them reveals their significant power. Only the stronger central government of the emperors would be able to monitor them more closely.

SKINNING THE SHEEP: EXTORTION

Selling verdicts and colluding with the tax collectors were not the only ways provincial governors could enrich themselves. Cicero reveals others in his remarks about his predecessors in Cilicia – especially Appius Claudius, whom he compares to a "savage beast." Daily expense allowances could be collected from every village on a road rather than just one. Communities could pay a bribe to prevent troops from being quartered with them: the people of Cyprus paid 200 talents, according to Cicero. The Verrine orations are filled with other schemes. For example, Verres demanded money to put up statues of himself throughout Sicily – a customary honor for governors – without putting them up, thereby pocketing 2 million sesterces. He also required the people of Syracuse to establish a festival in his honor, the Verres festival, the contracts for which he profited from.

The governor could use his immense power to help his friends financially too, to the detriment of provincials. Appius' willingness to entrust Brutus' agent Scaptius with troops is a chilling example. Brutus expected that Cicero would similarly oblige him, and other requests show what senators back in Rome thought they might get away with. Cicero's friend Caelius repeatedly begged for "help" from the provinces in funding the games he was planning as aedile; he even demanded that Cicero arrange for some panthers to be captured and sent to Rome (exotic animals being a crowd pleaser). Another senator was soon asking for the same. Cicero refused: to have provincial communities hunting publicly on his orders would harm his carefully groomed reputation.

Indignant at how senators were exploiting the *imperium* for their own ends rather than for the good of the People, citizens passed increasingly complex laws against extortion. Initially, provincials could sue for simple restitution of money illegally seized. Penalties were stiffened over time, ultimately forcing those found guilty to go into exile. Laws also increasingly included highly detailed regulations. As consul in 59, Caesar passed a new extortion law more than 100 chapters long, which Cicero refers to repeatedly in his Cilician correspondence. It placed strict limits on how much a governor could requisition to supply himself and his staff. It also required the governor to post copies of his accounts in the province and to submit a copy within 10 days of returning to Rome. At least in theory, governors were to be accountable to provincials and to citizens alike.

In practice, though, it could be hard to obtain justice. Taking on a powerful senator was a daunting enterprise for provincials. They would have to journey to Rome and find an advocate to represent them in the extortion court. The former governor would have powerful resources to muster against them – connections with *publicani* or high-ranking provincials whom he could summon to Rome to offer character testimonials. The current governor could make life miserable for those who dared to speak out against his predecessor. Some men who were almost certainly guilty were acquitted, thanks to the clever rhetoric of orators like Cicero, who himself defended far more often than he prosecuted.

There are different ways to read the record of extortion legislations and trials. On the one hand, however well intentioned the laws, they did not address the real problem of just how unsupervised governors were during their term of office. On the other, they show a willingness to criticize what was going on in the empire and to envision an alternative, in which the Roman People's interests still came first. The same was true of the law Pompey passed in 52 requiring a five-year interval between the holding of political office and a governorship, since it was intended to cut down on the large bribes that would then be recouped from innocent provincials. Cicero's own letters, while divulging the exploitation of Brutus, repeatedly show his own efforts to model integrity – and he expected the same from his staff. However dull he found the routine duties of governing, he conceded to Atticus that improving the conditions in his province gave him genuine pleasure. This is a sign of how the idea of *imperium* was moving beyond the earlier obsession with successful warfare.

THE ROMAN COMMUNITY OVERSEAS

Provincial societies were themselves changing too. While SPQR had no conscious policy of spreading Roman culture and provincial administration was remarkably minimal, Romans and Italians were settling overseas long before 50. One large group was that of former soldiers. Spain, one of the oldest parts of the empire, correspondingly provides the most examples. In 206, during the Second Punic War, Scipio Africanus founded the community of Italica for veterans wounded in battle. In 171 a Latin colony was created at Carteia, in response to a petition from the sons of Roman men who had married native Iberian women. In 152 M. Claudius Marcellus settled men in Corduba, and in 138, D. Iunius Brutus in Valentia. All of these settlements were on the Mediterranean coast or in the fertile lands of the Baetis River valley, accessible to the wider Mediterranean and similar in climate to Italy.

Joining the veterans in Spain were men dedicated to trade, banking, and related pursuits. Romans and Italians managed the mines for the *publicani*, and increasingly there were also agents of the firms to handle such jobs as collecting customs. There were independent businessmen, too, who ran profitable estates such as cattle ranches or traded overseas or both. Gades, on the Atlantic coast, was a hub of commercial activity, the home to many wealthy Romans as well as those of native background who had gained citizenship by Cicero's day. Its fish sauce became famous. Men successful in Spain made their way back to Rome. Catullus penned a funny poem about a Spaniard named Egnatius with "gleaming white teeth" who was always showing off his smile. Even at a mother's funeral for her only son, he would grin. Catullus claims that Egnatius was a Celtiberian – from a part of Spain where people allegedly washed their teeth with urine. The putdown is more devastating if we assume that Egnatius belonged to an old Roman or Italian family that had emigrated.

Southern Gaul, North Africa, and the lands around the Aegean Sea all had their share of Romans too, although settlement patterns varied regionally. Gaul, for example, had not experienced the decades of fighting that Spain had, and so fewer soldiers settled there. There were some, though, including at the garrison town of Aquae Sextiae (founded in 123). But by the time of Caesar's great war, the "Province" (as the south was called) and even areas north had plenty of Romans engaged in commerce. A brother of one of Cicero's legal clients, for example, had operations including ranching, agriculture, and slave trading. During his war in Gaul, Caesar undertook a campaign in the Alps to free a trade route from tolls the locals were charging to merchants coming from Italy.

The historical record reveals that by 50, Roman citizens across the empire had formed associations (*conventus*) with elected officials. With a few exceptions, these associations did not replace the governments of the urban settlements they took root in, but rather were parallel to them. Sometimes officially recognized by Rome, they inevitably had powerful connections with high-ranking Romans. By providing local expertise to provincial governors, for example, they were helped in turn by the governor in legal disputes they might have, or with business back in Rome. Extraordinary commanders like Pompey and Caesar formed strong bonds with the associations of Romans overseas in general, giving rise to hard decisions in the civil wars of the 40s (Chapter 11).

While detailed information about the associations is unavailable, it is clear that they were closely linked in the eyes of provincials with Rome and Roman power. Indeed, they almost perfectly exemplified the privileges that cooperation with Rome could bring. Provincials could see how Romans who soldiered well, or collected taxes, or facilitated trade gained in wealth and in prestige. Eastern cities of the *imperium* had their own distinguished Greek culture. Western Mediterranean cities, like the communities of Italian allies before the Social War, emulated Greek culture, just as the Romans themselves did. The unique attraction of Rome was its domination – and the tangible opportunities offered to those who helped in its imperial project. The associations of citizens were key in making those opportunities clear.

RESISTANCE, REBELLION, AND INTEGRATION

As Rome established control of territories overseas, there were challenges to its authority, just as there had been in Italy. The uprising of the Gallic peoples under the leadership of the charismatic Vercingetorix is a good example. Augustus would face similar rebellions in newly conquered areas (Chapter 14). Far more spectacular was the massacre of Romans and Italians in Asia organized by Mithridates in 88. According to later, Roman sources, instructions were sent out to kill the men, women, and children; to throw out their bodies unburied; and to seize all their property. Catalogues of atrocities were recorded. In Pergamum, for example, the Italians who sought refuge in a religious sanctuary were shot down with arrows as they clung to the statues of the gods. In Caunos, the children were killed first, before their mothers' eyes.

Piracy and brigandage also erupted in resistance to Roman rule. While piracy was endemic to the Mediterranean basin with its intricate coastlines, at least some of the men who embraced it in the late republican period belonged to communities destabilized economically by the arrival of the Romans in the east. The miniature states organized by the pirates in the 80s and 70s specifically sought to damage Roman prestige, not just to plunder. It is no wonder, then, that Mithridates collaborated with them. Mountain communities like those in Cicero's Cilicia – the "everlasting enemies of Rome" – were "enemies" in part because they might harbor runaway slaves of the Romans. Needless to say, the slaves had a different perspective than Cicero did. In the first century, oracles were disseminated in Greek proclaiming that the fall of Rome was at hand: "However much Rome has taken from tributary Asia, three times as much money will Asia take back from Rome, and will avenge Rome's deadly arrogance; however many from Asia who have served in the house of Italians, twenty times more Italians will be enslaved in Asia."

But while some communities joined Mithridates, others resisted his orders and took every opportunity to advertise their loyalty to Rome. The town of Stratonicea inscribed a letter from Sulla on the wall of its temple to the goddess Hecate. "You [Stratonicea] have on every occasion preserved unbroken your fidelity towards us . . . in the war against Mithridates you were the first of those in Asia to offer resistance," it said. Along with the letter was a Senate decree full of assurances of "good will, friendship, and alliance." The town's envoys were hailed as "gentlemen of character and honor," and the town itself as "an honorable people." All the territory and revenues Sulla had assigned to Stratonicea were confirmed by the Senate. The inscription neatly illustrates how communities cultivated relationships with the Roman state and with individual Romans, whose power was soaring in the first century.

The great challenges in the east ultimately strengthened the empire by providing an opportunity for Rome to demonstrate the value of loyalty. While Mithridates intermittently unified a number of communities against Rome, more typically they were inclined to vie with one another for preeminence. The various privileges Rome afforded, such as "freedom," conferred prestige and also could be economically valuable (e.g., tax immunities). This was especially so since those judged to have been insufficiently loyal were severely punished. Pergamum, for example, lost its freedom in 85 as part of Sulla's settlement and suffered financially for well more than a decade.

If whole communities looked for ways to express loyalty to Rome, so did individuals, in the east and also in the west. Taking their cues from Roman veterans and merchants – as well as the associations of citizens – Gauls, Spaniards, and others found ways to embrace aspects of Roman identity. They learned Latin and adopted Roman names. Even more important, they were willing to contribute to Roman imperial success, most obviously by joining the Roman army as auxiliary forces. From around the time of the Social War – when Roman citizenship was so boldly reimagined – commanders were authorized to grant citizenship to provincials in recognition of meritorious service. A bronze tablet survives revealing that Pompey's father did so for a number of Spanish cavalrymen in 89. Tellingly, several of them had already taken Roman names.

Ultimately, leading provincials and Romans had much to gain by joining rather than fighting one another. A superb example is that of Cornelius Balbus, a leading man of Gades on the Atlantic coast of Spain. Born around 100, he fought in naval and land campaigns against Sertorius in the 70s, ultimately winning citizenship from Pompey for the help he and his city furnished. He then joined the staff of Julius Caesar when Caesar was governor of Further Spain (61). In exchange for Balbus' local expertise, Caesar helped his ally tighten his grip on affairs in Gades. The two men together orchestrated an ouster of a group of local politicians not amenable to Balbus. The bond they formed proved an enduring one, and Balbus later served under Caesar in Gaul and also represented Caesar's interests in Rome in his absence.

Caesar's commentaries furnish another compelling example of how a provincial governor and provincials could reinforce one another's power. Throughout his Gallic campaigns, Caesar writes, he made use of two brothers from the Allobroges – Roucillus and Egus. Both were splendid cavalrymen, something Caesar badly needed. In exchange for their valiant fighting, he enriched them with captured land and ensured that they reached the highest political office in their own community. They went on to serve as cavalry officers for Caesar in the civil war with Pompey. When caught cheating their men of pay and embezzling plunder – so Roman had they become in their ways! – they deserted to Pompey.

It is revealing that during the great civil wars of the 40s and 30s there was virtually no attempt to eradicate Roman rule in the provinces – no repeat of the Asian massacre of 88. (There are reports of increased "banditry," in Sicily for example.) Failed rebellions and smashing military successes like Pompey's suggested that the Romans would always prevail. It was better to join them. The main question in the civil war, for provincials as well as Romans, was which side to join.

THE COURSE OF EMPIRE

In the first century, Romans were willing to critique their empire. This went beyond accusations against individual governors in court. In his speech in support of Pompey receiving command in the last Mithridatic war (66), Cicero was blunt: "It is hard to exaggerate how much we are hated among foreign nations because of the capricious and outrageous actions of those men we have sent to govern them in recent times." Writing in the 40s, Sallust was even more devastating. After the destruction of Carthage, he insisted, greed and the desire for empire grew to unbearable levels. Provincials were robbed of everything. In a later work, Sallust composed a speech for Mithridates to deliver that makes an even stronger indictment: the Romans are "a plague on the whole world; nothing human or divine prevents them from seizing and destroying allies and friends, those near them and those far off, weak and powerful alike."

Non-Romans made critiques too. Some of the most famous ones were issued by Poseidonius, a polymath born in Syria and educated in Athens who wrote a continuation of Polybius' history of the Mediterranean world. Only a few fragments survive, but we can recover something of his perspective from the partially extant history of the Sicilian Diodorus, finished around 30 BCE, since Diodorus relied on Poseidonius. Diodorus has harsh words about the Romans and the Italians. Driven by greed, Italian traders had made the Gauls addicted to wine, he claimed. Also, "A multitude of Italians have swarmed to the [Spanish] mines and carried off great wealth." A lurid picture of the contractors' inhuman treatment of the slave laborers follows. Gaius Gracchus is blamed for turning the provinces over "to the recklessness and greed of the tax farmers," thereby provoking the subject peoples "to a just hatred of their rulers."

Yet alongside criticisms there were celebrations. Cicero's speech for Pompey, like others of his writings, hails Rome's embrace of the entire world in its rule. Even in the last years of the Republic, Romans could still believe, as they had before, that they owed their success to their piety. The gods wanted the Romans to rule over all people, but victory imposed a duty on the Romans to care for those in their power. The abuses of bad governors required remediation. When Cicero's brother Quintus was serving as governor of Asia, Cicero sent him a letter with advice. "Let it be known to the whole province," Cicero urges, "that the lives, children, reputations, and property of all over whom you govern are most valuable to you."

Greeks had similar advice for their overlords. For all his criticisms, Diodorus upholds exemplars of good government, including Cicero's hero Scaevola. Along with his legate Rutilius, Scaevola "resolved that all expenditures for himself and his staff should be made from his own purse," Diodorus notes. Scaevola "redressed the unjust exactions of the *publicani*." He held trials of those accused of wrongdoing and enforced restitution of property where it was due, and so was able to reverse the "hatred that had earlier arisen against the ruling power."

The words sound much like Cicero's, even in his personal letters, and the similarity is revealing. Romans and non-Romans alike were shaping a vision of empire together. For all of its inequalities, empire itself was a shared experience. Mismanagement hurt provincials, but it hurt Romans too, as the Asian massacre showed most clearly. On the other hand, Romans were willing, as they had been with Italians, to let other peoples share in their successes. This could be military success, but it could also be the success of the trader who shipped his olive oil to one of the great cities of the empire, perhaps to Rome itself. While there sometimes was prejudice against others, such as the Celtiberians with their uncouth mouthwash, the reality was that foreigners could become Roman.

In his advice to his brother, Cicero gives one of the clearest expressions of the ideology of empire that was emerging: "Asia must reflect on this, that if she were not under our empire she would have suffered every disaster that foreign war and domestic strife can inflict. Since this empire can in no way be maintained without taxation, she should be content to give up a part of her revenues in exchange for permanent peace and tranquility." In the very years in which the traditional government by SPQR was unraveling, Romans were developing the majestic idea that universal Roman rule could offer universal peace, and the vision was one that provincials themselves could share in. Underpinning it were the connections forged between provincial aristocrats and Romans – the ties that bound the empire together.

FURTHER READING

The works on Cicero mentioned in the previous chapter have good discussions of his Cilician governorship and the earlier prosecution of Verres. For the geographical and historical context consult A. N. Sherwin-White, *Roman Foreign Policy in the East, 168 B.C. to A.D. 1* (London, 1984); S. Mitchell, *Anatolia: Land, Men, and Gods in Asia Minor* (Oxford, 1993).

Provincial administration is thoroughly discussed by A. Lintott, Imperium romanum*: Politics and Administration* (London, 1993), and more briefly by J. Richardson in chap. 13 of *The Cambridge Ancient History* (2nd ed.) Vol. 9, and J. P. V. D. Balsdon, *Rome: The Story of an Empire* (London, 1970). For exposés of the *publicani* and the governors, respectively, see E. Badian, *Publicans and Sinners* (Ithaca, NY, 1972), and *Roman Imperialism in the Late Republic* (2nd ed.; Ithaca, NY, 1982).

Recovering provincial cultures has been a priority in more recent research. Good insights are provided by N. Purcell, "Romans in the Roman World," and G. Woolf, "Provincial Perspectives," in K. Galinsky (ed.), *The Cambridge Companion to the Age of Augustus* (Cambridge, 2005), 85–105 and 106–29, respectively. R. MacMullen, *Romanization in the Time of Augustus* (New Haven, 2000), is full of vivid detail. Works on Spain include S. J. Keay, *Roman Spain* (London, 1988); J. Richardson, *The Romans in Spain* (Oxford, 1996); A. T. Fear, *Rome and Baetica: Urbanization in Southern Spain c. 50 BC–AD 150* (Oxford, 1996); S. Keay, "Recent Archaeological Work in Roman Iberia (1990–2002)," *Journal of Roman Studies* 93 (2003), 106–29. On citizens overseas there is much data in P. A. Brunt, *Italian Manpower, 225 B.C.–A.D. 14* (Oxford, 1971). An entirely different perspective is offered by B. D. Shaw, "Bandits in the Roman Empire," *Past & Present* 105 (1984), 3–52.

On changing ideas of empire see various papers in P. A. Brunt, *Roman Imperial Themes* (Oxford, 1990); C. E. W. Steel, *Cicero, Rhetoric, and Empire* (Oxford, 2001); L. Yarrow, *Historiography at the End of the Republic: Provincial Perspectives on Roman Rule* (Oxford, 2006); M. T. Griffin, "*Iure plectimur*: The Roman Critique of Roman Imperialism," in T. C. Brennan and H. I. Flower (eds.), *East & West: Papers in Ancient History Presented to Glen W. Bowersock* (Cambridge, MA, 2008), 85–111; S. Mattern, "Roman Imperial Power in the Republic," in D. E. Tabachnick and T. Koivukoski (eds.), *Enduring Empire: Ancient Lessons for Global Politics* (Toronto, 2009), 127–46; D. Hoyos (ed.), *A Companion to Roman Imperialism* (Leiden, 2013).

10

——————

WORLD CITY: SOCIETY AND CULTURE
IN ROME (85–45 BCE)

The city of Rome in the years following the Social War attracted extraordinary talents. One was the poet Catullus from the town of Verona in the far north of Italy, and another Catullus' friend and fellow poet Cinna, also from the north. Around 55 BCE Cinna finished a work nine years in the making, a miniature epic called *Zmyrna*. This story, of a beautiful woman who fell in love with her own father and then turned into a tree with weeping bark, illustrated a favorite theme of the young poets of this generation – the dark side of erotic desire. Cinna's well-polished poem also allowed him to display his attention to craftsmanship. Catullus proclaimed that *Zmyrna* would last for generations and be read far and wide, so refined was contemporary taste becoming. True, Catullus said, that plenty of bad poetry also was being written, like the bloated *Annals* of Volusius. But Volusius' dull rehashing of Roman history, Catullus predicted, would make it no farther than the River Po, and its many sheets used to wrap fish.

Other talents came less voluntarily to Rome than young Catullus and Cinna, including a number of Greek scholars taken prisoner during the wars with Mithridates. Prominent among them was Parthenius of Bithynia, perhaps brought back by Cinna himself or else his father. A champion of the scholar-poets of Alexandria, he produced the mythological handbook *Misfortunes in Love*, useful to aspiring versifiers in Rome. Similarly uprooted was the teacher Theophrastus of Pontus, renamed "Tyrannio" because of his overbearing manner. In Rome, he taught and helped Cicero and other prominent Romans with their book collections. He also found time to advance scholarship. Most notable was his involvement with the library of Aristotle, which Sulla had seized in Athens as war plunder and brought to Italy. Tyrannio assisted both in the organizing and editing of its contents, work of fundamental importance for scholars to the present day.

Contributions like Tyrannio's are well known thanks to references in Cicero's letters and the works of other ancient scholars. But many more who spent time in slavery shared their talents – however unwillingly – with Rome, as artists, chefs, musicians, actors, clothes designers, jewelers, and more. Some were enslaved because of their skills, but probably far more were given training as young slaves to increase their value. Epitaphs provide a few details, like that of the one-time slave C. Quinctilius Pamphilus: he supported himself and his household in the perfume business. Another former slave, M. Caedicius Eros, worked as a goldsmith on Rome's fanciest shopping street. L. Lutatius Paccius identified himself as a dealer in incense and a former member of the household of King Mithridates himself. As Mithridates was a renowned expert on poisons and their antidotes, Paccius' connection may hint that he had more than aromatics on offer – love potions, for example, if not lethal toxins.

Drawing new residents from ever farther away, Rome was becoming far less a city-state and more the capital of a world empire. The arrival of Greek experts transformed Roman education, and deeper familiarity with Greek scholarship led to the pursuit of Roman inquiries. The city that in Cato the Elder's day had expelled philosophers and suspected that all Greek doctors were murderers was by Caesar's death an intellectual hub. Further elevating the city's cultural profile was a growing expectation by the public of sophisticated entertainment, including theater, music, and visual art. A surging interest in satisfying individual pleasures, seen in poetry like Catullus', sometimes conflicted with the traditional image of the *res publica* but also helped integrate the diverse population of the world city.

As SPQR broke down, late republican Rome experienced its share of disorder, but its people were also making cultural innovations. New ways of keeping track of the city's population were developed. Residents found a means to express their views beyond the old assemblies. Dazzling cultural achievements such as public art displays proclaimed the power of Rome in ways battlefield victories alone could not – and would inspire later imperial capitals, such as London and Paris. Thanks to trailblazers like Catullus and Cicero, Latin language and literature were enriched with Greek words and viewpoints. Efforts such as theirs helped later writers in the age of Augustus craft canonical statements of what it meant to be Roman – accounts that were read for centuries afterward. Without the world city, there would not have been the world state.

LOST IN THE CITY

Already growing in the second century BCE, Rome exploded in size in the next hundred years, to become a bewilderingly large place. Immigrants from

Italy flooded in, including men and women far poorer than Catullus, attracted by Rome's amenities or driven by desperation. Captives of war, along with other slaves, also swelled the torrent. Some foreigners came freely, to make their fortune. Newcomers were crammed into tall and rickety apartment buildings. The city's twisting streets and ill-lit narrow alleys became almost proverbial. A disillusioned Catullus imagined the clever and beautiful woman he was obsessed with – he called her "Lesbia," a pseudonym inspired by the birthplace of the great love poet Sappho – engaging in sex like a prostitute "on the street corners and in the back alleys."

The old census system was entirely inadequate for keeping track of the city of Rome. The census was designed to categorize the Roman People, as voters and soldiers, wherever they resided. Its purpose was not to count all souls in Rome, many who might not be citizens. It did not seek to build a picture of how people in the city were living; it had no connection with public services. Moreover, from 85 until 28 BCE only one census was completed – in 70. Just as in earlier centuries the census ordered the Roman state by assigning citizens their roles, its breakdown was a visible sign of political instability.

An alternative system was needed for Rome, and politicians groped their way toward it. The key to life in Rome – and so to making sense of it – was its neighborhoods. Politicians went through them to recruit support and so had at least some knowledge of them. Clodius took this to the next level by supporting neighborhood organizations and the Crossroads festival they boisterously celebrated, and also by registering organizations neighborhood by neighborhood. His free grain distributions also gave him a grasp of the citizen population. Clodius is alleged to have burned the census records of 70 so that he could create his own lists.

In an effort to overhaul the grain dole, Julius Caesar, as dictator in the early 40s, instituted a new type of urban census. Neighborhood-by-neighborhood, officials collected information from property owners on all residents, in each building. Overall, Caesar is said to have cut the number of recipients from 320,000 to 150,000. While some of this reduction probably was achieved by sending city dwellers to new colonies, even more came from removing noncitizens who had snuck onto the distribution lists. Caesar's reorganization speaks to the huge size of Rome at that time, its large citizen population, and the inadequacy of traditional SPQR in handling it and its needs. Emperor Augustus would continue down the path of the late republican reformers.

BUSINESS: KEEP IT IN THE FAMILY

Rome depended on a large number of businesses to feed, clothe, and supply its large population. A wide range of foodstuffs was shipped or carted in,

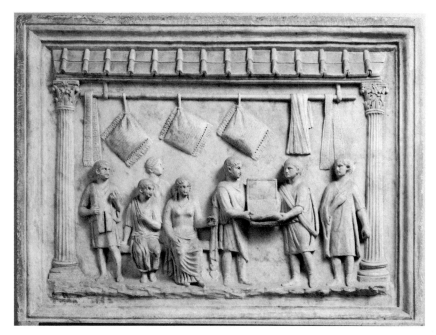

Figure 10.1 Cushions with fancy trim lure customers into this upscale textile shop. A bench is provided for potential customers to sit on as merchandise is exhibited by shop-workers wearing tunics, rather than full togas. The Uffizi, Florence, Italy. (Photo Nimatallah/Art Resource, NY.)

including fresh fruits, vegetables, meats, and fish cultivated in artificial ponds on nearby estates. Some items were sold in large open-air markets. But increasingly the city was full of shops selling freshly baked bread, bowls of expertly seasoned vegetables, hot pork sausages, and much more. There were workshops too, where clothes and footwear were manufactured, often made to measure, with materials ranging from the most basic wool cloth to water-resistant felt to silks interwoven with gold threads. Terracotta lamps, iron tools, bronze tableware, jewelry, and all sorts of other wares were made and sold.

Shops and workshops alike occupied the same type of structure, known as the *taberna* (pl. *tabernae*). The heart of it generally was a small rectangular room with a wide opening onto the street that allowed wares to be displayed on counters in front. Work could be done in the main room, or diners and drinkers might sit here (hence the meaning of the word "tavern" in later European languages). There was some informal zoning in Rome, with high-end jewelers like Caedicius Eros clustering on a busy street leading into the Forum called the Sacred Way. Yet there were *tabernae* throughout the neighborhoods of Rome. Wealthy Romans included them in the large buildings they constructed, since they could bring in regular income from any number of businesses.

The involvement of wealthy investors also helps account for the distinctive social profile of shopkeepers and craftspeople. Aside from the large firms of the *publicani*, which required the pooling of capital (Chapter 9), the household was the main unit of business in Rome. This was because most businesses were not capital intensive and also because slavery, as loathsome as it seems to us, actually solved many of the problems that small firms tend to face. Slaves could be trained as workers with less fear that the "employee" would go to a competitor. The prospect of freedom ensured good performance on the job. And after freedom was granted by a slave's owner, the ex-slaves would still be bound to their patron, making them trustworthy managers of branches of the business. Or they could open their own business, giving a cut of the profits to their former owners.

Senators tended to wash their hands of small-scale commerce. As senators saw it, those who earned wages were vulgar, selling at a retail markup was "dishonest," and catering to the sensual pleasures of others was "base." Of course, senators had other opportunities to enrich themselves, such as money lending, even to kings. They also had their own slave staffs to feed and clothe them. Other Romans of means happily invested in their slaves' commercial training and then freed them – and the freed in turn might do the same, thereby perpetuating a business. The freed slaves of Quinctilius Pamphilus, for example, likely took over his perfume business. The textile business of another *familia*, that of the Veturii, can be traced over several generations, starting with the freedwoman Veturia Fedra, seller of wool.

Epitaphs represent freed slaves in much larger numbers than freeborn Roman citizens. Those who escaped slavery, it has been suggested, were particularly eager to commemorate themselves, loved ones, and coworkers. But at least part of the explanation also must lie in the way slavery furnished access to education and capital. In some respects, freeborn immigrants to Rome must have had fewer opportunities, and so were likely to have taken less-lucrative jobs in construction, porterage, or street hawking. There were plenty of humble slaves too – working as maids, cooks, or litter-bearers, for example – and they have left little trace of themselves. The horrors of Roman slavery should not be minimized, but the institution must also be recognized as a flexible one that helped generate the sophistication the city of Rome achieved. The crowds that Cicero and Catiline spoke to in Rome included quite a few ex-slave shopkeepers.

THE ROMANS GO TO SCHOOL . . .

Unlike Greek cities, Rome made no provisions for public education. Yet Greek-style education took root in Rome – not surprisingly, as Roman literary culture was modeled so closely on that of Greece. A free young Roman of means would learn the rudiments of reading at home or at a neighbor's house, quite possibly from a slave. Next followed a more-advanced study of language and literature, normally consisting of the line-by-line examination of Homer's epics and other classic texts. Romans borrowed their term for this study, *grammatice*, from the Greeks. The teachers were called *grammatici* and were Greeks or trained in Greek methods. These men taught in their own schools or in the house of a prominent Roman.

Some of the *grammatici* had remarkable life stories, such as M. Antonius Gnipho. Born free in Gaul, he was at least briefly enslaved and received a good education. Some even thought he had studied in Alexandria, the leading center of scholarship in the early first century and renowned for its library. As a schoolmaster, Gnipho enjoyed a rare reputation for kindness. He set no fees but was rewarded generously by his pupils. He instructed young Julius Caesar in Caesar's house and then established his own school. Even adults attended his classes. He published two well-regarded books on the Latin language, while other works attributed to him were perhaps by his pupils.

After *grammatice* in the Greek educational system came study of rhetoric and philosophy, and among Romans these subjects especially concerned senators. In Caesar's and Cicero's day, the preference was to learn formal rhetoric from leading Greeks, perhaps in Greece itself. Aspiring politicians also would "intern" with distinguished Roman elders, as Cicero did with Q. Mucius Scaevola and L. Licinius Crassus, champions of political reform in the 90s (Chapter 5). Latin rhetoric professors emerged but were suspected of being subversive. Rhetoric could, in the mouth of a radical, overthrow the established order. Philosophy was left even more to Greeks. These tended to be distinguished men in their own societies, and it was not uncommon for Roman aristocrats after 80 to do a "grand tour" in the east, which would include philosophers' lectures. Other philosophers spent time in Rome, such as the Stoics the younger Cato liked to keep around to jolt his virtue. They helped politicians think about the Roman Empire in new and productive ways (Chapter 9).

The opportunities for education were distributed unevenly. Girls from wealthy families were certainly taught to read and given more-advanced instruction in literature, making them suitable addressees of the love poets. A few women went on to write poetry themselves, although precious little of it survives. While they did not study abroad, some cultivated knowledge of philosophy too, such as Caesar's last wife, Calpurnia. Male slaves, though, might end up being far better educated than freeborn women. A bright slave would be marked out at a young age for extensive schooling so that he could later help his master with household management, correspondence, speechwriting, and more. Cicero's friend Atticus was unusual in insisting that all of his slaves be highly trained. Even Atticus' footmen, a contemporary biographer noted with mirth, could read and copy finely. Normally footmen were valued for brawny good looks, not brains. As a man who spent much of his free time pursuing scholarship, Atticus developed a staff that could help him and his intellectual friends.

The growth of education in Rome stimulated intellectual life, especially since teachers were active as scholars and poets. It was not just Gnipho who published scholarly works. A freedman of Pompey translated King Mithridates' works on pharmacology into Latin. Another freedman teacher, P. Valerius Cato, nurtured aspiring poets, in part with his own work. Just as Catullus wrote a poem praising Cinna's *Zmyrna*, Cinna hailed Valerius Cato's *Dictynna*, probably another of the miniature epics pioneered in Alexandria and now becoming popular in Rome. Readings of new work provided an occasion for those with literary and scholarly interests to gather, as they also did in libraries. The best libraries were located in villas in the hills around Rome and in coastal retreats belonging to senators. Intellectual activity was better suited, many thought, to the leisurely pace of the villas, while in Rome one should focus on the urgent business of public life. But this was starting to change.

. . . AND BECOME MORE INTELLECTUAL

Scholarship flourished as never before in Rome in the 50s and 40s, a prime example being antiquarian studies. At a time when many traditional Roman institutions seemed to be crumbling, exploring history took on new urgency. Greek scholarship provided useful techniques, especially the close linguistic analysis of documents. It also allowed Roman scholars to compare their society with others, especially that of the Greeks themselves. This allowed a reexamination of Roman values – a way to define, or redefine, what those values were.

By far the most important work on the Roman past was done by Senator Varro. His masterpiece, now almost entirely lost, was his 41-volume *Antiquities*, dedicated on its completion in 47 to Julius Caesar, *pontifex maximus*. The tribute was appropriate, as the second part of the work dealt with religious matters, including priesthoods, holy places, festivals, rites, and the gods themselves. Other, better surviving works give a sense of Varro's method. Rome was thought to be a city of seven hills, although it had many more. Which were the genuine seven? Varro believed that he could establish this by studying an ancient document listing a series of shrines. The exercise can be seen as an attempt to make sense of the confusing sprawl Rome had become. Indeed, Cicero hailed Varro's *Antiquities* like this: "We were wandering and straying about in our own city as if we were visitors, and your books led us, so to speak, back home, enabling us at last to recognize who and where we were." Varro also produced biting satires proclaiming a decline in Roman values. A return to (an imagined) past offered an appealing alternative to the chaos he perceived around him – and it was a way to stake out a position in the debate on what Rome should be.

Contemporary ills drove other Romans to focus their leisure on serious scholarship. Atticus scored a triumph with his *Liber Annalis*, a book that gave a chronology of Roman history year by year, including important magistrates, laws, and treaties. The volume was so groundbreaking that it allowed Cicero to attempt the first history of Latin oratory (culminating, naturally, with the perfection attained by Cicero himself). Earlier, in the 50s, Atticus' friend Cornelius Nepos produced the three-book *Chronica*, inspired by an earlier Greek chronicle of human history from the fall of Troy. Nepos added Roman events to the Greek framework, thereby facilitating comparison. He then deepened his explorations in a major biographical work, *Lives of Famous Men*, which investigated the lives of Roman and foreign generals, historians, and more. Just as Pompey's triumph in 61 announced that Rome's empire had truly succeeded Alexander's, Nepos established that Rome was as worthy of investigation as Greece. Comparisons proved illuminating. The dangerous power acquired by the veterans of Alexander the Great, for example, helped explain what was happening in Nepos' own day.

Another advance of the 50s was the first major works of philosophy in Latin, which directly addressed contemporaries and their concerns. Nerve-racked Romans found inspiration in the teachings of the Greek Epicurus (341–270 BCE), who advised the wise man to give up the pursuit of wealth and to avoid political life. "Live unnoticed" was his catchphrase. In Athens, Epicurus established a secluded community of similarly minded men and women, known as the Garden. Romans started to do the same, especially on the Bay of Naples. Caesar's wife Calpurnia enjoyed Epicurean fellowship with a freedwoman of her family. To help spread the master's teachings, in the early 50s Lucretius produced a poem in six books, *On the Nature of Things*. Public life, it argued, had become hell on earth. The politician struggling for power is like Sisyphus, pushing the boulder up the hill, only for it to keep rolling back.

This repudiation of tradition alarmed some Romans, including Cicero, who struck back in philosophic works of his own, including dialogues inspired by Plato's. *On the Orator*, composed in 55, was set in the fateful year 91, just on the eve of the Social War. In it, prominent orators from Cicero's youth like his beloved teacher Licinius Crassus are made to discuss the proper training of the orator. Crassus insists that technical study of rhetoric alone is not enough. That could lead simply to demagogy. Oratory, and public life overall, must have an ethical foundation, and this can only come through philosophical

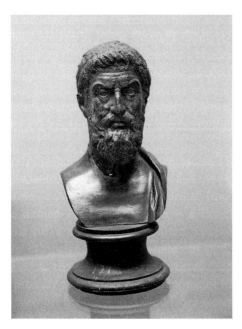

Figure 10.2 A small bust of Epicurus, found in a luxurious villa on the Bay of Naples. The anxious-looking philosopher helped Romans cope with their own anxieties. Museo Archeologico Nazionale, Naples, Italy. (Photo © Vanni Archive/Art Resource, NY.)

study. A slightly later work, *The Republic*, continues Cicero's investigations. This dialogue is set at the villa of Scipio Aemilianus in 129, and rather than proposing an ideal state (as Plato did), Cicero explores the actual Roman state. A key idea is that for Rome's mixed constitution to survive, an eminent leader (like Scipio Aemilianus) is needed – one who can stand up for the Senate, rally support generally, and resist the temptations of power.

While that leader failed to emerge, and while antiquarian and philosophical writings failed to turn the tide of political transformation as hoped, they broadened the Roman imagination. Rome's distant past provided a way of articulating present aspirations, Greek history a way of thinking about kingship and empire. Poets also widened horizons. Catullus created a novel type of love poetry in which the poet explored the highs and lows of his feelings for a single lover across a series of poems. Not even the great Sappho had done this. If at moments Catullus' Lesbia made him feel like a god, at others he desperately tried to overcome her rejection of him. His shortest poem is also his most memorable: "I hate and love. Perhaps you're asking why I do that? I don't know, but I feel it, and I am tortured."

Catullus' poems grab readers with their immediacy. Readers get to share the poet's life in the endlessly fascinating city, whether it is a lively dinner party where a guest jokingly steals a napkin brought to Catullus by friends from Spain or a day spent passing a writing tablet back and forth to his friend Calvus in a contest to outdo each other's verses. In one poem, Catullus is caught in the Forum by his friend Varus and introduced to Varus' new love (a prostitute, Catullus suspects). When she asks Catullus if he made any money while serving on a provincial governor's staff in Bithynia, he brags that he acquired a fine set of litter bearers. "Lend them to me, please, dear Catullus, just for a little," she replies, hoping to ride in style. He is forced to admit they belong to his friend Cinna. Being broke actually was a perverse source of pride for the poet and many of his friends; what counted was their talent and sophistication.

Oratory moved in new directions too. To later generations, Cicero stood out as the supreme practitioner of his day, but in fact he had a number of rivals, who increasingly found his speeches overblown – and were eager also to grab some attention for themselves. The leading proponent of a leaner style was Catullus' friend Calvus, himself lean and dangerously quick. Sadly, virtually nothing of his famous speeches survives, not even his renowned prosecutions of Vatinius (the tribune of 59 who obtained a super-command for Caesar). Catullus compliments them: "Somebody in the crowd made me laugh just now: when my Calvus had set out in splendid style his accusations against Vatinius, he lifted up his hands in surprise and said: 'Great gods! The little guy can talk!'" The poem neatly shows how oratory was savored by a wide audience, not just a few scholarly types.

Even Cicero's protégé Marcus Caelius adopted a punchier style. The son of an ambitious Equestrian from an Italian town in the foothills of the Apennines, Caelius had been entrusted to Cicero for training. Tall, handsome, and a sharp dresser – the purple band on his toga was unusually thick – Caelius grew bored with his teacher and, like other fashionable young men, had sympathies for Catiline. In 59, he prosecuted Cicero's fellow consul of 63 and ally, Antonius, for provincial maladministration. Here's how Caelius described one of the governor's orgies: "They found him lying prone in a drunken stupor, snoring with all the force of his lungs, belching repeatedly, while the great ladies who shared his quarters sprawled over every couch, and the other women were lying on the floor all over the place." As the enemy approached, the women tried desperately to rouse Antonius, shouting his name, then whispering sweetly in his ear, then slapping his face. "Half-asleep and in a daze, Antonius was thrown around by his centurions and his concubines." The sensational account must have riveted the audience.

Time and money were spent not just on scholarship and literary pursuits but also, increasingly, on art. Plundered masterpieces had been pouring into Rome for decades, along with architects who brought with them Greek materials and methods. By 45 Rome was a museum city – as it still is. The poor as much as the rich could enjoy great sculptures and paintings, Cicero

Figure 10.3 Amarble statue of a youngman carved by Stephanos, a pupil of the artist and scholar Pasiteles, as the signature on the tree trunk reveals. The evocation of the classical style in works like this appealed to Roman patrons. Villa Albani, Rome, Italy. (Photo Alinari/Art Resource, NY.)

wrote, so many were displayed in public. As the level of connoisseurship improved, the wealthy were eager to commission their own copies of great masterpieces or new works in the classical style. Like literature and scholarship inspired by Greek models, the new works announced Rome's arrival but also Roman priorities. A characteristic figure of the age was the versatile Pasiteles, a Greek from southern Italy who sculpted and engraved and also produced scholarship on the history of art. So transfixed was he studying the anatomy of a lion at the docks of Rome one day that he was nearly mauled by a panther.

Architectural projects also became more ambitious. Pompey's theater and Caesar's refashioning of the Forum, including an entirely new part named after himself as Caesar's Forum, gave the heart of Rome world-class buildings. On the outskirts of the city, the rich created "gardens," really huge estates with elaborate plantings, fountains, pools, and dining spaces – the perfect backdrop for a growing sculpture collection. Grandees might invite crowds of Romans to see the art here. Caesar left his gardens to the people of Rome in his will. Unrealized on his death was an ambitious plan for Rome's first public library, but this would soon come. Caesar's vision of a glittering new Rome that could equal or even eclipse Alexandria in its buildings was a fitting climax to an extraordinary period of intellectual and aesthetic achievement.

POPULAR PLEASURES?

Leisure was not just for aristocrats but also for ordinary Romans and thus was one of the city's main draws. Some of the amenities, of course, were familiar in Italy's other towns like Pompeii, but naturally those in "the City" (as Romans called Rome) were the best, or at least the most numerous. Any number of baths would welcome you, for just a penny, into their relaxing atmosphere. Every neighborhood had its taverns. Senators might sneer at them, with their awful food, the terrible stench, and the bar brawls that broke out, but they were lively places. Not only was there the chance for a hot meal and a hot (alcoholic) drink. There were games and gambling, perhaps music too – a Spanish or Syrian girl who played the castanets or flute.

Taverns offered the chance for a sexual encounter. Catullus skewers the swagger of the men at one tavern near the Forum: Do they think they are the only ones with pricks, and "the rest of us stink like goats?" Wealthy Romans assumed, no doubt unfairly, that any woman working in a tavern must be a prostitute. Yet certainly sex was available for purchase in bars, in brothels, or out on the streets. Like penny baths, there were penny whores. And there were more expensive options, "escorts" and "entertainers" with Greek names, female and male. The much-prized masculinity of Roman men did not preclude sex with another man, so long as the partner assumed the passive role.

Ordinary Romans were treated to a variety of spectacles. Neighborhoods put on their own entertainments, like slapstick theater and boxing matches. Poets performed in the Forum or in the baths; street entertainers told jokes and stories. Politicians desperate for attention, like Scaurus, displayed marvels such as massive wine jars or fights between elephants and bulls. They spent more money on the staging of plays. At the games inaugurating his theater, Pompey had a parade of live mules carry the plunder of

Agamemnon across the stage. In the first century the more traditional tragedies and comedies increasingly were edged out in popularity by a type of performance called "mime." With its realistic language and everyday settings, mime held up more of a mirror to life. The actors might shed their masks, even their costumes; and women performed as well as men. Ribald remarks and scenes of lovemaking were frequent. Also popular were "interludes" with dancing girls. The term for these (*embolia*) was Greek, as was much of the language of show business and the entertainers themselves. Rome drew in more than talented scholars.

Modern scholars sometimes lament the increasingly "popular" culture of first-century Rome in a way that would do Cicero proud. The reality, though, was that ordinary people's tastes were shared by the upper classes of society. Sulla is said to have enjoyed the company of mime actors and actresses, drinking with them on couches all day long. His favorite was the female impersonator Metrobius. Senators gambled, they hosted theatrical entertainments in their houses, and they hired popular musicians to perform. They even danced! The well-proportioned Caelius allegedly had some of the best moves in town. It is no wonder that he started to grow bored of Aristotle study sessions with Cicero. There were livelier ways to spend an evening.

Modern scholars – perhaps inadvertently betraying something of their own staid lifestyles – also nervously object that most of the evidence for Romans drinking, gambling, and dancing is rhetorical. This evidence stems from allegations like those that Caelius himself made against Antonius. How can we be sure that it really happened? One indication that the high living was probably not all fantasy is the way in which Catullus, in his own way, reacts against it. As much as his poetry revolves around an ideal of leisure, he rejects mere gluttony, drinking, or gambling as pastimes. The City appeals to him because it is where one can find the best literary companions (like Cinna and Calvus) or women who are not just beautiful but quick-witted.

Key to aristocratic leisure was sex. Cato the Elder would have been shocked by how much attention senators were paying (or were said to be paying) to their mistresses. According to the old censor, an occasional trip to the brothel was fine for the young man – and certainly better than sleeping with a freeborn girl or boy, or another man's wife. A generation or so later, Sulla is reported as being so intimate with the prostitute Nicopolis that she left her alarmingly large estate to him. In her old age, another prostitute named Flora reminisced about the teeth marks Pompey used to leave on her, such was the ardor of their lovemaking. When a friend of Pompey took a fancy to his bedmate, Pompey reluctantly let him take her. Exploits in the bedroom as much as on the battlefield could increase the popularity of politicians, with tavern goers seeing the great man as one of them or even as a role model.

Aristocratic women faced the same problem as men, and more. Marriages typically were contracted as alliances between families rather than love matches, which is not to deny that feelings of deep love could develop. But while the man was fully entitled to recreational sex, the woman was supposed to sleep only with her husband. Moreover, ideals of sexual virtue piled on further restrictions: the respectable woman should only be seen in public in certain settings, surrounded by a retinue of slaves, covered from head to toe. It would not be surprising if some women abandoned these conventions. Why not put on for dinner that practically see-through silk dress that could make a man crazy?

Most notorious is the middle sister of the patrician tribune Clodius, Clodia, a widow from the year 59 – when she was in her mid-30s. Unfortunately, she is known mainly through the words of her enemy Cicero, who basically called her a prostitute. Almost certainly she had an affair with Caelius, and there is also a very good chance that she is the woman lurking beneath Catullus' pseudonymous Lesbia. There is absolutely no doubt that she was willing to appear in public to support her brother. Her defiance of convention earned her attacks beyond Cicero's. When a young man – allegedly a spurned lover – sent her a purse full of the small copper coins used to pay common prostitutes, she became widely known as "Miss One-Penny." The slur points out the essential masculinity of Roman culture: while swagger was valued in men, women who dared to show it were upbraided, probably even by other women. Yet this does not mean that Clodia was simply a "victim." She, and other women like her, undeniably had a livelier time than their ancestors would have; if she horrified stern old moralists, others found her charming. Sober Atticus enjoyed dinner conversation with her.

THE CITY OF LOVE AND LAUGHTER

Moral decline concerned many of Rome's leading writers in the late Republic. Varro longed for the good old days, associated more with the Italian countryside than the city. Our uncouth great-grandfathers might have stunk of garlic and onion, he thought, but they were far less greedy. Lucretius went even further, claiming that greed and the "blind desire for offices" had pushed men beyond the bounds of law, even to the point of killing one another: "they double their wealth, piling slaying upon slaying." In his examination of the Catilinarian conspiracy, written in the late 40s, Sallust dwelled on similar themes: the "passion for illicit sex, gluttony, and other refinements" drove young men to crime "as soon as they had run through their family money." Civil war, rebellion, and periodic outbursts of violence in Rome gave allegations of immorality a sharp edge.

Politicians relied on such allegations in their cutthroat competition with one another, especially in the courts. Caelius did so in the trial of Antonius, and in 56 it was Caelius' turn to be prosecuted, on a variety of charges of violence, including the assault of ambassadors from Alexandria and the attempted poisoning of Clodia. According to his accusers, Caelius had asked Clodia for help in financing games and she lent him some gold jewelry. When she discovered that he was using the money to commit crimes, he then tried to murder her, and she was prepared to testify as much. Throughout the trial, the prosecution harped on Caelius' immorality. An old supporter of Catiline, he was up to his ears in debt, they said. More than once he had allegedly assaulted married women returning home from dinners on those notorious dark streets. With wild spending and reckless partying, Caelius' whole generation was a threat.

Against such charges Cicero came to the defense of his old pupil Caelius – and of Roman youth as a whole. The prosecution almost certainly concealed Caelius' affair with Clodia, assuming that the defense would not mention it because it was damaging to Caelius' character. Cicero dared to unmask it all, and by turning Clodia into a common prostitute, he managed to undermine her honor and so discredit her testimony. A highlight of Cicero's extant speech is two impersonations. First, he pretends to be her ancestor Appius Claudius Caecus ("the Blind"), censor in 312 and builder of the famous Appian Way from Rome to Capua. "Woman! What business have you with Caelius?" Appius shouts. "Did I build a road so you could parade up and down it accompanied by other women's husbands?" Then Cicero turns himself into Clodius, "the height of modern sophistication." "Why are you making such a fuss, sister?" this "Clodius" says. If Caelius has rejected you, don't keep bothering him. "Try somewhere else! You own gardens on the Tiber, carefully situated where all the young men come for a swim." Cicero knew his performance would bring gales of laughter from the audience that great trials like this one attracted. Their participation would help him win his case, as indeed he did.

Cicero's speech is a brilliant reminder that not all moralizing is entirely serious and that moralizing has a complex relationship with pleasure. Luxuriating in salacious details, some exposés actually end up glamorizing the vices they purport to attack. They might bring a smile as much as a frown. Rome's politicians knew this, and some almost deliberately flirted with scandal as a way to gain publicity and popular support. Young Julius Caesar delighted in walking around Rome in daringly loose clothing, he made no efforts to hide his extravagant tastes, and his affairs with married women were the talk of the town. His enemies never tired of claiming that he had even been the lover of King Nicomedes of Bithynia. Caesar was, according to one critic, "every woman's man and every man's woman" – a man of voracious sexual appetite in other words. Spending and sleeping around on his scale might have been Cato's worst nightmare, but a lot of Romans probably fantasized about doing the same.

While Rome's rival leaders used humor as a weapon against one another and it could be a distraction from more important issues, joking could also unite the city. Political jokes circulated well beyond the Forum – through the city's streets, shops, and taverns – and allowed everybody a way to participate. To kid about "the consulship of Julius and Caesar," for example, let one air anxiety about whether Caesar was pushing too hard – and could send a message to Caesar if the ribbing spread enough. Nicknames bestowed on society's most prominent figures made them more approachable, and so bound different levels of society more closely. To become Miss One-Penny was only in part an insult. It also confirmed the extraordinary popularity Clodia had achieved for herself by repudiating the role of the stiff matron. Politics was a spectacle, and the audience relished its role in making or breaking its stars.

Alongside the laments of Varro and Lucretius is the alluring image of a fun-loving city, able to absorb the best talents of the day. Over time, that image itself, as much as the real city, could draw in new recruits. Creative geniuses helped make Rome a world city, but so did all its people, telling jokes and spreading lampoons. The ability to do so did not depend on formal political assemblies, and it would survive under the emperors. By then, laughter was among Rome's most cherished traditions, one of the special pleasures that made it, at least for those who lived there, *the* City.

FURTHER READING

The best overall account of the city of Rome in this period is by N. Purcell in chap. 17 of *The Cambridge Ancient History* (2nd ed.) Vol. 9. The problem of "Knowing the City" is discussed in chap. 6 of A. Wallace-Hadrill, *Rome's Cultural Revolution* (Cambridge, 2008). There are many pertinent chapters in P. Erdkamp (ed.), *The Cambridge Companion to Ancient Rome* (Cambridge, 2013), including those by J. B. Lott on neighborhoods, W. Broekaert and A. Zuiderhoek on "Industries and Services," C. Hawkins on labor, and T. A. J. McGinn on "Sex and the City." Also consult the chapters by R. Saller on human capital, W. Scheidel on slavery, and C. Hawkins on manufacturing in W. Scheidel (ed.), *The Cambridge Companion to the Roman Economy* (Cambridge, 2012). On *tabernae* see C. Holleran, *Shopping in Ancient Rome: The Retail Trade in the Late Republic and the Principate* (Oxford, 2012). The distinctive role of ex-slaves is brought out by S. Treggiari, *Roman Freedmen during the Late Republic* (Oxford, 1969), and H. Mouritsen, *The Freedman in the Roman World* (Cambridge, 2011).

E. Rawson, *Intellectual Life in the Late Roman Republic* (London, 1985), is the standard work. A briefer introduction, with a good discussion of education, is provided by M. T. Griffin in chap. 18 of *The Cambridge Ancient History* (2nd ed.) Vol. 9. The excitement of literary developments is conveyed in G. B. Conte, *Latin Literature: A*

History (trans. J. B. Solodow; Baltimore, 1999), and also R. O. A. M. Lyne, *Latin Love Poets: From Catullus to Horace* (Oxford, 1980). J. H. Gaisser, *Catullus* (Malden, MA, 2009), introduces the poet, while T. P. Wiseman, *Catullus and His World* (Cambridge, 1985), evokes the period as a whole, including the trial of Caelius. See also M. B. Skinner, *Clodia Metelli: The Tribune's Sister* (Oxford, 2011). A lively work on Lucretius and his later rediscovery is S. Greenblatt, *The Swerve: How the World Became Modern* (New York, 2011). On artistic developments see J. J. Pollitt, *Art in the Hellenistic Age* (Cambridge, 1986), and M. Beard and J. Henderson, *Classical Art: From Greece to Rome* (Oxford, 2001).

J. P. Toner, *Leisure and Ancient Rome* (Cambridge, MA, 1995), explores changing concepts of leisure. More concrete is N. Horsfall, *The Culture of the Roman Plebs* (London, 2003). Moralizing is well handled by C. Edwards, *The Politics of Morality in Ancient Rome* (Cambridge, 1993), and also the delightfully irreverent T. Holland, *Rubicon: The Triumph and Tragedy of the Roman Republic* (London, 2004). Alternatives to traditional politics are discussed in C. Nicolet, *The World of the Citizen in Republican Rome* (London, 1980). Fruitful comparisons between Rome and pre-Victorian London can be made; for the latter, see V. Gatrell, *City of Laughter: Sex and Satire in Eighteenth-Century London* (London, 2006).

II

WAR OF THE WORLD (49–30 BCE)

"You will learn to obey orders!" bellowed the consul Mark Antony when the soldiers laughed at his offer of an extra 400 sesterces each. It was October, 44 BCE, just seven months after the assassination of Julius Caesar. In Apollonia, across the Adriatic Sea from Italy, Caesar had been amassing troops for a major campaign against the Parthians in the east. After Caesar's death, the plans had to be shelved, and Antony arranged for four of the six legions to be transferred back to Italy. At Brundisium, he encountered the troops' fury. Not only had Antony failed to avenge Caesar's murder, he also had dashed their hopes of the mountains of gold, pearls, and perfumes Parthia was legendary for. And the 400 sesterces? That was pathetic. Caesar's great-nephew and heir, the teenage Octavian, had agents circulating around Antony's camp offering five times that. Exasperated, Antony ordered the most disruptive soldiers to draw lots and then had a small portion of them executed. This was a decimation, the traditional response of a Roman commander to a mutiny.

But it was only now that the real mutiny began. The Martian Legion, named for the war god Mars, defected to Octavian while marching north from Brundisium. The Fourth Legion quickly followed. The legions fortified themselves in the town of Alba Fucens in central Italy, and when Antony appeared, they shot at him from the walls and forced him to flee. Octavian then collected the troops and had them carry out training exercises. Delighted with their performance, he paid out the promised handout and offered much more if they were victorious against Antony.

A hideous showdown would come several months later and is described in a letter by the commander of the Martian Legion. "At first the fighting was such that it could not have been fiercer on either side," he wrote. He soon found himself caught in the middle of Antony's forces and just managed to

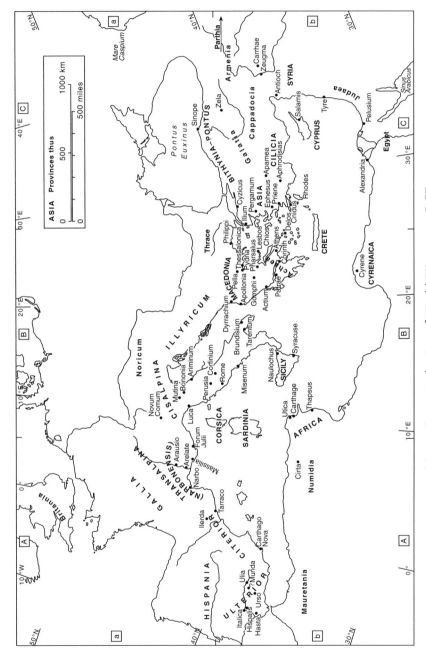

Map 9 Rome in the Age of World War, 49–30 BCE

gallop away, but then he was nearly pierced by a volley of javelins – from his own side. It was only "by some special providence I was saved."

These are just a few episodes in the civil war that began in 49 BCE and consumed the Roman world for the next 20 years. Extensive accounts of the campaigns survive, including eyewitness reports rare for other Roman wars. While often partisan, these accounts convey the particular horror of full-scale civil war – in which your own side might fail to recognize you. Massive armies and navies were mobilized and moved around the Mediterranean, creating logistical challenges but also bold and innovative strategies. Caesar and Pompey, two of the greatest generals in Rome's history, faced each other in battle more than once.

The long years of fighting led to major political change. Civil war, and the instability it brought, finished off traditional SPQR. Leaders like Julius Caesar, Mark Antony, and Octavian (the future emperor Augustus) exploited powerbases even more fully than politicians had in the 60s and 50s and experimented with autocratic government. Artists and poets crafted images that would define who the leaders were. Even tiny coins of Julius Caesar manage to show him with a penetrating gaze that suggests his power. Leaders also took new titles and names, such as "Augustus." As civil war spread, provincials were forced to pledge loyalty to one of these new-style leaders, and the leaders reciprocated with rewards such as grants of citizenship. The position of the emperor, who could form relationships with men and women living across the Roman world, was being forged.

Figure 11.1 A portrait of Caesar on a silver coin. He was the first Roman to have his image displayed on official coinage during his own lifetime. Of the many honors voted to him, the laurel crown he wears pleased him most: it helped to mask his receding hairline. (Photo © The Trustees of the British Museum.)

Closely bound up with the growth of one-man rule was the emergence of a standing army out of Julius Caesar's legions. Not only did soldiers in active service rally to Caesar's memory; others recently settled by Caesar in colonies reenlisted. Legions turned into permanent institutions, with fixed names such as "the Fourth." As Octavian and Antony's competing bids in 44 show, soldiering also became highly paid. It was detached from SPQR and the Republic that SPQR represented. While the end of civil war would stabilize the terms on which soldiers served, and the soldiers themselves would stabilize the vast empire after years of chaos, their loyalty would belong to the emperor. It is no coincidence that the very word for emperor, *imperator,* had earlier meant "victorious general." The soldiers were the ultimate powerbase.

POMPEY'S GRAND STRATEGY

At the start of the civil war in 49, each side had different strengths. Pompey had only two legions in Italy, but he had an army in Spain and control of the seas thanks to his ongoing grain commission obtained in 57. Caesar had one legion with him at Ravenna and a larger army in Gaul. Caesar marched down the eastern Italian coast with part of his troops, while Mark Antony was sent across the Apennines to cut Rome off from the north. Pompey quickly left Rome, along with the two consuls and many senators. Caesar's deadly enemy Domitius Ahenobarbus recruited troops, many off his own estates, and – defying Pompey – tried to block Caesar at Corfinium. But after a short siege, Domitius' army quickly surrendered. Caesar had the soldiers swear allegiance to himself, while letting Domitius and about 50 senators and Equestrians with him go free. As he wrote in an open letter, he was embracing a policy of clemency rather than the cruelty of Sulla. It was essential for him to show that he was not bringing the worst horrors of civil war to Italy. Pompey, meanwhile, had retreated to Brundisium, and from there crossed the Adriatic. He also instructed Cato to abandon Sicily, where he had been gathering ships and troops.

Caesar went to Rome, summoned the remaining senators, and lectured them on the wrongs done to him. The affront to his *dignitas* – his "standing" – was why he was fighting, he maintained. In keeping with his clemency, there were no proscriptions. But Caesar did break into the treasury to help fund his army. He also arranged for extension of citizenship to Italians north of the Po, something he had long pressed for and which would facilitate military recruiting since only citizens could serve in the legions. Then he left the praetor M. Aemilius Lepidus in charge. A pliable character – contemporaries thought he shifted as easily as the wind – Lepidus was useful for his patrician status and the air of respectability it lent him, as well as his skills in diplomacy.

The opening of the war raises the question of Pompey's strategy. Caesar suggests in his *Civil War*, a continuation of his earlier commentaries, that his speedy actions drove an unprepared Pompey from Italy. It is likelier that Pompey's plan from the start was to gain control of the seas to encircle Italy. As the food supply dwindled, Caesar would be forced to negotiate, while Pompey and his allies would not have the blood of citizen soldiers on their hands. The loss of Domitius' army in the siege at Corfinium was a major setback to this strategy. Caesar was able to send these troops to Sicily, under the command of the young noble Scribonius Curio. Pompey was forced to cede the island, important for its grain as well as its strategic location.

The ensuing series of campaigns in Spain, Africa, and the Balkans is easily understood once Pompey's attempted encirclement is grasped. Caesar would tackle Spain first. While an officer of his gained control of the Pyrenees passes, Caesar was held up at the old Greek city of Massilia. Officially, the Massiliotes were trying to maintain neutrality, but not trusting Caesar nor his long-term prospects, they had entrusted their defense to Domitius Ahenobarbus, who had not given up after Corfinium and was now in command of a small fleet. It was critical that Caesar demonstrate his strength, or he might lose all his provincial powerbases. He therefore put the city under a massive siege, which after several weeks was handed over to two officers from the Gallic War. It would drag on for a year, concluding only with Caesar's return. In Spain, a pair of experienced Pompeian officers had occupied favorable ground near Ilerda, on a tributary of the great Ebro River, and Caesar marched here. A huge storm led to river flooding, dangerously cutting him off from his supply lines. But then Caesar turned the tables, trapping the Pompeians in a camp with no access to food or water. After the Pompeian army surrendered, Caesar let soldiers and commanders alike go without penalty; as in Italy, his goal was not to destroy his opponents but ultimately to win them over.

Now Caesar had to deal with Farther Spain, where he and Pompey alike had networks of allies acquired during earlier commands. Pompey's officer, the great scholar Varro, had raised ships and an army and demanded large contributions from Roman citizens. But the Spanish communities one by one turned on him, backed up by the local citizens' associations, and Varro had to surrender to Caesar. Caesar spent time settling the province, rewarding those loyal to him. The residents of Gades, the hometown of his close associate Balbus, were granted citizenship.

Old loyalties were important in Africa too. Curio arrived to take it over from its Pompeian governor. But opposing him was King Juba of Numidia, a longstanding friend of Pompey who had grudges against Caesar. He also opposed Curio, who had earlier tried to make Numidia a tax-paying part of the empire. Caesar writes in his commentary that Curio, in his "youthful enthusiasm," allowed himself to be carried away by favorable rumors and false reports, leading his army to annihilation.

In the fall of 49 Caesar returned to Italy, with a view to crossing the Adriatic. Since both consuls had fled Rome, Caesar was briefly appointed dictator, so that he could hold elections in which he gained the second consulship he had long sought. He then left Rome for Brundisium. A strong fleet under the command of his old enemy Bibulus controlled the seas. By a risky crossing, Caesar made it with part of his army to Epirus, where the town of Apollonia tossed out its Pompeian commander and welcomed him. But the rest of the Caesarian force was held up for months by Bibulus, who died from overwork on one of his ships. Pompey, meanwhile, with the sizable army he had built up, moved west to meet Caesar. At Dyrrhachium, Caesar tried to surround Pompey's camp with fortifications, but Pompey slipped out by sea at night and surprised Caesar where his fortifications were unfinished. Caesar was forced to march east through the mountains to the plains of northern Greece.

The two great generals would soon have a rematch. Out of concern for his father-in-law, Metellus Scipio, who had been fundraising in the east and had just arrived in Greece, Pompey followed Caesar. Relying on his superiority in cavalry, Pompey decided to risk battle near the town of Pharsalus. Caesar proved his tactical genius by creating a secret fourth line of troops, who used their throwing javelins like spears to resist Pompey's horsemen. Pompey was defeated and fled, Domitius Ahenobarbus killed. Thousands more of their soldiers were left dead on the gory battlefield of civil war.

Those refusing to seek Caesar's forgiveness, including Cato, sailed for Africa, while Pompey himself travelled to Egypt, leading to an unexpected Egyptian interlude in the war. Hoping to collect a debt owed by the 13-year-old king Ptolemy XIII, Pompey instead was killed on the king's orders. His head was presented to Caesar several days later. Caesar decided to stay on to resolve an ongoing dispute between Ptolemy and his sister, Cleopatra. Summoned by Caesar, the beautiful as well as astute young woman (she was about 20) charmed him into helping her. Ptolemy's advisors, meanwhile, with backing from the fiercely anti-Roman Alexandrians, turned on Caesar, and fighting broke out in the city. For months Caesar was stuck in the palace quarter along with Cleopatra, a military setback that did wonders for one of history's most storied love affairs. Only when a major relief force arrived was Caesar able to go on the offensive. In the subsequent fighting, young Ptolemy drowned in the Nile, and Caesar installed Cleopatra and another brother as corulers and left Roman forces to protect them. A further legacy of his stay was a son born to Cleopatra, mockingly called "Little Caesar" (Caesarion) by the Alexandrians.

Caesar's detention in Egypt multiplied his challenges elsewhere. Pharnaces, son of the great Mithridates, invaded Asia Minor and defeated a Caesarian army. In Africa, Caesar's Roman enemies regrouped under the supreme command of Metellus Scipio. The highhandedness of Caesar's governor of Farther Spain also led to a resurgence of opposition. And in Italy, there was a mutiny of Caesarian troops, veterans of the Gallic War who had been promised land but had not yet received it.

Caesar made quick work of Pharnaces at the battle of Zela, the event that produced his famous boast "I came, I saw, I conquered." He then quashed the mutiny in Italy and finally made it to Africa in another of his risky crossings. Through generous promises, Caesar won the support of citizens and provincials. The King of Mauretania also helped him by invading Numidia and luring away Juba. At Thapsus, Caesar's army defeated Scipio's forces. Cato organized an escape to Spain for prominent survivors but then stabbed himself and died. A reorganization of Africa followed. Communities who supported Juba and the Pompeians were fined, as were, even more stiffly, Roman citizens' associations. Part of Juba's kingdom was annexed for Rome.

Cato's heroic suicide underscored – and was meant to – Caesar's inability to reconcile all Romans. As Cato saw it, to have to ask for mercy made him like a begging slave, and Caesar a tyrannical master. Returning to Rome, Caesar celebrated four magnificent triumphs, for his victories in Gaul, Egypt, Asia, and Africa. The *plebs* was thrilled at the lavish feasts, gifts of money, and entertainments (including theatrical performances in every neighborhood of the city). Yet there was dismay at paintings showing the deaths of leading Romans, including Cato.

Before the year was over, Caesar had to go to Spain to put down the Pompeian resurgence. Fighting was now much more vicious than it had been in 49. Caesar's army even decorated its fortifications with the heads of the enemy. Near the town of Munda, Caesar scored a major victory, and Pompey's elder son was killed afterward. The younger son, Sextus, escaped into hiding. Again Caesar settled the province, severely punishing Pompeian sympathizers before returning to Rome, where he would celebrate an even more controversial triumph. Sextus managed to strengthen his forces, and meanwhile at the other edge of the empire, Syria had fallen into the hands of an officer aligned with the late Pompey.

So civil war was not in fact over, but even the campaigns through 45 had lasting consequences. The extent of the fighting forced provincials, including citizens, to take the side of a leader, making SPQR even less relevant to them. Citizens living in the provinces and natives fought in large numbers, and natives gained citizenship for doing so. One of Caesar's most famous legions was recruited among Gauls and had the Gallic name *Alaudae* (meaning "larks" – a reference to the crests on their helmets). He gave soldiers land in Italy and also overseas, in colonies in Africa and Gaul, Spain and Greece. As had happened earlier in Italy, land was surveyed and divided among the settlers. Cities were created where they had not existed and stone buildings rose. Charters on bronze tablets established communal government. Measures like these sped up Rome's transformation from city-state with an empire into a more unitary world state.

BEWARE THE IDES OF MARCH

Civil war destabilized the city of Rome. As was typical in uncertain times, creditors called in loans and debtors were hard-pressed to pay. Coin itself was in exceedingly short supply. Late in 49 Caesar had a law passed against hoarding and arranged that property, which backed loans, should be valued at prewar prices. The financial crisis persisted anyway, and Cicero's former pupil Caelius used it to rally the *plebs* behind him. When expelled from Rome in 48 by Caesar's fellow consul, Caelius joined forces with Clodius' old rival Milo, who had come out of exile and reactivated his gangs. Both were soon killed by Caesarian forces, but in 47 Dolabella, a tribune in the mold of Clodius, stirred up further protest.

Caesar's absence was costing him the support of the *plebs*. After the battle of Pharsalus, he had been appointed dictator again, for a term of one year, and he sent his deputy in the office, Mark Antony, to restore order in Rome in 47. Antony succeeded to a degree, while also carrying out the difficult job of liquidating Pompey's estates. In his brief stay in Rome in late 47, Caesar passed new measures to resolve the debt crisis, including cancellation of interest and also of a year's rent (up to a limit of 2,000 sesterces). This helped restore his popularity.

Caesar had himself elected to another consulship for 46, along with Lepidus, but it was only after Thapsus that longer-term plans could take shape. Now he accepted a dictatorship for 10 years, to put the state (*res publica*) back together. Unlike Sulla, though, Caesar proved uninterested in pushing through coherent constitutional reform. Rather, he enacted a series of measures to bring some stability. Most impressively, he reformed the calendar. The Romans used a lunar year of 355 days, which required that an extra month be inserted every other year, but in recent years the pontiffs had failed to keep up. That meant that a festival to celebrate the harvest might take place in spring. With the help of the astronomer Sosigenes of Alexandria, Caesar switched Rome to a solar year of 365 days, requiring that only one extra day be inserted every fourth year. Hugely important too was his plan for overseas colonization. It involved not just veteran settlements in territories opposed to him but also the re-foundation of the ruined cities of Corinth and Carthage, where freedmen with good commercial instincts were sent, taking pressure off the city of Rome.

Caesar made no move to destroy the Senate or magistracies. He needed them to carry on the work of government across the ever-expanding Roman world, and indeed the Senate was enlarged to around 900 members and the number of magistrates below the consulship increased. This was a way to reward his own supporters, including (Romans joked) Gauls in trousers who needed directions to the Senate house. In reality, most of these new senators were Italians, including some living in Cisalpine Gaul. The recruitment intensified the integration of all of Italy into a wider Roman state – even if the Senate had less power now that Caesar personally set much policy.

Assassination cut short Caesar's grandest plans, to beautify the city of Rome and expand Roman supremacy (the two were interrelated in his mind). Sources report that he contemplated stupendous public works like a giant theater and a temple that would be the largest in the world. He commissioned Varro, who wisely had laid down his general's cloak, to collect all of Greek and Latin literature for a public library. Caesar was also planning, in addition to his Parthian war, campaigns along the Danube.

A largely compliant Senate heaped honors on Caesar that budged Rome further away from its republican traditions and closer to eastern monarchy. After Munda, Caesar was voted the right to wear the costume of a triumphing general whenever he wanted. The laurel crown particularly thrilled Caesar, since it masked his bald head. Later he was voted a golden chair and the all-purple clothing of Rome's ancient kings. Festivals were inserted into his new calendar to honor him; the month Quintilius was renamed "July." Senators swore an oath to protect him, just as Greeks had done for their monarchs. With Cleopatra now installed in Caesar's gardens across the Tiber, critics started calling him "king," and some felt that this was a title he actually sought.

Related to this were the divine honors that Caesar received. Greek rulers were traditionally worshipped as gods, and in the east, statues were put up to Caesar with such titles as "god manifest" and "god and *imperator* and savior of the inhabited world." In Rome itself, Caesar received honors similar to those that Roman gods did. For example, his statue was carried along with those of gods in the processions that opened games in the Circus. Shortly before he died, the Senate even decided that he should be worshipped as a god, with a temple built and Mark Antony to serve as his priest. No formal cult with sacrifices was in place, though, by his death, and it may be that as *pontifex maximus* Caesar never would have allowed one.

While Caesar dreamed of a Rome that could rival Alexandria in beauty and assented to many honors, he almost certainly had no interest in taking the title of king. He refused it on several occasions, most famously in February of 44 at the Lupercalia – an ancient festival in which men clad only in loincloths ran through Rome whipping half-naked women to insure their fertility. The consul Antony, after running with the other men, tried to crown Caesar with a diadem, unsuccessfully. Still, it was clear that free republican government was not going to be restored. The Senate did not enjoy open debate, and Caesar had control of foreign policy and finance. Caesar, not the assemblies, really chose the magistrates. By February of 44 Caesar had even taken the title of "Dictator for Life." It was emblazoned on the coinage, along with Caesar's own portrait – the first time a living man was so honored.

Some senators chafed at Caesar's growing domination and their own inability to compete for honors, and a conspiracy against him took shape. Its mastermind was Cassius, a talented military officer who had sought Caesar's pardon after the Pharsalus campaign. Joining him was Marcus Brutus, who traced his descent back to the Brutus who was reputed to have driven out the last kings of Rome in the sixth century – a legend with new resonance. A third key figure was the "other" Brutus, Decimus, a personal favorite of Caesar's since the Gallic War. Other Caesarians joined, showing that for all the Dictator's achievements, his increasing arrogance had alienated even some of his own supporters. Ultimately there were at least two dozen conspirators, and they chose a Senate meeting on the fifteenth of March (the Ides) to act. On the advice of his wife Calpurnia, Caesar almost decided not to attend but was shamed into doing so by Decimus Brutus. After Caesar entered the Senate, one of the conspirators approached him, ostensibly begging for a pardon for his brother in exile. This was the cue for the others to take out their daggers and stab Caesar. The rest of the Senate fled in horror.

FIGHTING FOR CAESAR

Caesar was dead, but what happened afterward showed that he had created a political movement that would outlive him. Friends, officers, and soldiers keenly defended his memory and sought to uphold his acts. The consul Mark Antony initially took the lead. Obtaining from Calpurnia important papers and money in Caesar's house, Antony also secured the support of Lepidus, who had troops in Rome. At a Senate meeting on March 17, Antony helped broker a compromise. There would be amnesty for the assassins, but Caesar's individual measures and appointments would be upheld and he would receive a public funeral. Separately, the *plebs* of Rome learned that Caesar had left them individual cash bequests as well as his gardens as a public park. Although Antony did not deliver the brilliant speech that Shakespeare wrote for him in *Julius Caesar*, he did cleverly stage the funeral to whip up the crowd. They cremated Caesar's body in the Forum on an improvised pyre and set up an altar on the spot. Fearful for their lives, by mid-April the leading conspirators had fled Rome. Decimus Brutus was able, though, to take up the command he had been already assigned – by Caesar – in Cisalpine Gaul.

The arrival in Italy of Caesar's great-nephew Gaius Octavius would increase the pressure on Antony. To the surprise of many, the dead Dictator had named the 18-year-old his heir. The young man was willing to accept the inheritance, which included the name C. Julius Caesar. (He could have added as a fourth name "Octavianus" but did not, although modern scholars call him "Octavian" for convenience.) Friends of Caesar, many upset with Antony for not avenging the assassination, gave support to the designated heir. Among them were the Spaniard Balbus, who now wrote a flattering memoir of his dead friend, and Hirtius, who worked to complete Caesar's unfinished commentaries. Others were far more skeptical and persisted in calling the young man "Octavius." To silence such critics, Octavian contrived to have himself posthumously adopted by Caesar.

Antony did not want to lose his preeminence. He refused to release Caesar's properties to the newcomer. He managed to block Octavian from displaying Caesar's golden throne at games, an honor previously voted by the Senate. Then, in early June, he tried to secure power through legislation giving him a five-year command over both Transalpine and Cisalpine Gaul, provinces to which the legions at Apollonia were then dispatched. But Decimus Brutus refused to leave his post and by the end of the year had entrenched himself in the city of Mutina, forcing Antony to put him under siege.

Octavian, meanwhile, despite only being a private citizen, worked at acquiring an army to counteract Antony, and he appealed especially to former soldiers of Caesar. He sponsored commemorative games for Caesar in July, during which a daytime comet appeared. Octavian said it was actually the star of his "father," as he was now calling Caesar, a god in the heavens. Complaining of Antony's failure to avenge Caesar and offering cash bounties, he started recruiting among Caesarian veterans settled in Campania. Two of Caesar's old legions, the Seventh and the Eighth, were reconstituted. In hindsight, this was a key moment in the formation of the imperial army. In earlier times, after their tours of duty were concluded, legions were dismissed and their serial numbers (like "First") reassigned as commanders enrolled new legions. Now, legions would have their own institutional identities, with fixed numbers, emblems, and sometimes titles, like "Martian."

While the reenlisted veterans marched to Rome with Octavian, they were more eager to reach some kind of reconciliation than to take up arms against Antony's soldiers. Antony and his brother Lucius, who was serving as tribune, attacked Octavian. Antony called him "boy" and "Spartacus." Lucius tried to discredit him with allegations about his sexuality, claiming that he had prostituted himself to Hirtius.

The young Caesar, who would soon be joined by the Fourth and Martian legions, badly needed legitimization, and obtained it through a surprising alliance with Cicero. While rejoicing in Caesar's assassination, Cicero had despaired at Antony's subsequent dominance. In September of 44, he went on the attack with his *Philippic Orations*, which circulated as pamphlets. The name came from the speeches the great Athenian freedom fighter Demosthenes had delivered against King Philip of Macedon around 340 BCE. By the end of 44, Cicero had paved the way for the Senate to grant Octavian a formal command and send him with the consuls of 43, Hirtius and Pansa, to relieve Decimus Brutus at Mutina. At Cicero's urging, the Senate undertook to pay the staggering 20,000 sesterces that Octavian had promised to the Fourth and Martian legions, whose defection had been such a blow to Antony.

Over Cicero's objections, the Senate still tried to broker a peace with Antony. None was achieved, and in spring of 43, Octavian and the consuls initiated full war. Antony lost in two bloody battles near Mutina, fleeing afterward to Transalpine Gaul. There Lepidus had a large army that included reactivated Caesarian troops, recruited from Gallic colonies. The Senate now declared Antony a public enemy. Cicero thought a return to the free Republic was at hand and that Caesar's heir could now be bypassed.

The Senate took measures to tighten its grip. Since Hirtius and Pansa had both died in the war, their troops were assigned to Decimus Brutus, at that time supreme commander in the north of Italy. The assassin Cassius, who had fled Italy late in the summer of 44 and gained control of Syria, had his command legalized. (Marcus Brutus, who had taken control of Macedonia and Greece, had already had his command there legalized in early 43.) Pompey's son Sextus was voted a naval command, having campaigned successfully in Spain, and was now in Massilia.

But neither Antony nor Octavian was deterred. By the end of the summer of 43, the "shifty" Lepidus changed direction and, with his army, joined Antony. So did two other former officers of Caesar, Asinius Pollio and Munatius Plancus, in command of the other major armies in the west. For his part, Octavian and his troops refused to obey the assassin Decimus. The Fourth and Martian Legions were further outraged when the Senate announced that it was cutting their bounties. With elections for replacement consuls underway, the still teenaged Octavian demanded the right to run, and marched on the city of Rome with his troops to make his point. Camped on the Field of Mars, the Fourth and Martian got the first part of their payout, restored to its full level by Octavian, who was duly elected consul. A law was passed establishing a court to exile those who murdered Caesar or had any knowledge of the crime. Among those condemned was Sextus Pompey, and so he, Marcus Brutus, and Cassius were all stripped of their commands. The Caesarian cause had rallied.

THREE'S A CROWD: THE TRIUMVIRATE

The reunion of the Caesarians ushered in a new experiment in autocracy. In October of 43, Octavian, Antony, and Lepidus met secretly in northern Italy and decided to rule as a board of three, a triumvirate. Essentially, this was a shared dictatorship. The triumvirs would have the power of consuls, the right to appoint magistrates, and the right to make laws. They also divided the western provinces among themselves, while the east remained in control of the republicans. The major immediate assignment of the triumvirs was to wage war on the conspirators against Caesar. They also had the formal charge "to put the state back together." Unlike the secret alliance of Pompey, Crassus, and Caesar in 60, this triumvirate was installed by law for a five-year term in November of 43.

Ratification of the triumvirate was accompanied by a spectacular act of terror, the revival of Sulla's proscriptions. The Caesarian conspirators, and many more, were instantly condemned. Their heads, if turned in, would fetch large rewards, leading bounty hunters to scour Rome and Italy. Adding to the shock, among those proscribed were Antony's uncle, Lepidus' brother, and Octavian's boyhood guardian. The death of the most famous victim, Cicero, haunted Romans ever afterward: according to his biographers, he was caught being carried in a litter, bravely extended his neck out, and fixed his executioners in the eye. Many men were proscribed simply for their wealth, like the scholar Varro. He escaped with his life, although his personal library was plundered. With the east out of their control, the triumvirs were desperate to raise money and imposed heavy taxation on citizens. Leading Roman women staged a demonstration in the Forum to protest, an event shocking in its novelty.

Eager to honor Caesar's memory, the triumvirate had him officially made a god at the start of 42. A temple was to rise on the spot in the Forum where he was cremated. It took some years for the temple and its cult statue to be completed, but designs for them soon appeared on coins. Octavian – he called himself Gaius Julius Caesar – took the chance to add "son of a god" to his official nomenclature, a way to enhance his authority. He also replaced

Figure 11.2 A gold coin of "Imperator Caesar, son of a god" (aka Octavian) from the mid-30s BCE reveals plans for the Temple of the Divine Julius. The star in the temple's pediment represents Caesar's ascent to the heavens as a god. (Photo © The Trustees of the British Museum.)

"Gaius" with "Imperator." Previously a victorious general had held this title only so long as he did *imperium*, although Julius Caesar had been voted its permanent use.

The terror unleashed by the triumvirs helped their already-formidable opposition. Brutus and Cassius continued building up forces and fundraising in the east. In the west, Pompey's son Sextus gained Sicily, and to his immense credit offered it as a refuge to the proscribed and others fleeing Italy, including Octavian's future wife, the highly aristocratic Livia, and her then husband. Sextus effectively exploited the memory of his father, who was represented on coins as Neptune, which made him the "son of a god" too. As had been true for the elder Pompey, control of the sea was crucial to Sextus' hopes and also those of the republicans in the east, who were building up naval resources.

It was only with great difficulty that Antony and Octavian and their massive army – including Caesar's Fourth Legion – made it across the Adriatic in the summer of 42. Marching east across the Egnatian Way, they found the republicans entrenched near the city of Philippi, with a strong supply line to the sea. Cassius' strategy was to starve out the triumvirs. Antony, trying to cut the republican supply lines, ended up precipitating battle. Mistakenly thinking that all was lost, Cassius killed himself prematurely. In fact, Brutus had defeated the forces of Octavian, who had abandoned his troops claiming illness. At a subsequent encounter, Brutus' forces were defeated, and he took his life.

After this major victory, Antony and Octavian reassigned the provinces. Antony would control all of Transalpine Gaul (Cisalpine was no longer to be

Figure 11.3 A silver coin issued by an ally of Sextus Pompey. The head of Pompey the Great is shown on the obverse (compare Fig. 7.1) but the dolphin and trident turned him into the sea-god Neptune. (Photo © The Trustees of the British Museum.)

a province), and he was given the east to reorganize. Octavian gained Spain from Lepidus and was to wrest control of Sicily from Sextus Pompey. He also was to settle Caesarian veterans in Italy on confiscated land. Lepidus would govern Africa.

Antony seemed the clear winner here, and as he made his way to Asia, he was greeted as a god, as Caesar had been after Pharsalus. Envoys from the Jewish high priest could not go this far, but they did offer a golden crown to commemorate Antony's victory, while also asking for some Jews enslaved by Cassius to be freed. Antony agreed and wrote back denouncing "the god-defying plots" of the republicans. "Through our victory, the body of Asia is now recovering, as it were, from a grave illness," he claimed. When he summoned Cleopatra of Egypt to account for her failure to help the triumvirs, she appeared in a magnificent gilded barge with purple sails, staffed by beautiful women. Captivated by the queen at least as much as Caesar had been, Antony was delighted to winter with her in Alexandria while Octavian fought for his own survival in Italy.

THE YOUNG CAESAR VS. THE YOUNG POMPEY

Veteran settlement in Italy was hideously disruptive. Huge swathes of territory were seized without compensation up and down the peninsula to provide farms for perhaps 40,000 men. A young poet from the north, Vergil, came from one of the towns affected and commemorated the displacements in his *Eclogues*, a work inspired by an earlier Greek poet, Theocritus, who celebrated the beauty of the countryside. "A disloyal soldier will have this fallow field, once carefully cultivated," one of Vergil's characters laments, "a brute these fields of grain. To what depth has strife brought us wretched citizens!" Of course, the soldiers had a different perspective. Funerary monuments they set up on or near their new farms recorded their service with pride, such as that of Vettius Tuscus, "eagle-bearer of the Fourth Legion Macedonica." (The Fourth Legion probably gained its extra name Macedonica after fighting at Philippi.)

Mark Antony's brother Lucius, consul in 41, along with Antony's wife Fulvia (the widow of Clodius), saw a chance to eliminate Octavian and end the hated triumvirate. Rallying support among victims of the land confiscations, they built up an army. Despite hoping to unite with commanders friendly to Antony in northern Italy, Lucius was cut off by the quick action of Agrippa, a childhood friend of Octavian and now his indispensable general. Lucius' army was trapped in the city of Perusia and starved into submission. Lead projectiles fired from slingshots have been discovered, and the messages inscribed on them help show what motivated the soldiers. On Octavian's side soldiers proudly announced their legion serial numbers; one bullet from the Eleventh Legion also mentioned "Divine Julius." The two sides taunted one another. Lucius is derided for his baldness, while Octavian is told, "You suck!"

After Lucius' failure, Antony rushed back to Italy. Collaborating with Sextus Pompey, he hoped that Octavian might still be defeated. Octavian, in response, contracted a marriage alliance with Scribonia, the daughter of one of Sextus' most important supporters; he also instructed his forces at Brundisium not to admit Antony's fleet into the harbor. Further war in Italy seemed imminent, but friends, officers, and soldiers of both triumvirs insisted on reconciliation. The so-called Peace of Brundisium (40 BCE) was the result. Fulvia had recently died from illness, allowing all the blame for the recent fighting to be assigned to her. Antony was now free to marry Octavian's sister Octavia to symbolize their accord. Writing a poem in honor of Caesar's old general Asinius Pollio, a key negotiator in the peace talks, Vergil held out the prospect of a new golden age.

Hopes were soon dashed. Betrayed by Antony, Sextus intensified his blockade of Italy, reducing the *plebs* of Rome to near starvation. Now it was their turn to demand peace. In one protest, Octavian was nearly stoned to death. In 39, he and Antony met Sextus and negotiated the so-called Treaty of Misenum. The terms were that Sextus would stop his blockade, receive a large provincial command (including Sicily), and later become consul. All political refugees could return to Italy, except for the actual murderers of Julius Caesar. The proscriptions were over. Antony was free to go east, to deal with the Parthians who had recently invaded Roman territory.

Octavian soon decided to reignite war with Sextus, accusing him of relying on pirates no better than those Sextus' father had fought. (Like the charges about Fulvia, this one strongly influenced subsequent history writing, and the burial of Sextus' side of the story is a real challenge for study of this period.) By early 38, Octavian had divorced Scribonia and married Livia. A member of the nobility whose father had died at Philippi, she herself had fled Italy with her first husband after the war at Perusia. She was six months pregnant with a child from him when she remarried, which set tongues wagging: "the lucky have children in three months." Still, a union with her would help Octavian win support from other aristocrats, many now returning to Rome. This, too, marginalized Sextus.

War with Sextus proved a great challenge for Octavian. In 38 his two main navies were badly defeated, and a sudden storm destroyed even more ships. The *plebs* faced food shortage again and circulated unflattering verses about Octavian: "After he has twice been beaten at sea and lost his fleets / He plays dice all the time – hoping to win something." In 37 Antony travelled briefly to Italy and met with Octavian at Tarentum, where they agreed to renew the triumvirate for five years: Antony would fight the Parthians, Octavian would oppose Sextus, and the remaining murderers of Caesar would be hunted down. In exchange for a promise of Italian legionaries, Antony offered Octavian some badly needed ships. The highly capable Agrippa built still more ships, engineered a huge artificial port in the Bay of Naples called the "Julian harbor," and drilled naval crews there. He armed his fleet with a new weapon, the "Snatcher," a grappling device with a cable that could hook onto ships and drag them.

In 36 Pompey's son was finally defeated by Caesar's. Agrippa and Octavian sailed to Sicily from Italy, and Lepidus brought an army from Africa. Sextus was trapped, had to risk a major battle just off Naulochus, and lost. Fleeing east, he was killed the next year by Antony's men. Records of the war are notable for revealing supporters of Octavian willing to fight with him. These included new men from the towns of Italy, like Statilius Taurus, for whom civil war was an opportunity. But there were also members of Rome's noblest families, like Paullus Aemilius Lepidus, nephew of the triumvir and equally "shifty." The triumvir himself had tried to seize control of Sicily after Naulochus, and Octavian had put him under permanent house arrest.

Octavian had prevailed in the face of many threats, but he now had to address the problem of his image and Rome's. Italians had suffered throughout the civil war, and the warring was a disgrace to Roman prestige. The poet Horace, who had fought for the republicans at Philippi and then returned to Italy, confronted his contemporaries with the paradoxical thought that "Rome is falling through her own strength." What Carthage had failed to do, wicked Romans would: "we will destroy

Rome ... and the ground will be taken over by wild animals again." Beginning in 36, Octavian responded vigorously to these sentiments. He campaigned against proper foreign enemies across the Adriatic, thereby securing northern Italy. A former consul was appointed to crush the bandit gangs that had menaced travelers for decades. In Rome itself, land Octavian had acquired for a palace was turned over for a temple. On the advice of the antiquarian Atticus, Octavian rebuilt the crumbling Temple of Jupiter Feretrius, and many other restorations followed. Multitalented Agrippa invested heavily in Rome, building a new aqueduct and hundreds of neighborhood fountains. He even cleaned out the city's sewers and to prove it proudly rowed down the central line in a boat.

Octavian also arranged in 35 for public honors for his sister Octavia and wife Livia, including statues and the right to administer their affairs without the customary guardian. Women had suffered much during civil war. A funeral speech inscribed on marble by one of the proscribed recalls how his wife saved his life by hiding him; in 41, she successfully confronted Lepidus at his tribunal about her husband's return. "What could have been more effective than this courage of yours?" he asked in his eulogy. With their families and their own interests threatened, women stepped up repeatedly in the civil wars to protest and to demand change. Despite lacking the vote, they became virtually an interest group in politics and were invited to celebratory banquets at which Livia presided along with her husband. Gradually, Octavian was building up the support that would be the basis for his personal rule.

THE TRAGEDY OF ANTONY AND CLEOPATRA

From 40 onward Antony's attention was occupied by the Parthians. That year, in collaboration with a republican officer left stranded after Philippi, Q. Labienus, they invaded Syria and overthrew the Jewish king in Jerusalem. Labienus soon extended his control to the Aegean coast of Asia Minor. Initially Antony struck back through his officers, especially Ventidius, one of the great new men of the age. In 38 Antony prepared to take over the command himself and reached a peace with King Antiochus of Commagene, who had collaborated with the Parthians. Antony was shrewd in his relations with client rulers, like Herod the Great, whom he placed on the Judean throne. They were key to his Parthian strategy.

In many ways Antony was like a Greek king himself. Already in Rome he had lived on a magnificent scale, winning favor for his joking, his swagger, and his reputation as a lover. According to the biography of *Antony* by Plutarch, the first winter Antony spent with Cleopatra in Alexandria (41/40) was consumed by revels – drinking, dicing, hunting, and more. He roamed the streets at night and joked with the city's people. While no doubt Antony enjoyed himself, the image he created as the "new Dionysus" was effective at winning local support. Cleopatra became one of his most important client rulers. In the eastern world, where kings had many wives, amorous relations with her that resulted in three children was normal foreign policy, although to Octavia it might have looked rather different.

The great Parthian expedition, launched in 36, was meant to seal Antony's reputation as the equal to that of Caesar (and Alexander), but it turned into a debacle. Avoiding the plains of Mesopotamia where Crassus' army had been mowed down by arrows, he marched through Armenia with the help of the Armenian king. Speeding ahead of his equipment wagons, Antony put the capital of Media (a Parthian ally) under siege. The wagons were seized, the men with them were slaughtered, and Antony's Armenian ally fled with all his forces. Antony was forced to march back to Syria, losing thousands of men on the way.

In the aftermath, he became more dependent on Cleopatra. After capturing Armenia and its treacherous king in 34, Antony celebrated his victory in Alexandria, not in Rome. And at the end of the ceremony, he named Cleopatra "Queen of Kings" and her son by Caesar "King of Kings." He also allotted their young children – decked out in royal costumes – territory allegedly including Roman provinces. As with Fulvia and Sextus Pompey, Antony's story came to be buried by Octavian's version of events, making one wonder if there might be some distortion in the surviving accounts of this spectacle.

Octavian's vilification of Antony began before their final confrontation, and helped cause it. Romans might not have worried too much about Antony's fondness for drink or even the foot rubs he allegedly gave Cleopatra. More alarming was the fear that he might replace Rome with Alexandria as the empire's seat of power. Octavian fueled rumors by breaking open Antony's will in 32 and reading aloud a clause stating that Antony wished to be buried in Egypt, with Cleopatra. By now, Antony had divorced Octavia, and a number of senators who supported him, including the consuls, fled to him from Rome. At the same time, Octavian arranged for loyalty oaths from the communities of Italy and then the western provinces. This formalized the pledges individuals had been making for years in the civil war, helping turn Imperator Caesar (as Octavian was known) into the head of state in all but name. Similar oaths would be sworn to him, and his family members, in years to come.

As he built up his land and sea forces in Asia Minor, Antony begged Cleopatra to return to Egypt, but she refused. She was fully a political actor in her own right now, and her presence undercut Antony's demand that

Octavian should agree to end the triumvirate formally and revert to traditional government. Annoyed by the queen, or by the political cost of her presence, Antony's supporters started abandoning him. By the fall of 32, Antony had moved most of his forces to western Greece, perhaps planning to invade Italy the next year. But swift action at the start of 31 by Agrippa hemmed in Antony and Cleopatra by Actium, at the entry into the Ambracian Gulf. On September 2 a naval battle was fought outside the Gulf. First Cleopatra escaped, then followed Antony. Their massive land army surrendered to Octavian a week later, sealing a decisive victory. In celebration, he restored the temple to Apollo at Actium, created a new festival there similar to the Olympic Games, and founded a new "Victory City" of Nicopolis.

Octavian was poised to take over the whole east and gain the spoils to pay for projects such as Nicopolis. Late in 31, envoys representing eastern communities came to him, recognizing his supremacy and seeking his favor. In the summer of 30, Octavian and his forces invaded Egypt and closed in on Alexandria. Told wrongly that Cleopatra was dead, Antony stabbed himself. He survived long enough to be brought to Cleopatra and die in her arms. According to one version of events, she then took her own life, too proud to appear as a captive in Octavian's triumph. Some have judged this as one final piece of mythology, masking Octavian's cold-blooded murder of the queen – which was the fate of her son Caesarion. Fantasy certainly could be useful to the victor: Horace wrote a poem vividly imagining Cleopatra "plotting mad ruin for the Capitol and funeral rites for the empire." Just the opposite had happened: Egypt with all its wealth was now part of the Roman *imperium*, an achievement in which Octavian could bask far more than in his Illyrian victories. But this aside, there were few alterations to Antony's arrangements, and rulers like Herod retained their thrones. Antony had done a good job running the east.

An even more urgent task than the takeover of Egypt was dealing with the massive armies of both sides. Those who had served their time – including Antony's men – would be given land, as had been customary now since Caesar's first settlements back in 47. Octavian's men were settled in Italy (although without the hideous dispossessions of 41), Antony's mostly overseas, where more colonies were created. By 28 BCE there were at least 55 overseas citizen colonies, in which an estimated 150,000 adult citizen men of Italian origin had settled. Their arrival integrated provincial societies more fully into the evolving Roman world state, a process already under way before 50. Their presence would spur further cultural transformation (Chapter 13).

A notable part of Octavian's reorganization of the army was his decision to keep some of Antony's legions in service, allowing them to retain their serial numbers and names. Since Philippi, Octavian had his own numbered sequence of legions. These included Caesar's old Fourth, but not the Martian Legion, which had been lost at sea. Now he would allow a few reduplications, adding a legionary name to prevent confusion ("Third Gallica," for example). Like the settlement of Antony's veterans, this was an act of reconciliation. Soldiers on both sides would be recognized through the perpetuation of their legions. There was a sense in which Caesar's army – made famous in the pages of his commentaries – was still intact, and it was all now fighting for a new Caesar. Like overseas colonization, this new conception of a permanent army was a product of the civil wars of 49–30 and another of its great legacies. In 30 the Fourth Legion was sent to Spain, where its men would serve for the next 70 years. They could look back with pride on how their predecessors took action in the year of Caesar's death to avenge his murder and support his heir.

But even as some could look back with pride, Romans also confronted the sin of civil war. "What field has not been fattened with Latin blood?" Horace asked in horror. It almost seemed as if Rome was under a divine curse, perhaps going back all the way to the founder Romulus' murder of his brother Remus, and made worse by all the recent atrocities. Much had to be done to restore the gods' favor. Focusing on that, Romans would be willing to experiment politically and culturally in the years ahead. Paradoxically, 20 years of civil war did not destroy the Roman world. It paved the way for what would be called, with some justice, its golden age.

FURTHER READING

K. Welch, *Magnus Pius: Sextus Pompeius and the Transformation of the Roman Republic* (Swansea, 2012), is an outstanding reinterpretation of this period. More general narratives are provided in *The Cambridge Ancient History* (2nd ed.) by E. Rawson in chaps. 11 and 12 of Vol. 9 and C. B. R. Pelling in chap. 1 of Vol. 10. R. Syme, *The Roman Revolution* (Oxford, 1939), drew inspiration from the rise of dictators in Europe in the 1920s and 1930s and, while open to challenge in its overall interpretation of politics, is full of useful information about the careers of individual politicians. For the rise of the standing army and the settlement of soldiers see L. G. F. Keppie, *The Making of the Roman Army: From Republic to Empire* (London, 1984), and *Colonisation and Veteran Settlement in Italy: 47–14 B.C.* (London, 1983), along with the foundational work of P. A. Brunt, *Italian Manpower 225 B.C.–A.D. 14* (Oxford, 1971). G. S. Sumi, *Ceremony and Power: Performing Politics in Rome between Republic and Empire* (Ann Arbor, 2005), explores new ways of articulating power.

Refer to Chapter 8 for works on Julius Caesar by Gelzer, Goldsworthy, Tatum, Stevenson, and Griffin. There are many fine articles on the problems of Rome in Caesar's absence and during his dictatorship, including these: M. Fredriksen, "Caesar, Cicero, and the Problem of Debt," *Journal of Roman Studies* 56 (1966), 128–41; K. Welch, "Antony, Fulvia, and the Ghost of Clodius in 47 B.C.," *Greece & Rome* 42 (1995), 182–201; J. T. Ramsey, "Did Julius Caesar Temporarily Banish Mark Antony from His Inner

Circle?," *Classical Quarterly* 54 (2004), 161–73; J. North, "Caesar at the Lupercalia," *Journal of Roman Studies* 98 (2008), 144–60.

The triumvirate is reinterpreted by C. H. Lange, *Res publica constituta: Actium, Apollo, and the Accomplishment of the Triumviral Assignment* (Leiden, 2009). J. Osgood, *Caesar's Legacy: Civil War and the Emergence of the Roman Empire* (Cambridge, 2006), focuses more on the social and cultural history of the triumviral period. Women's roles are discussed in J. Osgood, *Turia: A Roman Woman's Civil War* (Oxford, 2014). More generally on women, consult S. Treggiari, *Terentia, Tullia, and Publilia: The Women of Cicero's Family* (London, 2007); S. L. James and S. Dillon (eds.), *A Companion to Women in the Ancient World* (Malden, MA, 2012); A. Richlin, *Arguments with Silence: Writing the History of Roman Women* (Ann Arbor, 2014). There are many works on Cleopatra, among which can be recommended D. Roller, *Cleopatra* (Oxford, 2010), and A. Goldsworthy, *Antony and Cleopatra* (London, 2010); for an Egyptian perspective see J. Fletcher, *Cleopatra the Great: The Woman behind the Legend* (New York, 2008).

12

PRINCIPATE: GOVERNMENT
FOR THE WORLD STATE (30–6 BCE)

Octavian's victory at Actium in 31 BCE was immediately seen as decisive. After the battle, ambassadors from the small Syrian community of Rhosus sought him out at Ephesus and offered a gold crown and other honors. Leading the embassy was Seleucus, a sea captain who had served under Octavian in earlier campaigns and received Roman citizenship. Writing back to Rhosus to acknowledge the honors in late 31, Octavian promised, "I will try, when I come to your area, to be the author of some good to you and watch over the privileges given to your city, and all the more gladly will I do these things because of Seleucus." His letter was inscribed on a stone monument in Rhosus that survived into modern times. It is just one piece of evidence for the many new relationships forming between Octavian and the communities of the east.

In Italy and Rome, Octavian's victory was acknowledged too, especially after the deaths of Antony and Cleopatra. At the start of 29, the Senate voted to shut the Temple of Janus in the Forum, something only done – as Octavian later put it – "when peace had been secured by victories on land and sea throughout the whole empire of the Roman People." According to him, this was only the third time in Rome's history that the gates of war were closed. Vergil's four-book poem about agriculture, the *Georgics*, finished in 29, also emphasized victory. It concludes with the image of Octavian "thundering in war" in the east and then giving "the rule of law to willing nations, and making his way to Heaven." For the poet, Octavian was close to being a god.

Vergil read his poem in Naples in the summer of 29 to Octavian, who was resting in advance of the grandiose triumph held on August 13–15 to celebrate his campaigns in Illyricum, Actium, and Egypt. Octavian was careful to avoid the offense his father had caused in 46 by displaying paintings of dying Romans. The primary display at the Actian triumph

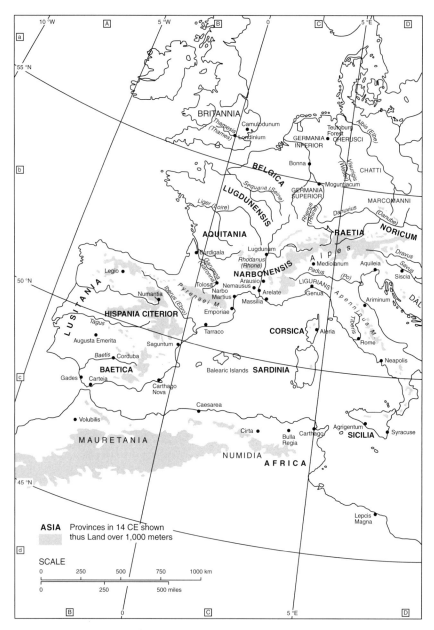

Map 10 The Roman World in the time of Augustus

appears to have been the huge bronze rams taken from Antony's warships. Permanent commemorations of the battle also relied not on images of the defeated but on more abstract symbols. One was the winged goddess Victory, often shown flying over a globe to symbolize Roman world rule made

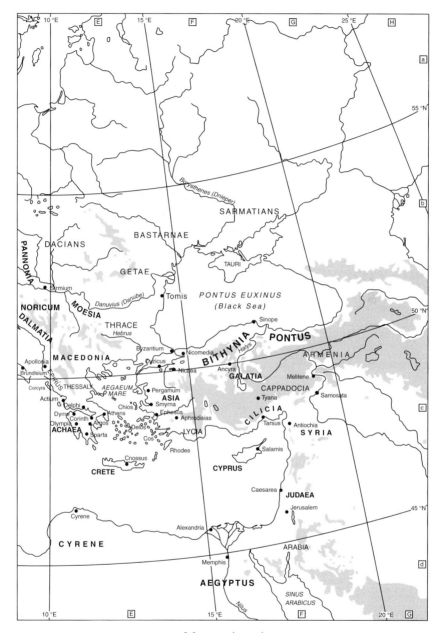

Map 10 (cont.)

possible by Octavian – or, as he should properly be called, Imperator Caesar. A statue of Victory was placed inside the new Julian Senate house, opened later in August of 29. A coin suggests that high on its roof was another statue of the goddess, for all to see.

Figure 12.1 The new Julian Senate house, opened in 29 BCE, on a silver coin of Octavian. On the apex of the roof stands the winged goddess Victory. (Photo © The Trustees of the British Museum.)

In reconstructing the history of these years – and indeed the period leading to the death of Imperator Caesar Augustus (as Octavian became in 27 BCE) – our only detailed narrative is a third-century CE account by Senator Cassius Dio. While accurately recording numerous events year by year, Dio very much wrote in hindsight, suggesting that in 27 Augustus practically created at a stroke a new form of monarchical government that would last centuries. A different picture emerges from contemporary documents, like the letter to Rhosus, in which Octavian already seems to be acting like (though not *as*) a king, as had Antony as triumvir in the east. Of course, documents tend to reflect an "official" version of events, casting Octavian in the best light – none more so than history's most famous résumé, the elaborate list of *Achievements (Res Gestae)* he personally composed to adorn his mausoleum by the Tiber River. But historians can use the remarkable volume of contemporary material – inscriptions and also coins, statues, buildings, works of poetry – to reconstruct how a new political culture actually developed more gradually, and dynamically.

There is one other key source: a biography of Augustus written by Suetonius in the early second century CE. This work, one in a series of the lives of emperors, reflects the great interest Romans had in their rulers. It is filled with memorable details. Suetonius depicts Augustus as a very ambitious man, one who personally vowed "to establish the state securely in its proper place" and to be "the author of the best constitution." Augustus, Suetonius writes, was eager to beautify the city of Rome and make it more secure, to reform Roman society, and to strengthen the empire. Two examples: "to fight fires he created nighttime watch groups; to control the floods, he widened the channel of the Tiber and cleared it out, for it had been filled for some time with rubbish."

Augustus was exceedingly careful. He liked to advise hotheaded generals "Hurry slowly." He compared risky wars to fishing with a golden hook, the loss of which could never equal any catch. Augustus never gave a speech without rehearsing it. He would not converse with anyone on serious matters, not even his wife Livia, without first writing his thoughts down in a notebook. He was a hard worker, staying up late at night on a couch especially equipped for study. Naturally reserved, he made himself into a great performer. He forced himself to pay total attention to public games, rather than read and answer letters as a bored Julius Caesar had. When he entered the Senate he made a point of greeting individual members by name and refusing to let anyone rise to greet him. He cast votes in elections "as one of the people."

Augustus' personality is bound to fascinate, and forming a view of it – as Suetonius tried to – is important. There can be no doubt that his particular vision of war and his zeal for administration had a profound impact on the Roman world. But it is also important to recognize the contributions of others in the development of a new style of government. Under Augustus there was never anything like a formal monarchy, nor even a legally defined position of emperor. The old political organs of the *res publica*, including the Senate, continued to function and helped shape the kind of head of state Augustus became. As he aged, he gave his younger male family members increasing prominence, especially as commanders, an essential element of his ambition of long-term stability for Rome. Yet he would find that Romans were eager to recognize these men more lavishly than he did. Some desired a more explicit monarchy than Augustus himself did.

AUGUSTUS AND THE *RES PUBLICA* (28–19 BCE)

Octavian had been holding a consulship every year since 31, but his power was really more extensive, as it had been in the triumvirate, and he sought now to change that. As he wrote in his *Achievements*, "in my sixth and seventh consulships (28–27), when I had put an end to civil wars, although by universal consent I had power over everything, I transferred the state from my own power to the control of the Senate and People of Rome." In 28, he ostentatiously shared all of the consular powers and privileges with Agrippa, ordered debt records burned, reviewed and cancelled some of the rulings that had been issued by the triumvirs, and fully reestablished the assemblies and courts. Octavian and Agrippa reduced membership of the Senate – swollen with some dubious members appointed during the civil wars. They also were specially empowered to conduct a census, at the end of which came the customary purification of Rome. This was the first complete census since 70, and an astonishing 4,064,000 citizens were counted. The number is so high that some historians think it must include women and children, excluded from earlier reported counts.

Then at the start of 27, Octavian summoned the Senate and gave a speech declaring that he was handing back all public business to the Senate and the People. Senators protested, and after some discussion finally agreed to give him *imperium*, to be exercised for 10 years over all of Spain, all of Gaul beyond the Alps, Syria, and Egypt, with the assignment of fully pacifying these areas. This was perfectly in tune with the now well-accepted view that Rome was the world ruler, although nobody could have failed to notice that almost all of the empire's troops would be stationed in these areas. Octavian would appoint senators as legates to govern his provinces (aside from Egypt, which would always be governed by an Equestrian prefect). The other, "public" provinces would be governed by senior ex-magistrates chosen by lot. Since Octavian would continue to hold the consulship, he would have *imperium* not just in his provinces but also in Rome. In other words, formally he retained quite a bit of power, but it now had nothing to do with the hated triumvirate.

In response to his renunciation of total control of the *res publica*, the Senate voted him fresh honors that would be confirmed by the People in assembly. Most important was the utterly novel name Augustus, which literally meant something like "Revered One." It derived from an adjective used to describe sacred places and things. Anything enacted after successful auguries was "august," since it was done by the will of the gods. The name put Imperator Caesar somewhere between man and god, exactly as poets like Vergil had. It was meant to confirm Romans' confidence that Augustus could establish and maintain order throughout the world.

Other honors similarly suggested Augustus' supremacy while drawing on the traditions of the *res publica*. As earlier generals had adorned the facades of their houses with the plunder of war, Augustus was voted the right to screen his front door with laurel bushes and place above it the civic crown. The evergreen laurel suggested permanent victory; the crown, traditionally awarded for saving a fellow citizen's life, suggested that Augustus was the savior of Rome. It was also voted to set up a golden shield in the Julian Senate house that, through its inscription, "testified that the Senate and the People of Rome gave it to me because of my courage, clemency, justice, and piety" (*Achievements*). All of these honors made Augustus into a kind of superman – or super-citizen. Yet they were clearly, calculatedly different from the much more regal purple robes and golden throne of Julius Caesar.

But as Augustus' consulships continued piling up, it must have struck Romans – especially senators eager for the glory of the top office – that for all he had given back, he was still holding on to a lot. After returning from a long tour of Gaul and Spain, in 23, Augustus became gravely ill. Thinking he would die, Dio later wrote, he summoned a number of senators and gave his fellow consul Piso "the list of the forces and of public revenues written in a book. He handed his ring to Agrippa," signaling his choice of a successor. Would others go along? Augustus himself had been visibly promoting his young nephew Marcellus. Married to Augustus' daughter Julia in 25, Marcellus was voted the following year the right to stand for office 10 years in advance of the legally appointed age, a very special privilege. A potential succession crisis was averted when, thanks to the cold baths prescribed by his physician Antonius Musa, Augustus recovered. It was time to think further about his position.

On July 1 of 23 Augustus gave up his consulship, and he would not regularly hold any formal office again. Free elections for the top office were to return. But Augustus would now hold continuous tribunician power – all the powers of the tribunes, without the actual office. His *imperium* outside of Rome was also made greater than that of others, so that if he appeared in a public province he could take charge if he wished. Augustus' position thus was detached from any office and embodied by ongoing powers – powers that could be conferred on others. Agrippa received his own five-year grant of *imperium* in 23 and later received tribunician power. In 23 Augustus probably hoped to see Marcellus reach a stature that would let him share, and ultimately carry on, Augustus' work. But it was in vain, since the younger man died before the end of the year.

The return to free consular elections was less than happy. Rome was suffering from one of its recurring plagues, there was Tiber flooding so extensive that people could sail through the city on boats, and food was scarce. People wondered, Was it all happening because Augustus was no longer consul? Were the gods angry? In his absence from Rome, the *plebs* protested, threatening to burn down the Senate house, with the senators in it. Many wished for Augustus to become dictator. With great theatricality he refused the post after returning to Rome, falling onto his knees and begging. He did, though, take measures to restore the grain supply before again leaving Rome in the fall of 22 for a three-year sojourn in the east. Still, elections in his absence were turbulent. In 20, for example, only one consul was elected for the next year, since voters were determined that Augustus should have one of the two posts.

The year 19 brought some resolution. When the sole consul, Sentius Saturninus, tried to hold elections for a colleague, a new champion of the *plebs* stepped forward. As aedile (probably in 22), Egnatius Rufus had organized a group of his slaves to fight fires and became so popular that he acquired a praetorship for the next year. When Sentius, following "the rigorous ways of the consuls of old," as one source puts it, refused to let Egnatius stand for the top office in 19, deadly riots ensued and were put down on orders of the Senate. Meanwhile, the Senate also sent envoys to Augustus. Augustus arranged for one of the envoys to be made consul, presumably by sending word that this was his wish. Upon his return to Rome later in 19, Augustus accepted the permanent right to exercise at least some consular prerogatives in Rome. Events of this year confirmed that Augustus would defend the *res publica* when called upon, and he had the supremacy to do so. But he would not be budged into assuming any extraordinary posts, like a dictatorship. A new political culture was clearly emerging.

THE NEW POLITICAL CULTURE

The institutions of the *res publica* endured. There was no legal position of emperor, no formal law of succession. The title Augustus preferred for himself was an informal one, *princeps*, which traditionally meant "leading man." His hope was that he would have successors who would prove themselves leading men (*principes*) too. In reality, though, he was the effective head of state, and Romans sought constantly to recognize that.

A key feature, then, of the new political culture was an ongoing dialogue between Augustus and Romans over the honors appropriate for him. After 27, the Senate continued to find new ways to honor Augustus. When he returned to Rome in 19 after his tour of the east, for example, the Senate voted that all the priests and Vestal Virgins should perform an annual sacrifice on October 12, to mark the day he reentered the city. Later, he would consent to call this yearly festival the "Augustalia." Many other constituencies beyond the Senate sought to honor Augustus. The *plebs* of Rome threw small coins in a fountain in the Forum to thank the gods for Augustus' continued safety. With the money collected, Augustus bought statues of the gods and dedicated them throughout the city's neighborhoods. The towns of Italy voted him gold crowns whenever he won a military victory, just as Rhosus had in 31, but according to the *Achievements*, Augustus declined them. Each side thus won credit, and the ongoing exchange defined what kind of leader Augustus was, while also integrating Italian towns into the political community.

Augustus' refusals of certain honors exemplified a new ideal of *civilitas* – the ruler comporting himself like a citizen (*civis*) rather than an absolute monarch. Like *clementia*, clemency toward political opponents or offenders, the virtue came to be associated with Augustus, and Suetonius in his biography offers many explicit illustrations. These include the dramatic refusal of the dictatorship in 22 and Augustus' effort to greet senators by name. The house Augustus lived in in Rome also showed his moderation. It was no palace but had previously belonged to a senator. It was not tricked out in marble and had simple furnishings. His villas were relatively simple too and were decorated less with valuable art than curiosities like "the incredibly large bones of massive sea creatures and wild beasts" noted by Suetonius. Even Augustus' clothing was simple. His normal attire was homespun garments, said to have been made by his wife, daughter, or granddaughters.

Yet for all this, wherever Augustus was, so too was the seat of power. He directly controlled appointments to virtually all the most important military positions. Even when there were ostensibly free elections, a word from him could be enough to determine their results. Over time, the patronage of the *princeps* became more and more important. This meant that those closest to him had great power too, including his wife Livia. When the Greek island of Samos sought freedom and tax immunity, Augustus wrote back, "I am of goodwill toward you and would be willing to favor my wife who is zealous in your behalf, but not to the point of breaking my custom . . . I am not willing to have the most valued privileges given to anyone without a reasonable cause." The response shows that Livia had intervened for the islanders, and Augustus wanted to make sure she got credit for that. Decisions were being hashed out not in the Senate, but in what was essentially a ruler's court.

Augustus sought for his household to be exemplary, and its male members to grow up to share his role with him so that they could take over when he died (Table 6). This was his succession policy. After the events of 23, Agrippa became more important than ever. He accumulated powers similar to those

Table 6 The House of Augustus

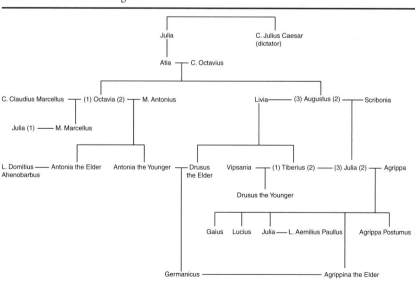

of Augustus and was married in 21 to Augustus' daughter Julia, who quickly bore a son, Gaius. Another, named Lucius, followed in 17, and Augustus would adopt both of them as his own and try to raise them to be worthy *principes*. Also important were Augustus' two stepsons from Livia, Tiberius and Drusus. Both were voted the right to stand for political offices five years earlier than was normally permitted and played major roles in Augustus' military campaigns – allowing them to win great recognition. Tiberius married a daughter of Agrippa, Vipsania. Drusus married a niece of Augustus, Antonia. As Antonia was the daughter of Mark Antony, her marriage was also a way to bind up the wounds of civil war.

The young "princes" were at the heart of the emerging principate and reflected its inherent tensions. They had no formal claim to succession, and their position was recognized only by honors voted to them such as the right to stand for office early. The promotion of the princes was a way to plan for the continuation of Augustus' policies without being too explicitly monarchical. Stability would be assured, or so it might be hoped. For there was a problem, already hinted at in 23: if Augustus died, could rivalries emerge among potential successors that would escalate into renewed civil war? The complex series of marriages following 23 – Agrippa to Julia, Tiberius to Vipsania, etc. – was designed in part to unite the all-too-powerful household, and through to the year 6 seemed to work reasonably well.

WAR AND PEACE (27–19 BCE)

After 27 there was campaigning in far northern Italy and the Balkans, but the main focus was on Augustus' provinces. Poets imagined great conquests in the style of Julius Caesar. "Augustus will be held a god amongst us," Horace proclaimed, "when to the empire he adds the Britons and grim Persians." The need to avenge Crassus' loss in 53 to the Parthians (Horace's "Persians"), as well as Antony's in 36, was indeed a pressing task. But the cautious Augustus would achieve results through diplomacy as well as war, set clear limits to his ambitions, and emphasize peace as the desired end result of fighting.

In 27 Augustus began his assigned job of pacifying Gaul and Spain. In Gaul he took measures to better organize the vast territory, including a census. In 26 he travelled to Spain and organized the conquest of the mountainous northwest, the one area not subject to Roman control. Augustus participated in some of the difficult fighting, before falling ill and then returning to Rome in 24. The Temple of Janus was closed as it had been in 29 to mark the peace that came through victories. But in fact there would be further resistance, only finally put down by Agrippa in 19.

An expedition to Arabia carried out by the prefect of Egypt, Aelius Gallus, was glamorous yet disastrous. Across the Red Sea from Egypt, Arabia was rich from trade in spices and scents and loomed as an appealing conquest. With a large army, including a force sent by Herod of Judea, Gallus marched down the Arabian Peninsula as far as Mariba in modern Yemen. Running low on water, he had to turn back and lost a large number of men to disease and starvation on the return march. His successor as prefect of Egypt, Petronius, was not sent back and instead marched south against the Ethiopians, who had attacked Egypt in Aelius Gallus' absence. He and his troops reached the royal residence at Napata, razed it, and left a garrison. When the Ethiopians marched against the garrison a couple of years later (around 21), Petronius successfully guarded it and sent Ethiopian ambassadors to settle final peace terms with Augustus, then on the island of Samos, en route to Syria. The Ethiopian campaign thus had more lasting value than the Arabian, although Augustus later bragged in his *Achievements* about his armies reaching Mariba in Arabia and Napata in Ethiopia "at almost the same time." This was a dash of glory in the style of Caesar – an assertion that there were no bounds Romans could not cross – that cost Augustus little.

Augustus' major focus after his near death in 23 was Parthia. Some years earlier, a pretender to the throne named Tiridates had fled the territory, bringing the son of King Phraates with him. Augustus offered shelter to Tiridates and took Phraates' son to Rome. In 23, Augustus sent the valuable hostage back to his father, asking in exchange for the return of the surviving prisoners and battle standards taken from Crassus' army in 53. Pressure was increased as Augustus made his way to Syria in 20. The king of Parthia's neighbor Armenia had been assassinated, and Augustus was supporting a candidate much friendlier to Rome, Tigranes. To assure the outcome, Tiberius escorted Tigranes to Armenia with troops. Fearful that he might suffer the same fate as the assassinated Armenian king, Phraates sent the standards and surviving Roman captives to Augustus, who brought them back to Rome with much fanfare.

The victory was trumpeted, but even more so was peace – peace brought by Augustus himself. Augustus chose not to celebrate a triumph but consented to a commemorative arch in the Forum, the design for which can be reconstructed through coins. A statue of Augustus stood on top of it, and on either side were Parthians, one of them surrendering a Roman battle standard. There was no image of defeat specifically, and this in a sense magnified Augustus' victory: the existence of the Revered One alone was enough to bring submission to Roman rule and universal peace, from west to east.

Returning from Spain in 19, Agrippa did not celebrate a triumph either – and the Parthian arch perhaps gave a hint that the old practice of individual commanders seeking the vote of a triumph by the Senate was at an end. On

Figure 12.2 A silver coin of Augustus shows the three-bayed arch voted to him by SPQR in 19 BCE after the Parthian settlement. Augustus rides in a four-horse chariot atop the arch, and on the right a Parthian hands over one of the Roman battle standards. (Photo © The Trustees of the British Museum.)

the arch was inscribed a list of all triumphs, going back to the legendary king Romulus, and virtually no space was left to add any after 19. Supreme command over armies resided with Augustus, meaning that all victories could be credited to him – or to male members of his family if they received their own special grants of *imperium*. Roman imperialism was coming into alignment with the new political culture.

ADMINISTRATIVE REFORM: ARMY AND EMPIRE

The booklet Augustus left his fellow consul in 23 with "the list of the forces and of public revenues" reveals how the *princeps* gained effective control over the finances of the whole empire and coordinated them with military needs. This was central to his goal of strengthening the empire. For Augustus and his contemporaries, empire was not conceived so much as a map as it was a list of provinces and friendly kingdoms brought into submission who owed the Roman People either taxes for their protection or military cooperation. A province, in turn, was a list of communities with their particular status, and their obligations. As much as he could, Augustus cultivated good relations with all of these communities as a way to bring stability.

The army was the key component of Augustus' vision of a more stable empire. After Actium, the army shrank significantly, settling at 28 legions. Some served as garrisons in recently conquered territories, while others were deployed to new campaigns. Wherever they were, an ongoing relationship with Caesar Augustus was emphasized. Legions kept their serial numbers, titles, and traditions, and every year swore loyalty to him. Augustus appointed a legionary legate to command each individual legion, and also an officer of Equestrian rank to supervise its camp. Further stability was introduced by a new system of discharge in 13 BCE. Legionaries would no longer receive land in colonies, but rather a large cash payment after 16 years in service. Later, in 5 CE, the term was changed to 20 years. A military treasury was set up to pay an increased discharge bonus, funded by a new 5 percent inheritance tax and a 1 percent tax on auctions. This perfectly illustrates Augustus' ongoing effort to balance military needs with financial resources.

There were significant forces beyond the legionary backbone of the army. Noncitizen auxiliaries were relied on heavily, organized more and more like legionary units with their own numbers and names. When Augustus died in 14 CE, there were probably as many auxiliaries in service as legionaries – around 150,000 of each. There was no standard set terms of service or rewards, but grants of citizenship were common. Standing navies, manned by noncitizens, were stationed in the Tyrrhenian and Adriatic Seas on either side of Italy and patrolled waters beyond. There were also forces in the city of Rome itself, including ultimately nine cohorts of Praetorians, who were Augustus' honor guard, and also nine urban cohorts, a sort of police force.

The armed forces were the main item in the state's budget, which was effectively controlled by Augustus and his personal staff. Other expenses were salaries for governors, grain for Rome and other forms of largesse, public building projects, and the maintenance of Augustus' own household. Income came from bequests to the *princeps*, the produce of his estates, gifts including gold crowns, and – above all – taxes. The *publicani* still collected indirect taxes like harbor dues (see Chapter 9), but their role in direct taxation became more limited. Periodic provincial censuses like the one made in Gaul in 26 BCE kept track of individuals' status and property and were used to help set overall taxation levels for communities. The difficult task of collection was largely left in the hands of local authorities.

Alongside the provincial census, another novelty was the growing presence of procurators. These were agents of Augustus who handled finances in his own provinces and managed the growing portfolio of imperial property, including estates, mines, and quarries. Usually Equestrians, procurators built up experience and expertise and to a degree replaced the *publicani* on which the Senate had relied in earlier days.

Fundamentally, provincials paid for the empire. As Cicero had already put it, they were owed fair government in return. Over time, the division of provinces in 27 between those of Augustus and those that were "public" was institutionalized, and thus there would always be two main types of governors: (1) legates of the *princeps* and (2) proconsuls chosen by lot from the Senate for public provinces. In addition, a few areas were administered by Equestrian prefects or friendly kings. Legates and proconsuls carried out the same tasks as governors had in the late Republic, with a priority on maintaining peace. Strabo, a geographer working in the age of Augustus, shows this arrangement in his description of the administration of Nearer Spain. Augustus' legate had three legions – commanded by subordinates – in the least pacified areas, and another subordinate oversaw the interior, protecting "the interests of those already called 'toga-wearing' or, as you might say, peaceably inclined." Strabo continues: "the governor himself passes his winters administering justice in the regions by the sea, especially in New Carthage and Tarraco, while in summer, he goes the rounds of his province, always making an inspection of things that need correction."

Augustus intervened in all provinces as he saw fit, and he considered his own pronouncements binding. A series of edicts inscribed on stone in Cyrene, a public province, is revealing. In one, Augustus told Roman citizens there that they must pay taxes too, unless they were awarded specific exemption, a good illustration of how Augustus concerned himself with state finances. Another edict introduced a senatorial decree Augustus helped pass, creating a streamlined procedure for accusing governors of embezzling money. "It will be clear to all inhabitants of the provinces," Augustus wrote, "how much concern the Senate and I have that no one of our subjects may suffer unduly any harm or extortion."

Problems were brought to Augustus' attention, and he sought to answer them as a good ruler. When Jews living in Cyrene had the tax they paid to the Temple in Jerusalem confiscated, they sent envoys to Augustus. He wrote back that the Jews must be allowed to preserve their customs, and anybody stealing their "sacred books or sacred monies" would have his property confiscated. In 6 BCE, envoys came to Augustus from the Aegean island of Cnidos. The house of a married couple had been under attack by neighbors, and the couple ordered their slave to dump excrement on the chief attacker and his brother. The slave let go of the chamber pot with its contents and killed the brother. Augustus sided with the homeowners and rebuked the men who "had launched an attack on another's house three times at night with violence and force and were destroying the common security of you all." He asked for his verdict to be inserted into the town's archives. The paternalistic tone was typical of earlier governors. What was new was the way in which one Roman could, and did, intervene in affairs across the empire. This was part of what made him "Augustus" – or, as Greek speakers called him, Sebastos (meaning "Holy").

ADMINISTRATIVE REFORM: THE CITY
OF ROME AND ITALY

Suetonius credits Augustus not only with a great beautification of Rome but also "keeping the city secure even for posterity, to the extent that can be provided for through human ability." While Augustus was reluctant to assume extraordinary powers himself, over time – and in response to popular demand – new positions were created to address chronic problems of fire, flooding, food shortage, and the need for fresh water. The end result was a more professional administration of the city. Senators or Equestrians held the top positions, but they could rely on the expertise of specifically trained slaves or freedmen.

It was not Augustus but Egnatius Rufus, aedile in the 20s BCE, who organized a fire brigade for Rome made up of his own slaves. Despite Egnatius' fate, his example was followed, and subsequent aediles were given a similar force. Still, terrible fires raged. In 7 BCE, Augustus presided over a massive reorganization of Rome, which divided the city into 14 main regions and over 200 formally recognized wards, each of which would elect its own officials. There was a profoundly religious element to this reform (Chapter 13). It was also intended to make Rome run better. Seven fire stations were created for the 14 regions, to which the local officials had access. Yet fires still remained a problem. And so, finally, in 6 CE the Vigiles were created – a standing fire brigade of seven cohorts, probably 3,500 men altogether. Overall command went to an Equestrian prefect appointed by Augustus, and he and the Vigiles (literally "Guards") were empowered to enter houses and penalize those who lacked appropriate firefighting equipment.

More than once Augustus came under pressure to take over the city's food supply. In response to a shortage of grain, he did briefly assume overall responsibility in 22, but quickly relinquished it. Two senators were then appointed to supervise the distribution of the free grain to registered citizens in Rome. Augustus himself continued making occasional extra distributions at his own expense but resisted further responsibility. At one point, complaints were made to him of the high price of wine, and he responded, "By having built several more aqueducts, my son-in-law Agrippa took sufficient care that men shall not go thirsty." Still, a grave shortage of grain in 6 CE finally led to the appointment of high-level officials to oversee the grain and bread supplies. Initially the job was assigned to two ex-consuls but then was transferred to a single Equestrian appointed by the *princeps*.

It was Agrippa who oversaw Rome's water supply until his death, building new aqueducts and training his own slaves to maintain the system. Agrippa left the force to Augustus in his will, Augustus made the force public property, and the Senate then established a board of three supervisors to manage the whole infrastructure with the aid of professional staff. Augustus himself contributed money to the building and repair of aqueducts – much as he continued giving out extra grain in his own name. He also made efforts to keep the Tiber clear to prevent flooding.

Italy experienced far less of an administrative revolution than Rome, since its towns largely continued to handle their own affairs. The peninsula was split up into II distinctive regions – not for direct administration but probably mainly to facilitate the census. Augustus did make a major investment in Italy through the establishment of colonies and he also, increasingly, paid for roads – important links not just among the towns but from Italy to the provinces and their armies. For a time he encouraged other senators to fund road repairs, but as this was typically done out of the plunder of campaigning, it became an ever-harder sell. In 20 BCE, a new post of road commissioner was created, thereby sharing at least the responsibility for overseeing the road network. Just as with provincial affairs, the administration of Italy and of the city of Rome reflected the emerging principate. Augustus avoided formal offices but essentially had great power, buttressed by the financial resources he controlled.

AUGUSTUS AND THE PRINCES (18–6 BCE)

With Augustus accepting a renewal of his provinces by the Senate in 18, his male family members would have important jobs to do in the years ahead. After jointly presiding over a special Centennial Festival in 17 that marked a new age of peace, prosperity, and piety (Chapter 13), Agrippa and Augustus left Rome the next year. Agrippa went to the east and handled business that arose there, such as relations with friendly kings. A tour of Jerusalem, lavishly being rebuilt by Herod, was a highlight. Augustus went to Gaul, which several German tribes had plundered after crossing over the Rhine.

The Alpine regions were unsettled too, and Augustus decided it was time to come to terms with the tough mountain warriors, especially in eastern Switzerland and Austria. In a brilliantly coordinated campaign in 15, Tiberius advanced from the west and Drusus from the south, and together they pressed on toward the Danube. Further campaigns followed in the Alps just north of the French Riviera, a region now put under a prefect. A monumental trophy was erected at La Turbie, now in the tiny country of Monaco, its giant inscription recording how "by his [Augustus'] leadership and under his auspices all the Alpine peoples stretching from the Adriatic to the Mediterranean were brought under the empire of the Roman People."

Figure 12.3 A seated Augustus receives the laurels of victory from his stepsons, Tiberius and Drusus, after their Alpine campaigns. The young men are in military attire, while Augustus wears the toga of a magistrate of the *res publica*. (Photo © The Trustees of the British Museum.)

In keeping with the new imperialism, the victories and the peace they brought belonged to Augustus. Coins showed his two stepsons handing their laurels to him. In a celebratory poem, Horace compared Drusus to the eagle of Jupiter, a way of tactfully expressing his subordination. And in another poem Horace wrote, "the troops, the planning, the divine assistance were supplied by you, Augustus." All marvel at the *princeps*, "ever-present guardian of Italy and imperial Rome." On Augustus' return to Rome in 13, the Senate voted that an Altar of Augustan Peace should be consecrated in the Field of Mars, where every year magistrates, priests, and the Vestal Virgins would sacrifice.

Thus the family of Augustus climbed to a new peak of eminence. In 13, Agrippa's powers were again renewed, as were the provinces of Augustus. Tiberius was consul, and young Gaius Caesar led Roman boys in a horse-riding display known as the Trojan Games. Next year came the great blow: after campaigning in the Balkans and returning to Italy, Agrippa died. A grand funeral was held, and he was buried in Augustus' own Mausoleum rather than a tomb of his own. In death as in life he was to be part of Augustus' house – the house that the emperor saw as ruling Rome, rather than he alone.

With Gaius and Lucius still so young, Tiberius and Drusus instantly became more important. In 12, Tiberius took over for the dead Agrippa in the Balkans, and for two years fought to gain control over the Pannonians, extending Roman rule just south of the Danube. Tiberius was also forced to divorce his wife and marry Agrippa's widow, Julia. Tiberius was becoming the new Agrippa. Meanwhile, Drusus carried out a new census in Gaul and then was sent on campaign against Germanic tribes across the Rhine. This was difficult fighting. Unlike in Julius Caesar's Gaul, it was hard to make alliances here, and keeping the army supplied was a challenge. A navy on the North Sea had to support the legions. Still Drusus successfully made it to the Weser River. At the end of 11, he and Tiberius were awarded triumphal ornaments, decorations that would now be given in place of the full triumphs that had ended in 19. Henceforward, both brothers would have their own separate *imperium*.

More successes followed, and again some setbacks. Tiberius and Drusus accompanied Augustus to Gaul, where he presided over the dedication of a grand altar for Rome and Augustus at Lugdunum (modern Lyon). Sixty Gallic tribes were named in the dedication – a list that well reflected Augustus' emphasis on a rigorously organized *imperium*. Tiberius left Gaul for yet more campaigning in Pannonia. In 9, Drusus, serving as consul, made it as far as the Elbe River and erected trophies on its nearer banks. Returning proudly to the Rhine, where most of his army camped in winter, he was pitched off his horse and died from wounds a month later. Tiberius escorted the body back to Rome for the funeral. Like Agrippa, Drusus was buried in the Mausoleum. The Senate voted him a number of posthumous honors, including an arch on the Appian Way and the name Germanicus, which his descendants also would have. Once more, death led to increased recognition of the importance of Augustus' family. In his eulogy for Drusus, Augustus said that he hoped his Gaius and Lucius would turn out like Drusus.

A huge weight now rested on Tiberius' shoulders. In 8 he finished the nominal pacification of Germany west of the Elbe, and returned to Rome to enter a second consulship at the start of 7 and celebrate a triumph. The people of Rome were feasted, with women attending a special dinner hosted by Livia and Julia. Soon Augustus would need Tiberius in the east: the king of Armenia had died and the new rulers were far less friendly to Rome. Thus in 6, Tiberius had his *imperium* renewed, and he received a five-year grant of tribunician power.

His transformation into the new Agrippa was complete – and he could not stand it. He told Augustus that he needed a break from his duties and sailed off to the island of Rhodes. His marriage to Julia had proved miserable, and he also might have been unhappy at how others, including apparently even Augustus himself, seemed to show greater favor to Gaius and Lucius. The boys were cheered loudly whenever they attended public games, and in 6, votes were cast for Gaius in the consular election, even though Gaius was only around 15 years old. Augustus angrily insisted that Gaius could not hold office now but hinted that he would not object in five years. Tiberius had had to wait until he was nearly 30.

Figure 12.4 Lucius Caesar received the same honors as Gaius, as this silver coin honoring the "*principes* of the young" shows. The brothers stand with the shields and spears presented to them by the Equestrian order. (Photo © The Trustees of the British Museum.)

Tiberius' departure spectacularly revealed the breakup of Augustus' house. Immediately Augustus and his constituents tried to repair the damage. Augustus held a consulship in 5 and in that office oversaw Gaius' official entry into public life. The Senate now let the teenager attend meetings. Senate and People marked out Gaius for a consulship when he was 20. The Equestrian order presented him with silver shields and spears and gave him the new honorific title of "*princeps* of the young" (the "young" specifically referred to younger members of the order but had a wider and more suggestive resonance). Surviving inscriptions reveal that in Spain and on the island of Samos oaths of loyalty were sworn to Augustus and his sons. Samos' mainland neighbor Sardis staged elaborate ceremonies in honor of Gaius' coming of age.

Tiberius' departure and the promotion of Gaius Caesar revealed that although the emerging principate might have been a fragile plant, it had sunk deep roots. With Tiberius gone, the Roman world suddenly felt less stable, but the Roman world rallied. The dialogue of honors that Senate and People, and many more, had with Augustus could be had with a much younger Caesar. Princes held out the promise of continuing the stability associated with Augustus. Because it served the interests of so many across the empire, the principate would survive.

FURTHER READING

The Cambridge Ancient History (2nd ed.) Vol. 10 provides excellent coverage of the political, military, and administrative history of Rome after the battle of Actium. J. Richardson, *Augustan Rome 44 BC to AD 14* (Edinburgh, 2012) offers a careful year-by-year narrative filled with insight, as does A. Goldsworthy, *Augustus: First Emperor of Rome* (New Haven, 2014). More thematic in approach are the valuable introductions by A. Wallace-Hadrill, *Augustan Rome* (London, 1993); W. Eck, *The Age of Augustus* (Malden, MA, 2007); K. Galinsky, *Augustus: Introduction to the Life of an Emperor* (New York, 2012); B. Levick, *Augustus: Image and Substance* (Harlow, 2010). G. Rowe, *Princes and Political Culture: The New Tiberian Senatorial Decrees* (Ann Arbor, 2002) brilliantly maps out the new political relationships.

Good collections of essays are F. Millar and E. Segal (eds.), *Caesar Augustus: Seven Aspects* (Oxford, 1984); K. A. Raaflaub and M. Toher (eds.), *Between Republic and Empire: Interpretations of Augustus and His Principate* (Berkeley, 1990); K. Galinsky (ed.), *The Cambridge Companion to the Age of Augustus* (Cambridge, 2005); J. Edmondson (ed.), *Augustus* (Edinburgh, 2009). Chaps. 10–16 of Fergus Millar, *Rome, the Greek World, and the East* Vol. 1 (Chapel Hill, 2002), offer an original view of "the Augustan Revolution." Other important essays are A. Wallace-Hadrill, "*Civilis princeps*: Between Citizen and King," *Journal of Roman Studies* 72 (1982), 32–48, and "Roman Arches and Greek Honours: The Language of Power at Rome," *Proceedings of the Cambridge Philological Society* 36 (1990), 143–81; J. Rich and J. H. C. Williams, "*Leges et iura p. R. restituit*: A New Aureus of Octavian and the Settlement of 28–27 B.C.," *Numismatic Chronicle* 159 (1999), 169–213; C. B. Rose, "The Parthians in Augustan Rome," *American Journal of Archaeology* 109 (2005), 21–75.

Particularly helpful are editions of the major sources: J. W. Rich, *Cassius Dio: The Augustan Settlement (Roman History 53–55.9)* (Warminster, 1990); P. M. Swan, *The Augustan Succession: An Historical Commentary on Cassius Dio's Roman History, Book 55–56 (9 B.C.–A.D. 14)* (Oxford, 2004); A. E. Cooley, *Res Gestae divi Augusti: Text, Translation, and Commentary* (Cambridge, 2009); D. Wardle, *Suetonius: Life of Augustus* (Oxford, 2014).

13

———

THE NEW AGE: REFASHIONING CULTURE
AND SOCIETY (30–5 BCE)

After the battle of Actium, the province of Asia decided to award a gold crown to "the person who found the greatest honors for the god" – the "god" being Augustus. A winner was named only about 20 years later, when the governor of Asia, an aristocratic friend of Augustus named Paullus Fabius Maximus, proposed that all the province's cities should start their calendars on the emperor's birthday, September 23rd. Time had seemed to begin anew with Augustus, Paullus said flatteringly. "He has given to the whole world a different appearance, a world that would have met its ruin . . . if he had not been born." In its decree putting Paullus' proposal into effect, the provincial council echoed his language. For them, Augustus was "a savior who brought war to an end and set all things in order" and surpassed all benefactors, in the past and even the future!

Perhaps surprisingly, similar claims were made several years later, around 1 BCE, in Ovid's *Art of Love*, a three-book poem instructing men and women in Augustan Rome how to find and win over one another in love. It is a work full of useful tips. Don't ask her age as a censor would, Ovid instructed his male readers. And avoid the woman who only thinks of her wool working during sex. Rome draws in pretty women from the whole world, the poet joyfully proclaimed, adding that Augustus' buildings and shows were some of the best pick-up spots. "In the past, there was rough simplicity; now Rome is golden and possesses the vast wealth of the conquered world," he wrote. And the city looked all the better for it. "Look at what the Capitol is now and what it was," Ovid enthused. "You would say the new one belongs to a different Jupiter." Compare the new Julian Senate house, marble clad, with the old one made of twigs and branches. "I congratulate myself that I was only born now; this age suits my nature well."

For all that Augustus emphasized the survival of the Senate and other traditional institutions after Actium, men and women across the Roman world increasingly thought they were living in a new age. The places they lived in really did look different. Architects transformed the appearance of Rome with dazzling buildings of marble, such as the Temple of Apollo on the Palatine. There were similar building programs in Italian and provincial cities. In Pompeii, a public priestess named Eumachia built a huge building on the eastern edge of the Forum that was dedicated to Augustan Concord and Piety. Houses were decorated with new types of paintings. Lamps, dishes, and cups – mass produced in clay and covered with a shiny red glaze – featured totally new designs. Brought out for use at dinner or drinking parties, these bright objects seemed literally to embody the peace and the sense of prosperity that had returned after civil war.

Augustus and his family were at the center of the emerging sense that Romans lived in a new era. Images of the imperial family could be seen everywhere. In setting up statues of the *princeps* or building temples for him, individuals and communities helped create new ideas of what it meant to be Roman beyond the old city-state activities of voting or fighting under the yearly consuls. Writers such as the poet Horace and the historian Livy – haunted by the long and terrible civil war – produced literary masterpieces that were also cornerstones of new Roman identities. They shared with Augustus an urgent feeling that good relations with the gods must be restored. The age of Augustus was not just a remapping of politics. It remapped religion too.

THE NEW CITY OF MARBLE

Part of what made Ovid's Rome and eventually many places beyond look so fresh was a proliferation of portraits of Augustus and his family in a radically new style. In earlier decades, Romans had preferred to show themselves old or at least middle-aged, their faces lined with wrinkles reflecting wisdom and experience. Augustus, by contrast, was always shown as youthful, mostly but not exclusively with idealized features. Only Suetonius' biography discloses that the *princeps* was actually quite short and wore high heels to compensate, that his teeth were rotten, and that as he grew older he sometimes limped. By always showing Augustus with a thick head of hair and smooth skin, artists were bestowing on him the near perfection of classical Greek masterpieces, even suggesting that Augustus was godlike. Portraits of his wife, Livia, and the rest of his family were in a similar style. They all retained enough individual features, though, like Augustus' jug ears or Livia's small but determined mouth, to make them clearly recognizable – and to this extent they appeared mortal. After Actium, official portraits in

Rome always depicted Augustus as a magistrate, general, or priest – never in the heroic nudity typical of Hellenistic kings.

Portraits proclaimed the dawning of a new age of peace. A prime example is a marble statue of Augustus found at a villa belonging to Livia in Prima Porta on the outskirts of Rome – quite possibly a copy of a bronze original made soon after the return of the Parthian standards in 20 BCE. At the center of Augustus' breastplate is shown a representative of Parthia – clearly identified by his un-Roman trousers – surrendering one of the standards. The historical event is given a cosmic significance: the personification of the

Figure 13.1 The statue of Augustus from Livia's villa at Prima Porta. Next to him on a scary-looking, piranha-like dolphin rides Venus' son Cupid, reminding the viewer that Augustus also claimed descent from the goddess. Vatican Museums, Rome, Italy. (Photo Alinari/Art Resource, NY.)

sky can be seen above, with the sun in his chariot, while below the Parthian is Mother Earth, with a cornucopia and two infants symbolizing increased prosperity. On either side of the central scene are western barbarians taken captive. The portrait thus suggests that world order depends on Augustus.

An even more ambitious articulation of the new age was the marble Altar of Augustan Peace. It was voted by the Senate in 13 BCE after Augustus' successful tour of the west and dedicated three years later, on Livia's birthday, in 9. The altar itself shows scenes of sacrifice – perhaps the ritual that was to be performed each year by all of Rome's priests and the Vestal Virgins on the anniversary of Augustus' return. Far more striking, though, is the sculpture on the walls surrounding the altar. On the lower levels, evergreen acanthus leaves intertwine with vines and flowers in an exuberant but balanced arrangement signifying the plentitude and order brought by peace. Above is a series of reliefs, including one of the Trojan ancestors of the Romans, Venus' son Aeneas, sacrificing after his arrival in the promised land of Italy. Down the two long sides streams a procession with dozens of figures: heralds, priests, magistrates, attendants, senators and their families, Augustus, Agrippa, Gaius, Lucius, Livia, and other members of the emperor's household. Quite possibly it is the festive thanksgiving on the occasion of Augustus' return in 13 being shown. But it is also a more timeless celebration of the peace that has come with Augustus and his victories, an event that depends above all on honoring the gods.

Figure 13.2 The new age proclaimed in marble, the Altar of Augustan Peace. In the upper panel on the right of the door, Aeneas can be seen sacrificing after his arrival in the promised land of Italy. (Photo Wikimedia Commons.)

Figure 13.3 A detail of the procession that unfolds along the southern side of the Altar of Augustan Peace. The veiled man is Agrippa, and holding onto his toga is a child who wears non-Roman costume, including a torque necklace and a royal diadem – most likely the child of one of the many client rulers Augustus relied on to maintain peace in the Roman empire. (Photo Wikimedia Commons.)

More than anything, the temples Augustus built showed his piety best, and among the most important of them was the Temple of Apollo on the Palatine. Augustus had been acquiring real estate on the prestigious hill to build a huge palace for himself, but in the later 30s decided instead to dedicate the land to the god he increasingly saw as his protector. The temple was finished in 28 and set new standards of lavishness. It was made of solid white marble from Luna in northern Italy (modern Carrara), where major quarrying had only begun under Julius Caesar. The column capitals were Corinthian – decorated with the same acanthus leaves seen on the Altar of Augustan Peace – a style Augustan architects made standard for grand temples in Rome and across the empire.

Only a few fragments of the Apollo temple now survive, but literary accounts, including enthusiastic descriptions by contemporary poets, round out the picture. From them we learn that the temple's doors were made of ivory and showed Apollo in his traditional role as avenger, driving out the Gallic barbarians who tried to spoil his famous sanctuary at Delphi. The main cult statue of the god – an original Greek masterpiece – showed him wearing flowing robes and playing the lyre in his role as a patron of poetry. In the portico around the completed temple, Augustus set up Greek and Latin libraries, open to the public. The whole complex thus was a proclamation of Augustus' piety and his devotion to culture. As he later boasted in the *Achievements*, he melted down silver statues of himself and used the money to make offerings of golden tripods in the temple. This was a vivid way to distance himself from the more open quest for supremacy of the triumviral years.

It would be impossible here to describe all of the buildings Augustus went on to sponsor in Rome, and that in a sense is the point. Until the year 18 BCE or so, other senators were sometimes allowed and even encouraged to build, just as they had for centuries before. Munatius Plancus, for example, used the spoils of his Alpine campaigns in the late 40s to rebuild the Temple of Saturn in the Forum, which also housed the treasury. Then, in a break with tradition that must have upset some senators, the opportunity was afforded only to Augustus' closest associates and was ultimately restricted to his family. While Augustus was in the west from 27 to 24, Agrippa carried out major construction on the Field of Mars. The old wooden Saepta was replaced with a much more elaborate marble structure. It was used not just for voting but also for gladiatorial shows and displays of art, arguably of more interest than elections to the hundreds of thousands living in the city. Adjacent to the Saepta was Agrippa's Porticus of the Argonauts, named after a cycle of paintings depicting the legendary band of heroes. And then, outdoing even himself, Agrippa constructed the city's first grand set of public baths with heated rooms. The women of Augustus' family built too. His sister Octavia memorialized her son Marcellus after his premature death in 23 with Greek and Latin libraries in his name, near the theater that Augustus built as his tribute.

Of course, the Senate as a body could still plan and execute monuments like the Altar of Augustan Peace. Augustus' permission was essential, though, and commissions like the Parthian Arch in the Forum (Chapter 12) obviously redounded to the glory of Augustus. One way or another, Augustus and his family came to overshadow the senators.

An account of Rome by the contemporary geographer Strabo, focusing on the Field of Mars, gives firsthand impressions of Augustus' urban interventions. A member of a prominent family of Pontus in Asia Minor, Strabo had travelled widely in the east and was well familiar with cities like Alexandria, whose attractions he celebrated in his work. In earlier days, he sniffed, the citizens of Rome set little store on the beautification of their city. "Later generations, however, and particularly those of today and in my time, have not fallen short in this and indeed they have filled the city with many lovely structures," he wrote approvingly. As Strabo saw it, Augustus and his family carried on the work begun by Pompey and Julius Caesar. The Field of Mars now held many of the city's finest buildings, such as Agrippa's baths.

It was littered with sculptures and boasted large grassy spaces for people to play ball games and watch grand entertainments be staged. The hilltops rising above the River Tiber made for splendid vistas. All in all, the Field was "a spectacle that one can hardly draw away from," he wrote, comparing it favorably with the old Forum.

Strabo almost seems to be suggesting here that Rome had turned into a Hellenistic city, but in fact Augustus was too zealous of Roman tradition ever to let that happen. While he rattled off his new works in his *Achievements*, he also recalled with great pride all the buildings he restored. In the year 28 BCE alone, he claimed, he refurbished 82 shrines. This set his urbanism apart from the planning of Caesar, which was focused on new and grandiose projects. Still, Rome had achieved an appearance that seemed worthy of the head of the world state, and its latest buildings were trendsetters. Even better than the lists of his *Achievements*, it was Augustus' boast that he had found Rome brick and left it marble that summed up the transformation. He spoke literally – the center of Rome was now a forest of marble columns – but also metaphorically. Marble asserted Rome's equality with cities such as Athens that had long used the stone for its buildings. The stone's fineness and prevalence testified to a new devotion to the gods and the prosperity of the people. The range of marbles used illustrated the breadth of Roman conquest. Their durableness suggested the stability brought by the *princeps* after years of civil war.

TAKING ON THE GREEKS: NEW LITERARY CLASSICS

Along with beautiful buildings came some of the most beautiful Latin poetry ever written. In the 20s BCE, Vergil produced *The Aeneid*, his epic masterpiece about Rome's Trojan founder Aeneas, while Horace wrote his first three books of *Odes*, lyric poems that often touched on the brevity of life and the consequent need to cherish happy memories. A later fourth book of *Odes*, finished around 13 BCE, dwelled more fully on the achievements of Augustus and his stepsons, Tiberius and Drusus, especially their Alpine campaigns. A distinct school of love poets also flourished in the 20s, the finest of whom was the Umbrian Propertius.

At least some of the credit for this outpouring is owed to another friend of Augustus, Maecenas, who provided financial and other support for Vergil, Horace, and Propertius. While content to operate behind the scenes politically – he always deliberately remained an Equestrian, like Atticus (Chapter 10) – Maecenas had no hesitation about flaunting his exquisite sense of taste. He strode around Rome in daringly loose clothing of the finest fabrics, built a palatial estate with the city's first heated swimming pool, and was notorious for love affairs with women and men alike, including the male erotic dancer Bathyllus. Yet like Atticus, Maecenas was eager to see Roman culture advance, gladly making available one of his freedmen to Augustus to help organize the libraries built by Octavia, for example. He encouraged poets because they would not only enhance Augustus' image and justify his authority as the artists did. They would bring glory to Rome.

In comparison with trailblazers of the previous generation, like Catullus, there is a more self-consciously monumental quality to the work of Horace and Vergil. As Horace proudly asserted in his *Odes*: "I have finished a monument more lasting than bronze and loftier than the pyramids of kings." Linking himself to the emerging idea of an eternal Rome, he promised, "I shall not wholly die . . . while pontiff and silent Vestal shall climb the Capitol Hill." Vergil makes no such direct claims in his *Aeneid* but does include descriptions of major works of art. These include a temple with a cycle of paintings depicting the Trojan War and also a shield created for Aeneas with scenes of Roman history. The shield's depictions culminate with Augustus' triple triumph in 29 and then Augustus on the Palatine, "seated on the snow-white threshold of shining Apollo." The various descriptions invite the reader to consider how Vergil managed to write an epic that was both mythological and contemporary at once – a sequel to Homer's classic *Iliad* that commemorated the new age.

For both poets a key theme is *pietas*: duty to gods, country, and one's family. *Sum pius Aeneas*, "I am dutiful Aeneas," Vergil's hero announces at the start, while clutching statues of the gods he snatched from Troy as it burnt to the ground. He goes on to tell the queen of Carthage, Dido, with whom he has a doomed love affair, the full story of his escape. He had to carry his father out on his back – an image that became a popular decorative device in Augustan art. Horace's early books of *Odes* are haunted by the idea that a lack of *pietas* led to Rome's civil wars. "Neglected, the gods have inflicted many woes upon sorrow-filled Italy," he laments. Crucially, Horace dwells on the horrors of civil war without taking sides – to do so might only reignite battle. Welcoming back to Italy a friend who had fought for Brutus and Cassius at Philippi, Horace subtly praises Augustus by asking, "Who has now restored you to citizenship, to your ancestral gods, and to the sky of Italy?" For Augustus' own return from Spain in 24 BCE, Horace wrote an ode that pictures a joyous thanksgiving, with men and women piously celebrating the success abroad – the proper kind of military victory. "This day, truly festal for me, will banish dark worries; insurrection or violent death I shall not fear while Caesar holds the earth." This is a poetic expression of what the artists of the Altar of Peace later rendered visually.

Horace and Vergil articulate the idea that the Romans have a special destiny to rule the world, despite the interruptions of civil war. Unlocking that destiny requires going back to early times, to the arrival in Italy of Aeneas with his son Iulus, the ancestor of the Julian family. Early in the *Aeneid*, Jupiter unfolds it all for Venus. Aeneas, he says, "shall wage a great war in Italy, shall crush fearsome peoples, and shall establish for his men laws and city walls." Later, Romulus, the son of the priestess Ilia and the god Mars, shall establish Rome itself. Finally, hundreds and hundreds of years later, "From this noble line a Trojan shall be born, Caesar, who shall extend empire to the Ocean and glory to the stars, Julius his name, handed down from great Iulus." The myth of Trojan origins allowed the Romans to think of themselves as equal to the Greeks, authorized to conquer the Hellenistic east.

The *Aeneid* was an extraordinarily ambitious undertaking, and it succeeded brilliantly. It is not simply a sequel to Homer. By telling of the wanderings of Aeneas and then the wars he had to fight in Italy, Vergil combines the plotlines of Homer's *Odyssey* and *Iliad* into one poem, and so arguably outdoes Homer. *Pius Aeneas* is neither an Achilles nor an Odysseus, but rather a man devoted to the welfare of his countrymen, even future countrymen. Rome's historical fate – also a totally un-Homeric concept – is not just to rule the world but also to fuse different peoples and traditions, to win over the Italians, and ultimately to integrate the civilized east with the brave but untutored west. It will take centuries, and Vergil suggests that the process is still ongoing: Jupiter's prophecy early in the poem is in the future tense. It is not for Aeneas to know, perhaps not even for contemporary readers fully to experience. Later, when Aeneas descends into the Underworld, his father shows him the souls of the future great men of Rome, including Augustus, "son of the deified, who shall again establish an age of gold in Latium." Note the future again: Vergil is inviting readers to think about the effort that goes into building a flourishing state. The poem succeeds because of its suggestiveness, and also the way it recognizes the toll that the quest for Roman greatness can take on individuals, beginning with Aeneas.

Love poets tended to engage with Augustus in a more detached way, while still ultimately contributing to the sense of a new age. Propertius' world revolved around his mistress, Cynthia, whose name provided the title for his first collection of poems, released around 29 BCE. As with Catullus, the reader gets the highs and the lows. Early on, Cynthia's beauty is celebrated – it lies not in her sporting the latest hairstyle or see-through silks that were all the rage, but simply in her naked form, like a goddess in a painting. But in a later poem, the rapture has given way to worry. Cynthia is dallying at the scandalous resort of Baiae, and the poet hopes she is only playing with a toy boat or swimming, not listening to the "seductive whispers" of a rival. Propertius is consumed by her and defiantly renounces any duties as a citizen-soldier. Let Augustus fight the wars! In a later work, Propertius contemplates the expedition to Parthia of 20 BCE and expresses hope that he will live to see a triumphal parade with "Caesar's chariot laden with spoils." But as he looks on, he will be "resting on my sweetheart's bosom." This can of course be seen as an ingenious way of celebrating Augustus, and Propertius' successor Ovid later used the same trick in his poetry.

Rivaling the poets in artistry was Livy, the major prose writer of the age. Working steadily beginning in about the year 30 BCE, he ultimately produced 142 books of Roman history, from Romulus to Augustus – the majority, including the later parts, sadly lost. From the start Livy knew it would be an "immense undertaking," but he hoped that immersion in the past could be an antidote to "the evils that our age has been witnessing for so many years." Like Horace, he was concerned especially with morality. What sort of lives had men lived in earlier ages? What qualities contributed to the growth of Roman power? Rome's vast history, Livy stated, allowed all to "behold lessons of every kind, as though they were displayed on a conspicuous monument."

The fourth-century BCE hero Camillus furnishes a fine example. When Rome had been nearly destroyed by Gallic invaders and citizens thought of moving away, Livy has him deliver a stirring speech. In Rome, Camillus successfully argues, "no place is not filled with a sense of religion and gods . . . here are all the gods who will be favorable if you remain." This is a clear echo of the antiquarian scholarship of Varro (Chapter 10), heeded closely by Augustus as he undertook to recover what were thought to be lost religious traditions.

RELIGIOUS AND MORAL REFORM

Preserving and even reviving Rome's religion was a top priority for Augustus and made him seem sacred. He brought out of obscurity several minor priesthoods, such as the Arval Brethren, by holding them himself or recruiting distinguished members of society to fill them. Augustus also held membership in all four of the major priestly colleges, something no Roman had ever done before. When his colleague in the triumvirate Lepidus died in 12 BCE, opening up the post of *pontifex maximus*, Augustus secured that too. Traditionally, the *pontifex maximus* lived in a special residence in the Forum, next to the shrine of Vesta. Augustus dedicated a new shrine for the hearth goddess adjacent to his own house on the Palatine, thereby giving it a sense of sacredness. As *pontifex maximus* Augustus showed even more zealous concern for Roman religion – throwing out unreliable books of prophecies, for example, or ensuring that there were good candidates to serve as Vestal Virgins – and the post essentially was turned into an overall head of religion. All succeeding emperors took it.

Rituals were revived, reinvented, and newly created. The Lupercal – the cave at the foot of the Palatine Hill where Romulus and Remus were said to have been nursed by the she-wolf – was restored, and the festival of the Lupercalia on February 15 altered. Probably the young priests were now made to wear more than loincloths and women did not bare themselves. The annual sacrifice at the Altar of Augustan Peace, on the other hand, was a typical new ritual, involving not just one set of priests but all of them, as well as the magistrates. New rituals tended to be less associated with the old gods and instead focused on the successes of Augustus and his house. Augustus' various returns to Rome after his provincial tours provided prime opportunities for creating them. The yearly calendar gradually was filled up with days honoring the *princeps* and his family, observing their birthdays and other personal milestones.

Holidays, anniversaries, and rituals mattered to a wide range of Romans. Calendars inscribed on marble have been discovered in the towns of Italy, marked with entries such as this one for January 16th: "Imperator Caesar was called Augustus, when he himself, for the seventh time, and Agrippa for the third time, were consuls." Local officers of one ward of Rome set up a monthly calendar along with a list of the consuls from 43 BCE, the year of Augustus' first consulship. Also included was a list of the local officers from 7 BCE, the year Augustus reorganized the city into 14 regions and more than 200 wards, in each of which his own protecting spirits (*lares*) were now worshipped as part of the traditional crossroads cult.

New cult altars – fashioned out of marble, of course – survive and show how ex-slave officials attached themselves to Augustus and perpetuated the emerging mythology of the new age. On one, we see the officials themselves sacrificing, Aeneas' arrival in Italy, and the goddess Victory carrying the golden shield awarded to Augustus by the Senate and the People of Rome in 27 BCE. Shared stories and symbols like these gave Romans a new collective identity.

Restoring the favor of the gods was crucial to Rome's success, as Augustus saw it, and so too was reversing a perceived collapse in morality. Troubles began in the home, Horace proclaimed in one of his sternest *Odes*, with young women thinking only of sex. "While her husband is in his cups," he wrote of one, "she seeks out younger men as lovers," and her husband even approves. It was not by people like this that the Punic Wars were won! By 18 BCE Augustus felt ready to confront the issue with major legislation requiring all adult citizens to be married, even widows and widowers. Those who failed to comply were penalized financially, especially by the loss of inheritance rights, while rewards were offered to those who did marry and have children.

At least in spirit, this legislation recalled speeches by the censors of the good old days, who harangued male citizens on the need to marry. Far more radical was a law passed in 18, which for the first time made adultery a criminal offense. Adultery was strictly defined as sexual activity with a married woman. The law also forbade men sexual activity with widows, unwed girls of respectable status, and boys and men of respectable status. This meant that males or females of low status were still available to men, whereas the respectable woman could only be with her husband. Respectable women's sexual activity, in other words, was to be controlled with the utmost rigor. A court was set up to try the accused, and the penalties were stiff. Those found guilty were formally disgraced, banished to separate islands, and heavily fined. A husband who knew his wife was committing adultery and failed to divorce and prosecute her could be charged with pimping.

Both laws were intensely disliked, especially by the high-status Romans they were most clearly aimed at. Men and women alike relied on tricks to evade them. Men would declare their engagement to infant girls, since betrothal provided an exemption from penalties on the unmarried. Or they might marry in advance of an expected inheritance and then quickly divorce. At least one woman belonging to a senatorial family, Vistilia, registered as a prostitute, so she could have extramarital sex. In 9 CE, amidst efforts to tamp down on some of these evasions, members of the Equestrian order protested publicly at the games, and Augustus was none too pleased.

His persistence is to be explained, ultimately, not just by an aversion to immoral behavior but by a conviction that the crackdown was essential to preserve the social hierarchy. Augustus wanted the top members of society to be role models for all. Thus he not only wanted senators married and having children, he also forbade them or anyone in their family to marry an ex-slave. He also instituted stricter rules about their participation at Senate meetings. In exchange, he gave members of this more precisely defined senatorial order front-row seats in the theater, just ahead of the Equestrians. Ultimately, Augustus' own notion of the "new age" was wrapped up closely with morality – much more so than it was for somebody like Ovid.

Still, by the end of 18 BCE many could agree that Rome was on a new path. Old temples were restored, gleaming new ones built. Civil war was a memory, Spain was fully conquered, and the shame of Parthia was erased. The meaning of Rome's earliest days was powerfully reinterpreted. It was time formally to announce the new age, and a means was at hand to do so. By tradition, "Saecular" games were supposed to be held once a century (*saeculum*, in Latin), but now an oracle conveniently turned up, redefining the *saeculum* as a period of 110 years.

That permitted the celebration of 17. Augustus and his son-in-law Agrippa led it, presiding over three days and nights of sacrifices – some more traditional, others quite new. They asked the gods to grant "safety forever, victory, and good health" to the Roman People, to favor the legions, and to be well disposed to their own family. Horace was commissioned to write a hymn sung separately by choirs of boys and girls in front of the Temple of Apollo on the Palatine. "Now Faith, Peace, and Honor, along with old-fashioned Modesty and Virtue so long neglected, venture to return, and blessed Plenty with overflowing horn is visible," the children chanted. In his last book of *Odes*, Horace used the same style, assembling long lists of Augustus' achievements. The future tenses of Vergil's *Aeneid* disappeared. The Golden Age is here, he wrote: "your time, Caesar."

LIVING IN A GOLDEN AGE?

The décor of private residences in Rome and Italy was transformed in the age of Augustus. The painted frescoes that were the ancient equivalent of wallpaper were in a totally new style. Bombastic depictions of grandiose architecture receding deep into the background gave way to simpler views of more natural landscapes. Single scenes would be framed by a painted architectural niche, inviting the viewer to look in more closely, as if to be suffused with feelings of serenity. Some walls were painted to evoke whole picture galleries, with paintings in a range of styles and subjects that would make the owner of the house look cultured and could invite learned discussion of the art. In some rooms, artists gave up the quest for three-dimensional depth altogether, flattening out the architecture, making columns impossibly thin, and adding quite elegant but artificial decorative motifs such as vines, birds, and Egyptian sphinxes. Central scenes showing bucolic landscapes dominated in their calmness. The decorative stuccoes on ceilings, created with stamps, featured similar contents: more rustic sanctuaries, with sacrifices in progress. Overall, decorations seemed to harken back to the *pietas* of earlier days now being restored, while also sometimes featuring symbols familiar from official monuments, such as flying Victories or Apollonian tripods.

Furniture and serving vessels from the period have similar motifs. Marble tables that would have been proudly displayed in a house's atrium used sphinxes as supports and were decorated with acanthus and vines similar to those on the Altar of Augustan Peace. Bronze braziers also were propped up by sphinxes or were fashioned to look like tripods. A huge silver service, found in a villa at Boscoreale just north of Pompeii in 1895 – probably hidden for safekeeping during the eruption of Mt. Vesuvius and then never retrieved – includes Augustan-era dishes decorated with plants and animals, as the Altar of Augustan Peace and other monuments were. One of the cups shows Augustus' stepson Tiberius riding in a triumphal chariot. Another features Augustus himself, seated, granting a pardon to a barbarian on his knees, while the other side depicts Venus presenting Augustus with a statue of

Figure 13.4 A painted bedroom from a villa at Boscoreale, near Pompeii, now on display in the Metropolitan Museum of Art in New York. The elaborate architectural vistas are typical of a style in favor down to around 15 BCE. The Metropolitan Museum of Art, New York, USA. (Image © The Metropolitan Museum of Art/Art Resource, NY.)

Victory. Passed along at drinking parties, cups like these literally unfolded scenes of the new mythology of Augustus as the creator of peace.

Even for humbler consumers there were new styles of lamps and pots, manufactured in large numbers out of clay from molds. The lamps were now covered in a shiny red glaze – evoking the sheen of more-precious metals – and featured a large central space that could be decorated. Sometimes there were overt references to the *princeps*, for example an image of Victory holding the Shield of Virtue awarded in 27 BCE, inscribed "FOR SAVING CITIZENS." Other lamps used the same design, but the shield was inscribed with wishes for a prosperous new year. These likely were made for the traditional exchange of gifts Romans made on January 1.

Red glaze for pottery now totally eclipsed the earlier black glaze. At least for a time, production was centered in Maecenas' hometown of Arretium,

Figure 13.5 A painted bedroom from a villa in Rome, now on display in the Palazzo Massimo in Rome. The style is typical of the Augustan period: the overwhelming architectural vistas are gone, and viewers can lose themselves in the details of the individual paintings, many of which evoke earlier Greek masterpieces. Museo Nazionale Romano, Rome, Italy. (Photo Scala/Art Resource, NY.)

perhaps not coincidentally. Even after production spread, it was still called "Arretine," as a sort of brand name, just like Champagne today. Small workshops – staffed largely by freedmen – made a good profit exporting their dishes to the provinces. Especially popular were those with erotic scenes.

Clearly even objects of everyday life took on a new appearance in the age of Augustus, and historians have wondered how consciously adopters of these items were expressing allegiance to the *princeps*. Whoever bought or commissioned the first lamps with Victory and the Shield of Virtue or the Boscoreale cup with the *princeps* must have been. And the same is probably true of those who decorated their houses or tombs with copies of the crown of oak leaves awarded to Augustus and displayed on his own house. But much of the imagery, including that of the new wall paintings, is not overtly political and could spring more from a desire for something new and different that would reflect the growing sense of tranquility and economic prosperity after the turbulence and destruction of civil war.

Figure 13.6 Tiberius rides in a triumphal chariot on this silver drinking cup found at a villa at Boscoreale. A slave crowns him with laurel and behind him follow several officers including one wearing a torque: he might be a Gaul. Louvre Museum, Paris, France. (Photo © RMN-Grand Palais/Art Resource, NY.)

A comparison could be made here with the love poets Propertius and his successor Ovid. In their works, Augustus and his new buildings are essentially in the backdrop, parties and erotic encounters in the forefront. "I was born unsuited for glory, unsuited for war," Propertius boasted. Poets were offering new definitions of what it meant to be Roman, and so were the manufacturers of the pots. Of course, after the legislation of 18 BCE, writers had to be more circumspect – which is why in the *Art of Love* Ovid insisted, unconvincingly, that he was writing only about legally permitted love affairs.

More than expressing allegiance to Augustus, Romans enjoying new luxuries or even their cheaper versions might have been asserting their own status. Veterans settled in colonies or ex-slaves holding new offices or provincials recognized with Roman citizenship could celebrate their enhanced position in society by dining off fine Arretine dishes, drinking at lamp-lit parties, or decorating their walls with the latest designs. Even Maecenas, whose own career would hardly have been possible a generation earlier, or the many Italians joining the Senate for the first time, had reason to celebrate their arrival in society, and their tastes were especially important in shaping the new culture. But even if new styles and new goods were less about political allegiance than has sometimes been thought, they were politically important because they satisfied Romans of many different social levels. The days of stern senators telling the *plebs* that stone theaters would corrupt them were over. It was left to Augustus to play the role of censor, with results not entirely happy.

MARBLE CITIES MULTIPLIED

Just as they embraced new dishes or lamps, communities across Italy, and ultimately the empire, embarked on building projects inspired by Rome's. When it came to temples for Augustus or statues of him and his family, expressing allegiance was a clear goal. But once again, new buildings, which also included theaters and baths, allowed those who commissioned and paid for them to elevate their own and their communities' status. In the process, communal identity was redefined so that more and more men and women across the empire could feel that they were Roman – thus further carrying out the city's transformation into a world state.

The urban makeover of Pompeii in the lifetime of Augustus is especially well known and gives a vivid sense of what was possible. (For its earlier history, see Chapter 6.) As in Rome itself, old temples were restored and new ones were built. The local magistrate and priest Marcus Tullius built a temple to Augustan Fortune that was faced in marble. "Augustan" deities (like "Augustan Peace" in Rome) became widespread. Another major building in Pompeii, built and paid for by the priestess Eumachia, was dedicated to Augustan Harmony and Piety. Its magnificent marble door, decorated with acanthus scrolls, was in the finest Augustan style.

One well-established Pompeian family, the Holconii, paid to rebuild the town's theater, tricking it out in marble and restructuring the seating to make sure the town's leaders were most prominent – including of course the Holconii themselves. Preserved in the town is a marble statue of one member of the family, M. Holconius Rufus, made out to look like the war god Mars. Although he almost certainly never served in the army, Holconius was granted an honorary military office by Augustus that brought with it Equestrian status. The inscription on the base of his statue reveals this and also shows that Holconius served as a priest of Augustus in Pompeii, leading worship of, or on behalf of, the *princeps*. His story shows how, just like freedmen in Rome or veterans, local notables were recognized by Augustus, and they recognized him in turn, while also emulating the emperor's glorious beautification of Rome. An important basis for Augustus' success was the way the principate provided opportunities for men like Holconius to elevate themselves, marble statue and all.

Figure 13.7 The Pompeian bigwig M. Holconius Rufus. Though he probably had no military career, he is made to look like Mars. Romans of many statuses enjoyed being depicted as gods. Museo Archeologico Nazionale, Naples, Italy. (Photo Scala/ Ministero per i Beni e le Attività culturali/Art Resource, NY.)

With a far less developed tradition of urbanism, the transformation of the western provinces beyond Italy was more radical. Augusta Emerita, founded in Lusitania in 25 BCE, and other colonies established for veterans were trailblazers. The name "Augusta Emerita," which has partly survived in the town's modern Spanish name (Mérida), is one of many that honored Augustus.

Figure 13.8 New styles of architecture spread across western Europe in the age of Augustus, as the Maison Carrée at Nîmes shows. It in turn inspired Thomas Jefferson's State Capitol in Richmond, Virginia. (Photo Wikimedia Commons.)

Others included Augusta Praetoria, modern Aosta in Italy; Augustodunum, modern Autun in France; and Augusta Vindelicorum, modern Augsburg in Germany. The colonies themselves were also meant to aggrandize Augustus. Augusta Emerita was established at the confluence of two rivers and given a deliberately imposing appearance, with walls of stone and a formidably long bridge leading to one of the main gates. In the years that followed, the city acquired a theater built by Agrippa, according to an inscription over one of its doorways, as well as an amphitheater, a temple for the imperial cult, and a marble Forum inspired by a new Forum Augustus himself opened in Rome in 2 BCE (Chapter 14). This ambitious building campaign ultimately took decades to complete. But it – and others like it – inspired quicker and less-elaborate transformations of already-existing communities. A tiny town in Portugal, Conimbriga, built a new forum, a temple for the cult of the emperor, and also a set of baths. When it comes to Africa and Gaul, a similar story could be told. Cities founded or refounded in southern France in the age of Augustus and settled with veterans boast some of the best-preserved Roman buildings anywhere, such as the massive theater at Orange or the stunning Maison Carrée at Nîmes.

The pattern in the east was different. A few veteran colonies were designed and built from scratch to look more like new Roman towns, such as Pisidian Antioch in modern Turkey. But otherwise Greek traditions proved resilient, and builders – while eager to honor Augustus and even at times to assert a quite Roman identity – tended to enhance what was already there. In the city of Aphrodisias, in modern Turkey, an ex-slave of Caesar or Augustus named C. Julius Zoilos, who had helped protect his town during the civil wars, funded a refurbishment of the local theater's stage building in marble. It was an upgrade, even though marble architecture was nothing new in this part of the world.

An exception is Herod the Great of Judea, who consciously created Roman-style buildings in his kingdom. Excavations of Herod's palaces reveal vivid wall paintings in the Roman style, heated baths, and even storerooms that held wine imported from Italy to be served at his banquets. Herod also built in non-Jewish parts of his kingdom whole cities in honor of Augustus, such as Caesarea on the Mediterranean coast. It included a hugely impressive artificial harbor made out of concrete. A lavish temple for the *princeps* overlooked the scene, with a colossal statue modeled on that of Zeus at Olympia. A new quadrennial festival like the Olympics was established to honor Augustus.

While Herod aroused discontent with some of his Jewish subjects for these projects, he was showing himself to the wider world as an up-to-date Roman – like Holconius Rufus in Pompeii or the veterans of Augusta Emerita or the freedmen of Rome. Marble buildings, heated baths, even Arretine pottery: all were becoming badges of Roman identity. So too was the expression of loyalty to Augustus and also, increasingly, to members of his family. He was credited with forging a new age, and the younger generation would perpetuate it. Statues of them all were set up across the empire, usually made locally but reproducing closely the features of official portraits first created in Rome. Just as important days in the lives of Augustus' family made their way into local calendars, communities might also erect a statue in response to some good – or bad – news. A splendid pair of statues of Gaius and Lucius from Corinth, showing them in heroic nudity, may well have been commissioned after their shockingly early deaths just 18 months apart in 2 and 4 CE (Chapter 14).

Religion provided the fullest framework for honoring Augustus. In the east, already in the second century BCE, Roman generals, like Hellenistic kings, had received the same recognition that gods did from individual communities, including sacrifices, priests, and hymns of praise. The honoree might be envisioned as a god himself and so venerated in his own cult, but cult could also be offered to other deities on his behalf. It was easy enough, then, for individual communities to find ways to honor Augustus that best suited them, just as they had honored Pompey and Julius Caesar. But a notable development after Actium was the establishment of cults for Augustus by provincial councils

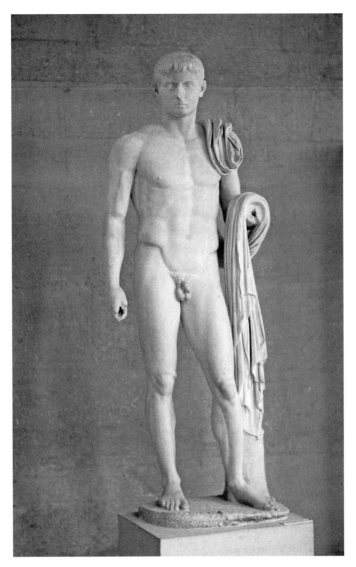

Figure 13.9 Gaius or Lucius Caesar?Augustus' adopted sons were practically carbon copies of the princeps and can be hard to tell apart. This statue from Corinth, part of a pair, probably shows Gaius. Archaeological Museum, Corinth, Greece. (Photo © Vanni Archive/Art Resource, NY.)

of both Asia and Bithynia-Pontus. In Asia, the cult of which is better attested, a temple for Augustus along with the goddess Rome was built in the leading city of Pergamum. The council, comprised of delegates of the member cities, met yearly to discuss business – such as Paullus Fabius Maximus' proposal to honor the "god" Augustus by restarting all local calendars. Delegates annually chose a chief priest, among whose duties was presiding over a yearly festival for Augustus and Rome that drew large crowds. The gatherings gave those living in Asia a way to celebrate not only Augustus but also their own special place in the wider Roman world.

Just as urbanism was less rooted in the western empire, so was the tradition of formal cult for rulers. But Italian towns like Pompeii started to worship "Augustan" deities and sacrifice on behalf of – or even sometimes to – Augustus, and provincial communities did as well, with citizen colonies often taking the lead. At Lugdunum (modern Lyons), a hugely important colony in Gaul that served as the hub of an ambitious road network planned by Agrippa, a sanctuary was established to Augustus and Rome in 12 BCE, with a provincial cult modeled on those of the east. Every year, representatives from 60 tribes around Gaul were to come to Lugdunum on August 1st. Each of the tribes was listed on an altar and represented visually with a statue. For a tribe to have one of its members elected chief priest would be a great honor. In what is now southwestern France, the Cadurci set up a statue for Marcus Lucterius Leo after he was priest. As his name shows, he was a Roman citizen – but only a recent one, like other chief priests of his generation. Men like him were key intermediaries between native populations and Rome and are known to have equipped their own communities with new buildings in the latest Roman style. The province-wide cult was a vehicle for spreading Roman culture.

Ultimately, what was novel about the age of Augustus was not just the way politics and warfare changed, but also the invention of new symbols of what it meant to be Roman, the most important of which was the image of Augustus himself. Historians can see this with great clarity, since they know that many of the symbols would endure for centuries. But contemporaries were also aware of the changes, and their perceptions coalesced around the idea of a "new age" or an "Augustan age." Of course, the new age would not really have been possible without earlier developments like the massive spread of Roman citizenship after the Social War, the creation of a more stable provincial administration, the rising cultural ambitions of the city of Rome, and a growing appreciation for leisure. The troubles of the recent past also weighed on the minds of contemporaries, just as they did on Vergil's Aeneas as he set out to build a new life for himself, his followers, and future generations. He could only succeed by looking forward. In many ways he was the perfect hero for the new Romans.

FURTHER READING

Viewing the age of Augustus as a cultural, as much as political, revolution is now standard, and is well argued by A. Wallace-Hadrill, *Rome's Cultural Revolution* (Cambridge, 2008).

A groundbreaking study of visual imagery is P. Zanker, *The Power of Images in the Age of Augustus* (trans. A. Shapiro; Ann Arbor, 1988). Valuable discussions of art and architecture, literature, and religion are included in K. Galinsky, *Augustan Culture: an Interpretive Introduction* (Princeton, 1996). Cultural history is also a strength of K. Galinsky (ed.), *The Cambridge Companion to the Age of Augustus* (Cambridge, 2005), including the chapters by A. Wallace-Hadrill, N. Purcell, G. Woolf, R. Beacham, J. Scheid, D. Favro, J. R. Clarke, A. Barchiesi, J. Griffin, P. White, K. Galinsky, and L. M. White. On literary developments G. B. Conte, *Latin Literature: A History* (trans. J. B. Solodow; Baltimore, 1999), is exciting.

P. Zanker, *Pompeii: Public and Private Life* (trans. D. L. Schneider; Cambridge, MA, 1998), documents the Augustan transformation of the city, as does A. E. Cooley and M. G. L. Cooley, *Pompeii and Herculaneum: A Sourcebook* (2nd ed.; Abingdon, 2014). On cultural developments in the provinces of the empire, consult G. Woolf, *Becoming Roman: The Origins of Provincial Civilization in Gaul* (Cambridge, 1998); R. MacMullen, *Romanization in the Time of Augustus* (New Haven, 2000); S. Keay and N. Terrenato (eds.), *Italy and the West: Comparative Issues in Romanization* (Oxford, 2001); A. J. S. Spawforth, *Greece and the Augustan Cultural Revolution* (Cambridge, 2012).

For religious history, influential studies are M. Beard, J. North, and S. Price, *Religions of Rome* (2 vols.; Cambridge, 1998), and D. Feeney, *Literature and Religion at Rome: Cultures, Contexts, and Beliefs* (Cambridge, 1998).

14

———

THE WORLD STATE TESTED (4 BCE–20 CE)

One night in the year 12 CE, Ovid tells us, he was awakened by a sudden rush of air and the creaking sound of a window opening. Before him stood the young god Cupid, looking unusually sad, his hair messy and the feathers of his wings ruffled. Ovid, who had been banished to a Black Sea town at the edge of the Roman world by Augustus four years earlier, complained to the boy that he was to blame for the exile. If only Cupid had let him write something other than the *Art of Love*, Ovid never would have angered Augustus. "You know there is another thing that did you more damage," Cupid replies – an unspecified crime that Ovid tried to pass off as simply a mistake. Still, Ovid should take hope. Cupid has come because Augustus is finally in a good mood, as is his whole house. Tiberius is celebrating a triumph, "and throughout Rome every altar burns with fragrant flames."

As Ovid's Cupid hints, the preceding years had been marked by challenges for Augustus. By 4 CE, Tiberius had withdrawn from public life and both of Augustus' adopted sons were dead, raising the question of who would take over for him when he died. Two years later, a rebellion broke out in the Balkans – the most serious war Rome had faced since the wars with Carthage, it was said. It had only just ended when three legions were annihilated in Germany, with the loss of over a tenth of the whole Roman army. On top of the military crisis, a bad spate of fire, flooding, and food shortages had set the city of Rome on a razor's edge. Augustus banished members of his own family, leading to street protests. The peace and prosperity that men and women across the Roman world had come to count on seemed no longer secure.

The world state would prevail, thanks to some important innovations. An elaborate set of adoptions in 4 CE, including the emperor's adoption of Tiberius, revitalized the house of Augustus. And loyalty was no longer expressed just to Augustus but to his whole "house" – precisely since it would outlive him. Poems that Ovid wrote in exile, such as his *Letters from the Black Sea*, offer some of the clearest testimony for this. Another change, encouraged by the loss of the German legions, was an increased sense that the empire had reached its limits and that further wars of conquest meant unnecessary risk. It was in the final years of Augustus' life, too, that a more robust administration for the city of Rome was created (Chapter 12).

Augustus' death in 14 created new anxiety. "There was the greatest fear," wrote the contemporary historian Velleius Paterculus, who for long years served as a military officer under Augustus. Like the poems of Ovid, his work is invaluable for its firsthand perceptions. He did not know – as we do – that the principate would endure for centuries. He was just glad that Tiberius agreed to assume the position that Augustus had held for so long.

Still, anxieties continued. When Tiberius' adopted son, the wildly popular Germanicus, died in 19, a major crisis ensued. A close friend of Tiberius was accused of murdering the prince and went on trial in the Senate. Extensive documents have been discovered in recent times that have shed much light on the affair. More important, they also reveal the relationships that linked the *princeps* and the whole Augustan house to key constituencies across the Roman world, including the army. We see more clearly than ever how the principate was able to command the loyalty of far more Romans than the old government of SPQR. For this reason, this book extends slightly beyond the more conventional stopping point of Augustus' death.

DYNASTIC TRIUMPH AND TRAGEDY

At the end of his life, Augustus looked back to events early in the year 2 BCE as the highpoint of his political career. To preside over his adopted son Lucius' official coming of age, Augustus held the consulship, just as he had in 5 BCE for Gaius. Lucius received the same honors that Gaius had. Coins show these two "sons of Augustus" holding the spears and round shields voted to them by the Equestrian order as "leaders of the youth." Meanwhile, Augustus himself was awarded the new title "Father of the Fatherland," which recalled language used to describe the great saviors of Roman history such as Camillus. The *plebs* offered it first, sending a delegation and then crying it out at games, where the Equestrians in their prominent seats joined them. Messala Corvinus, who had fought for Cassius and Brutus back at Philippi in 42 BCE, spoke last, for the Senate: "May there be good fortune and favor to you and your house (*domus*), Caesar Augustus! For in this way we believe that we are praying for everlasting happiness and blessings for this state." The hope of ongoing prosperity was starting to be linked not just to

Augustus alone but to the House of Augustus (*domus Augusta*). The Father of the Fatherland had clear heirs in his sons.

Augustus opened his most elaborate building project in Rome, an entirely new "Augustan" Forum, in 2 BCE, and it held out a vision of Rome's past, present, and future intertwined at every point with his Julian family. At the rear of the huge colonnaded square rose Augustus' Temple of Mars the Avenger, with massive Corinthian columns of white Carrara marble. Envisioned in 42, during the war to avenge Julius Caesar's killing, the temple almost certainly included cult statues not only of Mars and divine Julius but also the ancestress of the Julii, Venus. Also displayed were the legionary standards lost by Crassus to the Parthians and then recovered by Augustus in 20. Augustus had avenged not just Caesar, but the Roman People's honor. Augustus ordered the new Forum's long porticoes filled with statues of great Romans: the founders Aeneas and Romulus, others of their time, and the later generals who had built up the empire to its present greatness. Accompanying inscriptions recorded their specific deeds. "I did this," Augustus proclaimed, "so that both I, as long as I live, and the leaders (*principes*) of future generations should be required by citizens to conform to them as a model." The reference to Gaius and Lucius was unmistakable.

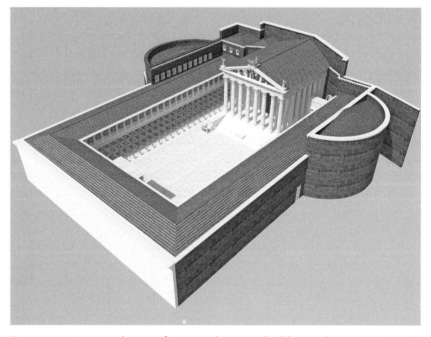

Figure 14.1 A restored view of Augustus' greatest building endeavor in Rome, his own Augustan Forum. Mars the Avenger almost certainly shared his temple with Venus, his adulterous lover in Greek myth. (Image from Virtual Rome, a digital model © 2016 University of Reading. Virtual Rome was developed by Dr. Matthew Nicholls.)

Lavish spectacles allowed Augustus to strengthen loyalty to himself and his family. Leading boys rode on horses with Gaius' and Lucius' younger brother, Agrippa, in the so-called Trojan Games. Even more impressive was the reenactment, in a huge artificial lake with room for 30 warships, of the Greek naval victory over the Persians at Salamis in 480 BCE. The spectacle was designed to recall Augustus' defeat of the "oriental" Cleopatra at Actium and his subsequent humiliation of the Parthians, the heirs of the Persians. For Ovid, then finishing up his *Art of Love*, the show also anticipated Gaius Caesar setting out for the east to win a major victory over the Parthians. "Leader of the youth, one day of the elders," Ovid called him. The show happened to be a splendid opportunity for picking up girls as well, he could not resist adding.

Of course, Ovid said, he was only writing about prostitutes. But adultery was at the heart of a scandal that broke out by year's end. It destroyed Augustus' daughter and several leading aristocrats, including Iullus, the son of Mark Antony. Julia was alleged to have made herself available to "swarms of adulterers," to have wandered the streets in nighttime orgies, even to have solicited sex in the Forum. Ashamed by the revelations, or so he said, Augustus stayed at home and sent a letter to the Senate with a list of the names of her lovers. Iullus took his own life, while others were sent into exile. Julia was among them, banished to the tiny island of Pandateria, in the Tyrrhenian Sea, accompanied by her mother, Scribonia. Nobody could visit without Augustus' permission, and she was even denied the minimal comfort of wine.

Julia's crime was regarded not simply as adultery but treason, which was being redefined to include treason against Augustus. Indeed, at least one ancient author suspected that Julia was actually plotting against Augustus' life, and some modern historians have shared these suspicions. Maybe, some even suggest, she intended for her son Gaius to take over, with herself as a kind of regent. But there were simpler ways for Augustus to get rid of Julia if he truly feared her. The point, really, was that adultery by Julia was worse than another woman's because it was a stain on the House of Augustus, and so it was dealt with like treason. By all accounts, Julia was a free spirit, as were Iullus and her other friends. If she did carry on love affairs, especially after being compelled to marry Marcellus, Agrippa, and then Tiberius (who abandoned her in 5 BCE), who could blame her? Certainly members of the *plebs* were angry with Augustus over Julia's fate and protested on her behalf. In an assembly, Augustus called on the gods to curse his critics with daughters like his own.

Gaius, at least, seemed willing to play his assigned role in the east. The pro-Roman king of Armenia had died, Rome's new candidate was driven out, and the Parthians were backing a rival, Tigranes IV. Parthia also had a new king, Phraates V, an illegitimate son of the Phraates who had restored the standards to Augustus in 20 BCE. Augustus wrote Phraates V a letter, refusing to call him king and ordering him out of Armenia. Gaius, meanwhile, slowly made his way toward Syria, along with senior advisors sent by Augustus. When the Roman nominee for the Armenian throne died, Augustus accepted new overtures from the Parthian-backed Tigranes IV and instructed him to meet with Gaius for official recognition. Phraates V was now willing formally to renounce Parthian claims to Armenia in exchange for Augustus promising to keep the king's unsupportive brothers in Rome. At a meeting on the Euphrates, Gaius and Phraates celebrated the accord with lavish feasts.

Mission accomplished, it seemed. But in fact Augustus had unwittingly sent Gaius to his death. When Tigranes IV was killed, perhaps by men angry over his turn to Rome, Gaius was ordered to install Tigranes' replacement, a Mede whom some Armenians resisted. An unsuspecting Gaius was lured to a parley on the pretext that Parthian secrets would be revealed to him – and was then attacked and wounded. Gaius felt totally incapacitated and was brought even lower by the news that his brother Lucius had died suddenly of illness while journeying to Spain in August of 2 CE. Gaius wrote Augustus asking to be relieved of his duties. All Augustus could do was persuade him to return, but in February of 4 on his way back to Rome, Gaius died of complications from his wounds. He was 22 years old.

Two decrees from the veteran colony of Pisa in northern Italy record an overwhelming response to the loss of the young men. After Lucius' death, the town council planned construction of an altar at which yearly offerings would be made to his spirit. Envoys were authorized to go to Rome to seek permission from Augustus. Two years later, the Pisans voted a lengthy mourning, yearly sacrifices, and construction of an elaborate arch on the top of which would stand a statue of Gaius in triumphal dress. Again, envoys led by the local priest of Augustus were to transmit the proposals to the emperor. The decrees show how Gaius and Lucius were understood as the intended successors of Augustus and the position he had achieved. For the Pisans, Gaius in particular was "designated *princeps*, most just and most like his father in manly excellence."

Augustus himself, of course, never let a word like "successor" cross his lips. It was too overtly monarchical. Writing to Gaius, he spoke of his two sons "taking over my post (*statio*)," using a military metaphor. Indeed, acquisition of some kind of military glory by his sons struck Augustus as essential; they had to measure up to all those generals in Augustus' Forum. The effort to do so ended up destroying Gaius. Augustus' plans lay in ruins, and yet paradoxically the deaths of Gaius and Lucius would strengthen support for a clear succession to Augustus. Constituencies across the Roman world were mourning. In the city of Rome itself, lavish honors were voted for the dead young men. The grief was for a lost future, and Augustus responded to the deep sense of anxiety.

THE HOUSE THAT WILL HAVE ETERNAL SWAY

Augustus would have to rehabilitate his stepson Tiberius, despite Tiberius' decision to leave public life in 6 BCE. As member of several of Rome's noblest families, Tiberius had proven himself time and again campaigning and can only have been dismayed at the popular acclaim Gaius and Lucius had received as mere boys. Tiberius was the consummate aristocrat. A tough general who liked to sleep in the open air while on campaign, he detested the political intrigues of Rome and preferred in his free time to read difficult Greek poetry, collect art, and garden. He had little time for public religion or festivals and was practically addicted to astrology. Though an impressive-looking man with broad shoulders and chest, he usually frowned and often stayed silent. He was poorly suited to play the role Augustus did.

After he withdrew to Rhodes, he came under suspicion of plotting against Gaius. He was forced to beg Augustus to be allowed to return to Rome, with the support of his mother, Livia. Finally in 1 CE he was allowed back – but only as a private citizen, and only after Gaius had given his consent. The good news came just in time to save the astrologer Thrasyllus, whom Tiberius was ready to push off a cliff for his seemingly unreliable predictions.

Now, the deaths of Gaius and Lucius transformed Tiberius' life. On June 26 of the year 4 CE, Augustus adopted him and Agrippa Postumus, the last surviving son of Julia and Agrippa, born after the father's death in 12 BCE. The adoption of Tiberius, Augustus publicly announced, was "for the good of the state" – the closest he would come to explicitly anointing a political successor. Yet by also adopting the teenage Agrippa, Augustus avoided too strong an impression of one-man rule. And indeed, before he adopted Tiberius, Augustus made Tiberius adopt Germanicus, the 18-year-old son of Tiberius' late brother Drusus – even though Tiberius already had his own slightly younger son, also named Drusus. Handsome and much better with a crowd than Tiberius, Germanicus himself was married to the sister of Gaius and Lucius, Augustus' granddaughter Agrippina. There could be little doubt that Germanicus – and whatever sons he had – would attract support for Augustus, Tiberius, and the whole House.

The adoptions, then, did more than simply rehabilitate Tiberius. Along with the marriage of Germanicus, they reasserted the unity of the House of Augustus, after it had been undermined by the departure of Tiberius and the disgrace of Julia. At the same time, they gave the House a clear sequence of three generations that promised stability for years to come. Ovid's poems of exile show this, and were meant to. In the poem about Cupid's appearance, for example, Ovid proclaimed how everyone rejoiced at Tiberius' triumph in 12: the "House and the children"; "mother Livia"; Augustus, "great father of our fatherland"; and the people. In an earlier poem, anticipating Tiberius' celebration of a triumph for campaigns in Germany, Ovid imagined the Palatine being decorated and sacrifices being prepared by "both Caesars." It was a reference to Augustus and Tiberius, since Tiberius' adoption meant he now had the magical name of "Julius Caesar." Sacrifices were also prepared "by the youths who are growing up under Caesar's name to give that House eternal sway over the earth" – that is, Germanicus and Drusus. Whereas before 4 it was simply the next generation of Augustus' family that mattered, now it was multiple generations who would bring everlasting success.

Key to Tiberius' rehabilitation, as Ovid also shows, were his campaigns in the north, fought more or less continuously from 4. Regaining tribunician power and *imperium*, he was sent that year by Augustus to Germany, where there had been recent troubles. Velleius Paterculus accompanied Tiberius as prefect of cavalry and described the moment: "the people beheld again their commander of old, by his merits and fine qualities a Caesar long before he received the name . . . Tears of joy sprang from the soldiers' eyes at the sight of him." By 5 Tiberius had regained control over Germany between the Rhine and Elbe. A grand assault was planned for the following year on the increasingly powerful kingdom of the Marcomanni, in Bohemia, just north of the Danube. Tiberius would bring an army from the south, and the experienced commander C. Sentius Saturninus would come from the west, with the Rhine legions.

But then one of the greatest challenges of Augustus' final years intervened. A revolt erupted in Illyricum, arising in part from preparations being made for the Marcomannic campaign. Such was the scale of it, Velleius later wrote, that "the spirit of Caesar Augustus was shaken with fear." Peace had to be made with Maroboduus, the king of the Marcomanni.

"GIVE BACK MY LEGIONS!"

The Illyrian revolt spread quickly and widely, and this unnerved the Romans. It began with the Dalmatians along the Adriatic coast, already restive because of the taxes they had to pay, and further upset when Rome's governor of Illyricum, Valerius Messallinus, demanded extra troops for the Marcomannic war. Once raised, this force revolted under the leadership of a local chief named Bato, who ordered raids far down the coast of Macedonia. To the north, in Pannonia, another insurgency formed, led by a man also called

Bato. The key Roman fort at Sirmium was almost captured. Panic struck in Rome. Augustus told the Senate that unless immediate precautions were taken, the enemy could be in sight of the city in 10 days. Veterans were recalled. Quite unusually, even ex-slaves were enlisted, this being a significant part of the urban population. Velleius Paterculus, newly elected as quaestor, was ordered by Augustus to bring some of the reinforcements to Tiberius.

With great effort, Tiberius gradually crushed the uprising. The two Batos had joined forces and established themselves near Sirmium, while Tiberius and Messalinus waited at the other critical fortress of Siscia for Velleius' reinforcements. Then began a painful war of attrition. By the year 8, the Pannonians turned on their Bato and ultimately surrendered, but the other Bato kept the revolt alive by withdrawing to Dalmatia. After difficult campaigning the following year by Tiberius, Germanicus, and other generals, the Dalmatian Bato finally surrendered. Henceforward, Illyricum would be split into the two provinces of Dalmatia and Pannonia and run by experienced generals.

The successful end of the war should have been a glorious moment for the House of Augustus, and indeed it briefly was. Augustus and Tiberius were awarded triumphs, while Germanicus was granted triumphal ornaments. He was also given the rank of praetor and the right to hold the consulship early. Even Tiberius' son Drusus – who had not campaigned – was elevated in status. Scarcely had the honors been voted, though, when the terrible news reached Rome that three legions in Germany had been slaughtered, along with a large number of auxiliaries.

In essence, it was another provincial rebellion. After the earlier campaigns across the Rhine, the governor of Germany, Quinctilius Varus, was now trying to consolidate Roman rule by organizing the territory into tax-paying units – an activity no doubt related to recent financial strains. The attempted transformation has been revealed by the excavation in the past few decades of a half-completed Roman town at Waldgirmes 60 miles east of the Rhine, including a forum with a bronze statue of Augustus on horseback. Advising Varus was Arminius, a noble of the Cherusci who had earlier been rewarded for his successful command of auxiliary soldiers with a grant of Roman citizenship and Equestrian status. With Rome worn out by the Illyrian rebellion, and Germans unhappy with their occupiers, Arminius saw an opportunity to drive the Romans out of Germany, and he secretly built up a powerful network of allies.

After touring his province with his troops in the summer of 9, Varus was preparing to return to winter quarters on the Rhine when word of a small rebellion – contrived by Arminius – reached him. Varus was enticed to march against the rebels, with a promise of support from leaders in Arminius' network. In reality, the Roman was being led into an ambush in the

Teutoburg Forest. The major battle site was discovered in the 1980s, by a British army officer stationed in Germany whose metal detector uncovered Roman coins and bits of military equipment. The legions were spread out along a narrow path, with swamp on one side and a wooded hill on the other, further reinforced by Arminius. It was a total massacre. Most of Varus' troops were killed – "slaughtered like cattle," wrote Velleius. Varus and his senior officers took their own lives. Arminius sent Varus' head to Maroboduus to encourage him to join the rebellion, but Maroboduus refused. Augustus was devastated. According to Suetonius, he stopped shaving, kept banging his head against the door, and cried out, "Quinctilius Varus, give back my legions!"

Varus' surviving nephew acted quickly to prevent the revolt spreading across the Rhine, where Tiberius now travelled. Over the next couple of years, Tiberius built up a much larger army of eight legions and made brief campaigns with Germanicus, never straying too far east of the river. The goal was to reassert Roman prestige in the region – and the prestige of the House of Augustus across the Roman world.

When Tiberius finally returned late in 12 to celebrate his deferred Illyrian triumph, Germanicus took over the Rhine command. He had held his first consulship the same year, and Augustus took the occasion to tell the Senate that because of his own advancing age, senators must take care of Germanicus, while Tiberius would take care of the Senate. The message was read out by Germanicus, since Augustus could no longer make himself heard and had stopped attending Senate meetings. As fearful as it had been, the crisis seemed to vindicate claims that Rome's well-being depended not just on Augustus but his whole House. Meanwhile, as much as possible the loss of the legions was blamed on Varus. A funerary monument for an officer killed in the Teutoburg Forest labels the uprising simply as "Varus' war."

While it was convenient to blame Varus, the bigger truth was that the empire was in danger of overexpansion. To conquer more territory, Rome would need a bigger army, and that meant more taxation; the wilds of northern Europe simply were not going to yield much wealth any time soon. Along with a will and other documents that Augustus left with the Vestals for safekeeping until his death was a recommendation not to enlarge the empire beyond its present limits. Certainly this would be Tiberius' own policy. Germanicus did continue campaigning in Germany after Augustus' death through the year 16. He buried Varus' army, recovered two of the legionary eagles, and put Arminius on the run. That was sufficient for Tiberius, who saw that if the Romans drew back to the Rhine, German would turn on German and could be played off one another by Rome. Indeed, Arminius attacked Maroboduus, driving him permanently from his kingdom in 19, and Arminius himself was killed by his own kinsmen in 21. Of course, later emperors did fight wars of conquest and boasted of expanding the empire. But the overall shape of the empire changed little in the centuries after Augustus, and his counsel – not to mention the horror-filled memory of the Varian massacre – justified the abandonment of aggressive imperialism.

TREASON: THE OPPOSITE OF LOYALTY

The outbreak of the Illyrian rebellion in the year 6 coincided with trouble elsewhere, as could happen in a vast empire like Rome's. There was rebellion in Sardinia, increased brigandage by the Isaurian tribes of southern Asia Minor, and attacks on Roman interests in Africa, all requiring increased military investment. That same year, Augustus decided formally to annex Judea, and his legate Quirinius carried out a census immortalized in the Gospel of Luke: "and all went to be taxed, everyone into his own city." Luke places Jesus' birth in the reign of Herod the Great, who died in 4 BCE, creating a puzzle for historians, since Quirinius' census was certainly in 6 CE. A small rebellion over the new taxes ensued. It is no accident that it was now that Augustus set up the new military treasury, funded by an inheritance tax on citizens. Provincials alone could not front all the costs of keeping the empire secure.

There were problems in the city of Rome too. In 5 there was terrible flooding and a grain shortage, and the following year an even more severe grain shortage, forcing Augustus to increase free distributions. The year 6 also saw many parts of the city destroyed by fire. It was now that the night watchmen were established, to be funded by a new 2 percent tax on the sale of slaves. Two years later, after yet more grain shortages, a prefecture for the food supply was established. As earlier in his principate, Augustus himself avoided acquiring new offices for himself, but the scale of government was becoming more ambitious in response to crisis.

Not surprisingly, in the face of all these challenges there were rumblings of protest among the urban population. In 6, plans for an uprising were discussed, and notices calling for action went up at night. A certain Publius Rufus was said to be behind it all, but as others came under suspicion, a full investigation was initiated by the Senate. Rewards were offered for anybody with information to share. The easing of the grain shortage calmed the situation, as did gladiatorial games presented by Germanicus – always good for distracting the public.

Still, the unrest raised the all-too-familiar dilemma of how to balance security with freedom of expression. The final years of Augustus' life were marked by an increasingly broad definition of treason. When ongoing stability was predicated on the well-being of Augustus and his House, to attack them in any way – or even to be, as Velleius put it, one of those "who hated this prosperous state of affairs" – could be deemed seditious.

Members of Augustus' own family were caught in the net. In 6 or 7, Augustus disinherited Agrippa Postumus and confined him to the town of Surrentum. Slightly later, Agrippa was banished to the island of Planasia and placed under permanent military guard by the Senate. His property was turned over to the new military treasury. Historical sources are full of accusations against Agrippa: he was prone to anger, he spent all his time fishing, and he criticized Augustus and also his stepmother, Livia. His version of the story does not survive, leading scholars to wonder if something more was afoot. Criticism of other family members, though, might be enough to explain his fate. Like his mother, Julia, he would have been seen as harmful to the House – and so to Rome.

The next to fall was Agrippa's sister Julia. In 8 she was banished to a small Adriatic island after being accused of adultery with D. Iunius Silanus. Because her husband is included in a separately recorded list of conspirators against Augustus, modern scholars have speculated that she (perhaps along with the banished Agrippa Postumus) was really scheming to topple the *princeps*. As with her mother, adultery was quite possibly her only crime, yet her status made it tantamount to treason. The point was reinforced when Augustus refused to let the child born to his granddaughter after her condemnation live.

Ovid's exile around this same time might have been linked to Julia's. According to the poet – the only source – he was banished to Tomis on the Black Sea by an edict of Augustus. There were two charges against him: "a poem and a mistake." The poem was the *Art of Love*, published some years before. Unwilling to swallow Ovid's line that he was only writing about prostitutes, in his edict Augustus charged Ovid with inciting adultery, possibly even Julia's. Augustus had copies of the *Art* banned from Rome's public libraries. As for the "mistake" that Cupid told Ovid had done more harm, the poet remains studiously vague, but it apparently had to do with Ovid accidentally seeing something – to do with Julia? – and not reporting it. To say anything more would evidently undermine his protestation of loyalty to Augustus, which Ovid maintained to the end. In one of his last poems, he describes a shrine in his house with statuettes of Augustus, Tiberius, Livia, and "both of the grandsons" (Germanicus and Drusus). Every morning, he says, he offered them incense and prayers. His devotion was complete.

Another sign that questions of loyalty, treason, and freedom of expression were increasingly dominating political discourse was a crackdown on the sort of defamatory writings that were so common in the age of Cicero. Augustus became particularly irritated with Cassius Severus, such a ferocious-looking man with an equally ferocious tongue that people compared him to a gladiator.

Probably in 8 CE, Cassius was sent into exile for writings against illustrious men and women, and the formal charge was treason. Note, though, that it was the Senate, not Augustus personally, who banished him. In 12, the Senate ordered that defamatory literature be searched out and burned by the aediles. Also burnt were books of the historian T. Labienus, who was specifically described by a contemporary as recalling the era of the late Republic and out of touch with the tranquility of the new age. The same observer pointed out that Labienus' "freedom of speech was so great that it went beyond the definition of freedom." Societies that prize freedom of speech do have to treat defamation and incitements to immediate violence seriously. Still, at least some Romans thought something was being lost. After seeing his books burnt, Labienus had himself carried to the tombs of his ancestors and walled up, to ensure that he would be buried with them and not in exile abroad.

THE LAST DAYS OF AUGUSTUS

Toward the end of his life, Augustus appeared in public less and less, conducting much of the business of state from his couch. Still, he felt well enough to travel to Campania in the summer of 14, accompanied by Tiberius, to enjoy some time at the imperial villa on Capri and then attend an athletic tournament in Naples. At Beneventum, he said goodbye to Tiberius, who was heading to Illyricum for a tour of inspection (his *imperium* was now equal to that of Augustus). Augustus started back to Rome but collapsed at Nola, at an old family property. On his last day, August 19, he called for a mirror and had his hair combed. He then called in his friends, jokingly compared himself to an actor, and asked for a round of applause. He died a happy man.

Tiberius, who had been summoned to Nola, sent a dispatch to all the provincial governors and armies with the news. He also issued an edict summoning the Senate to meet to discuss the funeral arrangements. Augustus' body was carried at night by local town councilors to the outskirts of Rome, where the Equestrians took over. It was probably on September 4 that the Senate met. Augustus' will was read out, with provisions naming Tiberius and Livia chief heirs and leaving cash legacies for the *plebs* of Rome and the soldiers. Other documents also were read, including a copy of Augustus' *Achievements* and his own wishes for his funeral. In response, the Senate granted a parade with statues of Rome's legendary founders and all the heroes of later times, just as in Augustus' Forum. Tiberius and his son Drusus delivered the eulogies. The body was then carried to the Field of Mars in a massive procession, with senators, Equestrians, and *plebs*, men and women alike. Livia stood vigil by the lit pyre for five days. A senator was ready to testify on oath that he had seen Augustus ascend into heaven.

For the events of 14 onward, an account survives by the most brilliant historian Rome ever produced, Tacitus. A senator who wrote in the early second century CE, Tacitus was especially concerned with how senators responded to the rule of emperors. Whereas the biographer Suetonius tended to depict emperors as corrupted by power, Tacitus suggested that it was those around the emperor who were most corrupted. Thus when news of Augustus' death reached Rome, Tacitus claimed, "there was a rush into slavery by consuls, senators, Equestrians." The order of his list is significant: as Tacitus saw it, everybody did their part to ease Tiberius' takeover of Augustus' position, but consuls and senators led the way.

Related to this are frequent allegations by Tacitus of individuals acting criminally behind the scenes. Tacitus reports suspicions that Livia, determined to protect Tiberius' interests, hurried along Augustus' death after the old man allegedly visited Agrippa Postumus on Planasia early in 14 with a view to restoring him. Immediately after Augustus' death, when Agrippa was killed by a centurion acting under orders of unknown origin, Tiberius was shocked and called for a Senate investigation. But then, wrote Tacitus, Sallustius Crispus, "a partner in secrets ... found out." Sallustius, the great-nephew and adopted son of the historian Sallust, is a quintessentially Tacitean figure – an unsavory Equestrian, prone to luxury, and not afraid to do the emperor's dirty work. Alarmed by Tiberius' demands, he warned Livia that the "mysteries of the household should not be divulged." Tacitus' implication is that Sallustius had disposed of Agrippa by sending orders to the centurion under Augustus' name and that Livia was willing to help with a cover-up. But there can be no certainty – which in a way is exactly Tacitus' point: the principate resulted in chilling mysteries like the death of Agrippa.

More practically, Tacitus can be read for a sense of how senatorial debate proceeded. This is because he almost certainly consulted the record of minutes directly. Since he reports selectively, in keeping with his own interpretation of events, he should be supplemented with other accounts wherever possible.

When the Senate reconvened on September 17, it first acknowledged Augustus' divinity. Measures were passed for the cult of the new god. A temple would be built, a new priestly college established, and Livia would be a priestess of the cult and was to have the use of a lictor when attending to her duties. Then came a discussion of Tiberius' position in the state. The Senate was eager to see Tiberius "succeed to his father's post (*statio*)," according to Velleius. Tiberius responded that it was too big a job, one only Augustus was able to do. The senators could not accept this and "burst into complaints, tears, and prayers" until finally one asked what part of the job Tiberius did want. He preferred to be excused totally, or so he said, but finally accepted the "post," while also making it clear that at some point old age would force him to resign.

In the absence of explicit succession – something Augustus was never willing to allow – the Senate wanted some reassurance about the future, as did others across the Roman world. The little harbor town of Gytheion in Greece, for example, communicated with Tiberius and Livia in 15 a plan for a new civic festival. On successive days Tiberius, Livia, Germanicus, and Drusus would be honored; a bull would be sacrificed "on behalf of the safety of our rulers and gods and the eternal continuance of their rule." It was an anxious time. After Augustus' death, armies in Pannonia and Germany staged mutinies, mainly over the terms of their service. These were handled by Drusus and Germanicus, respectively, in part by judicious concessions. The German soldiers also became ashamed when Germanicus sent away his pregnant wife, Agrippina, with their little son, who was a sort of mascot in the camp and given the nickname "Caligula" because of the little boots he wore. With support from all the armies as well as other key constituencies now confirmed, it was clear that the Augustan model of government was holding. The position of *princeps* was becoming an institution.

"GUARD, PRESERVE, PROTECT"

Germanicus stayed on in Germany until Tiberius recalled him and let him celebrate a triumph in May of 17. He was then sent east, where he had the now-familiar job of installing a new king in Armenia and also the task of annexing two former client kingdoms. Tiberius also sent out as governor of Syria an experienced ex-consul, Cn. Calpurnius Piso, ostensibly to support Germanicus. But Piso was an old friend of Tiberius, and his wife, Plancina, was close to Livia. Tacitus cannot resist suggesting that Piso and Plancina were actually supposed to thwart Germanicus and his wife, in an attempt to advance the cause of Tiberius' own son Drusus.

Germanicus was all too successful and, without Tiberius' permission, detoured to Egypt, causing a stir. When he returned to Syria, he found that Piso had tried to cancel some of his arrangements, and the two quarreled. By this point, Germanicus had become badly ill, and he was convinced that Piso was poisoning him. Piso left the province in a huff – and Germanicus promptly died. His corpse was autopsied, and while no conclusive proof of murder was found, a suspected poisoner named Martina was taken into custody and sent to Rome, only to die en route. Piso tried to reenter Syria but was turned back by the acting legate, while Agrippina sailed home to Italy with her husband's ashes after the funeral.

Romans had been alarmed to learn of Germanicus' failing health and had themselves started to suspect not just Piso and Plancina but Tiberius and Livia. When a false report arrived that the prince had recovered, there was a mad rush through the streets. Tiberius awakened to crowds of Romans chanting through the streets: "Rome is safe, the country's safe, Germanicus – safe!" But the euphoria was soon dashed. An anxious Senate voted lavish honors for the dead Caesar and decreed that tributes to Germanicus composed by Tiberius and Drusus should be inscribed publicly in Rome; this would help counter any hostile rumors about them. So too would the wide distribution of the decree that the Senate ordered, copies of which have turned up in modern times on bronze tablets.

As Agrippina with her young children got off the boat in southern Italy, clutching the urn with Germanicus' ashes, an extraordinary outpouring followed her into Rome. "The streets of the city were crowded," Tacitus wrote, "torches were blazing out across the Campus Martius. There the soldiers with arms, the magistrates without their symbols of office, and the people in their tribes kept shouting that the state was ruined and no trace of hope remained." Complaints were rife. Why was there no funeral in Rome? Why didn't Tiberius and Livia come out and acknowledge the people's grief? Under pressure, the *princeps* finally issued an edict. Many illustrious Romans had died before, he said, and it was time to show a stiff upper lip.

The *plebs* were starting to recover, it seemed, when Piso made his return to Rome. Fearless, he deliberately brought his boat down the Tiber to the Mausoleum of Augustus – where Germanicus' ashes had been interred – and disembarked. His clients met him there, Plancina's female friends joined her, and they all proceeded to Piso's house overlooking the Forum for a noisy welcome-back party. The next day, Piso was arraigned before the consuls, and Tiberius agreed that the Senate should hear his case. Piso was charged not only with the murder of Germanicus but also with treasonous activity, especially his attempt to reenter Syria by force after Germanicus' death. As the trial got under way, the outraged cries of the *plebs* could be heard in the Senate house. Recognizing the danger he faced, Piso killed himself, while Plancina was subsequently acquitted of any wrongdoing. Tacitus wrote that she had secured pardon through the influence of Livia and had given up on Piso, thereby convincing him that he was finished.

Historians used to believe that Tacitus exaggerated the strong emotions so many Romans felt after Germanicus' death. But the grief and anger make sense. Romans had grown devoted to the whole House of Augustus, not just the individual *princeps*. And resentment was starting to build up against Tiberius, who was not keen to play the part Augustus had, slavishly attending games and putting on new spectacles.

What really demonstrates that the loss of Germanicus was a crisis, though, is the recent discovery, in Spain, of multiple copies of a massive decree by the Senate concerning Piso. In it, the Senate attempted to lend all the support it could to Tiberius and to set him apart from Piso. The Senate gave thanks to the gods "because they did not allow the wicked plans of Piso to disturb the present tranquil condition of the state, than which no better could be desired and which the beneficence of our *princeps* has made it possible to enjoy." Tiberius' grief for Germanicus is recognized as extensive, and appropriate. Praise is heaped on all the other members of the imperial house, including Livia and even Germanicus' young children.

From hindsight, Tacitus was inclined to see all this as just more servile adulation. Reading through the whole decree, you may agree with his conclusion. But should we entirely dismiss the sense of anxiety that pervades the document? For the writers of the decree, Piso raised the hideous specter of renewed civil war: entering Syria, he tried to turn Roman against Roman, he gave out cash in his own name, and soldiers were being divided into "Pisonians" and "Caesarians." This was a glimpse of the bad old days that no sane person would want back – the time of Marius and Sulla, of Caesar and Pompey.

Adding to the Senate's worry in 20 was the unexpected loss of so important a member of the House of Augustus. So many had now been taken before their time: Marcellus, Lucius, Gaius, and now Germanicus. The Senate hoped "the immortal gods will devote all the care more to the one who remains" (Drusus). "All hope for the post which his father holds," it added, ". . . rests for the future on one person alone." Drusus too would die in 23, apparently of illness, leaving Velleius to pray anew, at the end of his history, for Jupiter, Mars, and Vesta, "the guardian of the eternal fire," to "guard, preserve, protect the present state of affairs, this peace, this *princeps*. When he has filled his post of duty with the longest term possible for mortals, mark out, as late as can be, successors for him, but only successors whose shoulders are strong enough to support the weight of the world empire." The prayer perfectly encapsulated the political ideas of the new state.

The Senate decree of 20 set out even more fully the framework that had emerged over the previous 50 years. The Senate expressed its loyalty to Tiberius. The Equestrian order "declared with repeated acclamations its sentiments and its grief for the wrongs of our *princeps* and of his son." The *plebs* "joined with the Equestrian order in demonstrating its devotion to our *princeps*," while the soldiers showed continued "loyalty and devotion to the House of Augustus," the decree said. The relations among all these different constituencies and the *princeps* together with the House tied the Roman world together, and widespread distribution of the decree reaffirmed the ties. There may be a sense of fragility, but it is precisely because a realistic ideal of stability and security was now in place.

The new political framework could stop violence from spiraling out of control where traditional SPQR could not, despite the role Senate and People each played in 20. But what also prevented civil war breaking out was the decades of administrative work done by Augustus, encapsulated in one of the documents he left for Tiberius – a summary of the condition of the empire. Its contents included the size of all military forces and their disposition, the provinces and their revenues, and moneys in the treasury. Needs and resources were balanced with maximum efficiency; soldiers could count on their yearly pay and their large discharge bonus. Any handouts Piso might have offered were less impressive than they would have been 50 years earlier. The empire, and the structures supporting it, had a greater solidity.

By 20 Ovid was dead. To the end, he kept up hope that he might return to the city he loved. But in the earlier days of his banishment, in a poem he wrote to his stepdaughter, he consoled himself with another thought. Maybe Augustus had deprived him of his home, maybe Ovid would even be killed, "Yet when I am dead my fame shall survive. As long as Mars' Rome surveys victorious from her seven hills the conquered world, I shall be read." Even in his remote Black Sea town, he could still claim to be a proud member of the world state.

FURTHER READING

The general titles referred to in Chapter 12 are again relevant, including Richardson, Goldsworthy, Wallace-Hadrill, Levick, and Rowe, as well as *Cambridge Ancient History* (2nd ed.) Vol. 10. Also refer to R. Seager, *Tiberius* (London, 1972); B. Levick, *Tiberius the Politician* (London, 1976); A. A. Barrett, *Livia: First Lady of Imperial Rome* (New Haven, 2002); G. Rowe, "Tiberius," in A. A. Barrett (ed.), *Lives of the Caesars* (Malden, MA, 2008; a useful collection), 38–60; A. G. G. Gibson (ed.), *The Julio-Claudian Succession: Reality and Perception of the "Augustan Model"* (Leiden, 2013, including an important chapter by R. Seager). Politics after 4 CE are discussed, sometimes differently than here, in a lively book by A. Pettinger, *The Republic in Danger: Drusus Libo and the Succession of Tiberius* (Oxford, 2012). For the risk of overstretch and much more, see the stimulating study of E. Luttwak, *The Grand Strategy of the Roman Empire* (2nd ed.; Baltimore, 2016).

K. Volk, *Ovid* (Malden, MA, 2010), introduces the poet. E. Cowan (ed.), *Velleius Paterculus: Making History* (Swansea, 2010), introduces the historian. J. B. Lott, *Death and Dynasty in Early Imperial Rome: Key Sources, with Text, Translation, and Commentary* (Cambridge, 2012), includes the Senate decree concerning Piso as well as a valuable introduction; consult also the special number of *American Journal of Philology* concerned with the decree, vol. 120.1 (1999), edited by C. Damon and S. Takács.

Three particularly helpful essays are F. Millar, "Ovid and the Domus Augusta: Rome Seen from Tomoi," in *Rome, the Greek World, and the East* Vol. 1 (Chapel Hill, 2002), 321–49; K. A. Raaflaub and L. J. Samons, "Opposition to Augustus," in K. A. Raaflaub and M. Toher (eds.), *Between Republic and Empire: Interpretations of Augustus and His Principate* (Berkeley, 1990), 417–54; J. Matthews, "Tacitus, *acta senatus*, and the Inauguration of Tiberius," in *Roman Perspectives* (Swansea, 2010), 57–84.

SOURCES OF QUOTATIONS

The translations in this book of literary sources are based on those in the Loeb Classical Library, Penguin Classics, Oxford World Classics, and Focus Classical Library series. Translations of documentary sources are credited below.

CHAPTER I

"became the worst" etc.: Sallust, *War with Catiline* 5.9–13 *passim*
"When this fellow": Cicero, *Letters to His Friends* 7.30.2

CHAPTER 2

"I shall do . . . ": Livy, *History of Rome* 45.12.6; cf. Polybius, *Histories* 29.27
"the Romans succeeded": Polybius, *Histories* 1.1.6
"an organic whole": Polybius, *Histories* 1.3.4
"universally accepted": Polybius, *Histories* 3.4.3
"to settle differences": Polybius, *Histories* 6.13.6
"the fiery war": Polybius, *Histories* 35.1.1
"Carthage must be destroyed!": Plutarch, *Cato the Elder* 27.1 etc.
"Only he has wits": Plutarch, *Cato the Elder* 27.4 (quoting Odyssey 10.495)
"some wretched old Greeks": Plutarch, *Cato the Elder* 9.2
"fallen from the sky": Polybius, *Histories* 36.10.2
"near to the sea": Cato, *On Agriculture* 1.3
"could admit and send away": Strabo, *Geography* 14.5.2

CHAPTER 3

"to cut away the hydra-like luxury": Plutarch, *Cato the Elder* 16.5
"If we could exist": Aulus Gellius, *Attic Nights* 1.6.2 (quoting Q. Metellus Numidicus)
"stirred up a great question": Plutarch, *Gaius Gracchus* 5.3
"the Senate stands": Polybius, *Histories* 6.16.5
"Citizens, please": Valerius Maximus, *Memorable Deeds and Sayings* 3.7.3
"the nobility passed the consulship": Sallust, *War with Jugurtha* 63.6
"since there was famine": Obsequens, *Book of Prodigies* 22

CHAPTER 4

"The wild animals": Plutarch, *Tiberius Gracchus* 9.4–5
"the wealth": Plutarch, *Tiberius Gracchus* 9.5
"this foul crime": Appian, *Civil Wars* 1.17
"those scoundrels" H. Malcovati, *Oratorum Romanorum fragmenta liberae rei publicae* (3rd. ed; Pavia, 1953) no. 48 frag. 17
"clearly saved the lives": Plutarch, *Tiberius Gracchus* 5.4
"will you then": Plutarch, *Tiberius Gracchus* 14.5
"the first outbreak": Plutarch, *Tiberius Gracchus* 20.1
"I brought back": quoted in Aulus Gellius, *Attic Nights* 15.12.4
"You should increase": quoted in Aulus Gellius, *Attic Nights* 11.10.3
"If you give": Malvocati, *Oratorum Romanorum* no. 32.3
"at Rome": Sallust, *War with Jugurtha* 20.1
"the nobility passed the consulship": Sallust, *War with Jugurtha* 63.6
"A work of mad Discord": Plutarch, *Gaius Gracchus* 17.6
"the masses": Cicero, *For Sestius* 96
"That man [Nasica]": *For Herennius* 4.68

CHAPTER 5

"unknowns of low origin": Valerius Maximus, *Memorable Deeds and Sayings* 9.7.2
"Every year": Appian *Civil Wars* 1.33
"would take the government": Plutarch, *Sulla* 6.7
"the din of warfare": Plutarch, *Marius* 28.2
"the Roman People": Cicero, *On the Orator* 3.5
"Marius nearly lost it": Plutarch, *Marius* 32.2
"neither law": Appian, *Civil Wars* 1.60
"for three years": Cicero, *Brutus* 308
"I was not sent to Athens": Plutarch, *Sulla* 13.4
"Remove this cruelty": Cicero, *For Roscius of Ameria* 154

CHAPTER 6

"Maras Atinias": A. E. Cooley and M. G. L. Cooley, *Pompeii and Herculaneum: A Sourcebook* (2nd ed.; Abingdon, 2014) no. A13
"or mended their patchwork": Cato, *On Agriculture* 2.3
"sell the oil": Cato, *On Agriculture* 2.7
"the merchants and those": N. Lewis and M. Reinhold, *Roman Civilization: Selected Readings* Vol. 1 (3rd ed.; New York, 1990) no. 169.vi
"citizens of Rome": Lewis and Reinhold, *Roman Civilization* Vol. 1 no. 131

CHAPTER 7

"The wild animals": Plutarch, *Pompey* 12.4
"the common enemy": Lewis and Reinhold, *Roman Civilization* Vol. 1 no. 82
"by grace": Plutarch, *Sertorius* 24.4
"and all under myself": Plutarch, *Pompey* 22.6
"their business and property": Cicero, *For the Manilian Law* 17
"In his three triumphs": Plutarch, *Pompey* 45.5

CHAPTER 8

"still alive": quoted in Asconius, *Commentary on Cicero's "In His White Toga"*
"There are two bodies": quoted in Cicero, *For Murena* 51
"How long, I ask you": Cicero, *Against Catiline* 1.1
"an immigrant citizen": quoted in Sallust, *War with Catiline* 31.7
"it was not the quarrel": Plutarch, *Caesar* 13.5
"in the consulship": Suetonius, *Divine Julius* 20.2
"it is through": Cicero, *Letters to Atticus* 2.19.3
"a fallen star": Cicero, *Letters to Atticus* 2.21.4
"Caesar marched": e.g., Caesar, *War in Gaul* 1.37
"at top speed" and "hastened back": Caesar, *War in Gaul* 1.10
"the worthiest man": Caesar, *War in Gaul* 1.53
"could men, especially of so tiny a stature": Caesar, *War in Gaul* 2.30
"beneath his and the Romans' dignity": Caesar, *War in Gaul* 4.17

CHAPTER 9

"The Forum": Cicero, *Letters to Atticus* 5.15.1
"full of everlasting enemies": Cicero, *Letters to Atticus* 5.20.3
"Pindenissum?": Cicero, *Letters to Atticus* 5.20.1
"in arms" and "We threw": Cicero, *Letters to Atticus* 5.20.5
"screwed": Catullus 28.10
"the first lesson": Cicero, *Letters to Friends* 15.2.7
"the staff of Q. Scaevola": Cicero, *Against Verres* 2.2.34
"I am their darling": Cicero, *Letters to Atticus* 6.2.5
"savage beast": Cicero, *Letters to Atticus* 5.16.2
"gleaming white teeth": Catullus 39.1
"However much Rome has taken": *Sibylline Oracles* 3.350–55
"You have on every occasion" etc. Lewis and Reinhold, *Roman Civilization* Vol. 1 no. 124
"It is hard to exaggerate": Cicero, *For the Manilian Law* 65
"a plague of the whole world": Sallust, *Histories* fr. 4.60 Loeb
"A multitude of Italians": Diodorus, *Library of History* 5.36.3
"to the recklessness": Diodorus, *Library of History* 34/35.25.1
"Let it be known": Cicero, *Letters to Quintus* 1.1.13
"resolved that all" etc.: Diodorus, *Library of History* 37.5
"Asia must reflect on this": Cicero, *Letters to Atticus* 1.1.34

CHAPTER 10

"on the street corners": Catullus 58.5
"We were wandering": Cicero, *Academica* 1.9
"I hate and love": Catullus 85
"Lend them to me": Catullus 11.25–26
"Somebody in the crowd": Catullus 53
"They found him lying": quoted in Quintilian, *The Orator's Education* 4.2.123–24
"the rest of us": Catullus 37.5
"blind desire for offices" etc.: Lucretius, *On the Nature of Things* 3.59–63
"passion for illicit sex": Sallust, *War with Catiline* 13.3–4
"Woman! What business": Cicero, *For Caelius* 34
"the height of modern sophistication": Cicero, *For Caelius* 36

"every woman's man": Suetonius, *Divine Julius* 52.3 (quoting the elder Curio)
"the consulship of Julius and Caesar": Suetonius, *Divine Julius* 20.2

CHAPTER 11

"You will learn": Appian, *Civil Wars* 3.43
"At first the fighting": quoted in Cicero, *Letters to Friends* 10.30.3
"youthful enthusiasm": Caesar, *Civil War* 2.38
"I came, I saw, I conquered": quoted in Suetonius, *Divine Julius* 37.2 etc.
"god manifest" and "god and imperator": R. K. Sherk, *Rome and the Greek East to the Death of Augustus* (Cambridge, 1984) no. 79
"the god-defying plots": quoted in Josephus, *Jewish Antiquities* 14.306–13
"A disloyal soldier": Vergil, *Eclogues* 1.70–72
"eagle-bearer": H. Dessau, *Inscriptiones Latinae Selectae* (Berlin, 1892–1916) no. 2340
"Divine Julius" etc.: L. Benedetti, *Glandes Perusinae: Revisione e Aggiornamenti* (Rome, 2012)
"the lucky have children": Cassius Dio, *Roman History* 48.44.5
"After he has twice been beaten": quoted in Suetonius, *Divine Augustus* 70.2
"Rome is falling through her own strength": Horace, *Epodes* 16.2, 9–10
"What could have been more effective": J. Osgood, *Turia: A Roman Woman's Civil War* (Oxford, 2014) Appendix 2
"plotting mad ruin": Horace, *Odes* 1.37.7–8
"What field has not been fattened": Horace, *Odes* 2.1.29–30

CHAPTER 12

"I will try": Sherk, *Rome and the Greek East* no. 86
"when peace had been secured": Augustus, *Achievements* 13
"thundering in war": Vergil, *Georgics* 4.561–62
"to establish the state securely": Suetonius, *Divine Augustus* 28.2
"to fight fires": Suetonius, *Divine Augustus* 30.1
"Hurry slowly": Suetonius, *Divine Augustus* 25.4
"as one of the people": Suetonius, *Divine Augustus* 56.1
"in my sixth and seventh consulships": Augustus, *Achievements* 34.1
"testified that the Senate": Augustus, *Achievements* 34.2
"the list of the forces": Cassius Dio, *Roman History* 53.30.2
"the rigorous ways": Velleius, *History of Rome* 2.92.2
"the incredibly large bones": Suetonius, *Divine Augustus* 72.3
"I am of goodwill": R. K. Sherk, *The Roman Empire: Augustus to Hadrian* (Cambridge, 1988) no. 3
"Augustus will be a held a god": Horace, *Odes*
"at almost the same time": Augustus, *Achievements* 26.5
"the interests of those" etc.: Strabo, *Geography* 3.4.20
"It will be clear to all": Sherk, *Rome and the Greek East* no. 102
"sacred books or sacred monies": quoted in Josephus, *Jewish Antiquities* 16.162–65
"had launched an attack": Sherk, *Rome and the Greek East* no. 103
"keeping the city secure": Suetonius, *Divine Augustus* 28.3
"By having built": Suetonius, *Divine Augustus* 42.1
"by his [Augustus'] leadership": quoted in Pliny, *Natural History* 3.136–37
"the troops, the planning" and "ever-present guardian": Horace, *Odes* 4.14.33–34 and 43–44

CHAPTER 13

"the person who found": Sherk, *Rome and the Greek East* no. 101
"In the past" etc.: Ovid, *Art of Love* 3.113–22
"Later generations" etc.: Strabo, *Geography* 5.3.8
"I have finished a monument" etc.: Horace, *Odes* 3.30.1–2, 6, and 8–9
"seated on the snow-white threshold": Vergil, *Aeneid*
"I am dutiful Aeneas": Vergil, *Aeneid* 1.378
"Neglected, the gods": Horace, *Odes* 3.6.7–8
"Who has now restored you": Horace, *Odes* 2.7.3–4
"This day, truly festal": Horace, *Odes* 3.14.13–16
"shall wage a great war": Vergil, *Aeneid* 1.263–64
"From this noble line": Vergil, *Aeneid* 1.286–88
"son of the deified": Vergil, *Aeneid* 6.792–93
"seductive whispers": Propertius, *Elegies* 1.11.13
"Caesar's chariot" and "resting on": Propertius, *Elegies* 3.4.13 and 15
"immense undertaking" etc.: Livy, *History of Rome preface*
"no place is not filled": Livy 5.52.2 and 5.54.7
"Imperator Caesar": M. G. L. Cooley, *The Age of Augustus* (London, 2003) C7
"While her husband": Horace, *Odes* 3.6.25–26
"safety forever": Sherk, *The Roman Empire* no. 11
"Now Faith, Peace": Horace, *Centennial Hymn* 57–60
"your time, Caesar" Horace, *Odes* 4.15.4
"I was born": Propertius, *Elegies* 1.6.29

CHAPTER 14

"You know there is" and "and throughout Rome": Ovid, *Letters from the Black Sea* 3.3.72
    and 89–90
"There was the greatest": Velleius Paterculus, *Roman History* 2.123.1
"May there be good fortune": quoted in Suetonius, *Divine Augustus* 58.1
"I did this": quoted in Suetonius, *Divine Augustus* 31.5
"Leader of the youth": Ovid, *Art of Love* 1.194
"swarms of adulterers": Seneca, *On Benefits* 6.32.1
"designated princeps": Sherk, *The Roman Empire* no. 19
"taking over my post": quoted in Aulus Gellius, *Attic Nights* 15.7.3
"for the good of the state": Velleius, *Roman History* 2.104.1
"House and the children" etc.: Ovid, *Letters from the Black Sea* 3.3.87–88
"both Caesars" and "by the youths": Ovid, *Tristia* 4.2.8 and 9–10
"the people beheld again": Velleius Paterculus, *Roman History* 2.104.3–4
"the spirit of Caesar Augustus": Velleius Paterculus, *Roman History* 2.110.6
"slaughtered like cattle": Velleius Paterculus, *Roman History* 2.119.2
"Quintilius Varus": quoted in Suetonius, *Divine Augustus* 23.2
"and all went to be taxed": *Luke* 2:3
"who hated": Velleius Paterculus, *Roman History* 2.91.2
"a poem and a mistake": Ovid, *Tristia* 2.207
"both of the grandsons": Ovid, *Letters from the Black Sea* 4.9.109
"freedom of speech": Seneca the Elder, *Controversiae* 10 praef. 5
"there was a rush": Tacitus, *Annals* 1.7.1
"a partner in secrets" and "mysteries of the household": Tacitus, *Annals* 1.6.3
"succeed to his father's post": Velleius Paterculus, *Roman History* 2.124.2

"burst into complaints": Tacitus, *Annals* 1.11.3

"on behalf of the safety of our rulers": Sherk, *Roman Empire* no. 29

"Rome is safe": quoted in Suetonius, *Gaius* 6.1

"The streets of the city": Tacitus, *Annals* 3.4.1

"because they did not allow": M. G. L. Cooley, *Tiberius to Nero* (London, 2011) P3d (adapted)

"the immortal gods" and "All hope for the post": Cooley, *Tiberius to Nero* P3 j

"the guardian of the eternal fire" etc.: Velleius Paterculus, *Roman History* 2.131

"declared with repeated acclamations": Cooley, *Tiberius to Nero* P3 k

"joined with the Equestrian order": Cooley, *Tiberius to Nero* P3 m

"loyalty and devotion": Cooley, *Tiberius to Nero* P3 n (adapted)

"Yet when I am dead": Ovid, *Tristia* 3.9.50–52

INDEX

Notes: (1) this index is not intended to be exhaustive but to lead readers to the most significant discussions of particular topics or to the clearest definition of a technical term; (2) Roman men are typically identified by their more familiar *cognomen;* (3) major Roman authors are listed under their familiar English names, e.g., "Sallust"; (4) to help distinguish Romans, especially those of the same or similar names, further information sometimes is included in parentheses (e.g., a significant magistracy or magistracies)